The Primary Textile Industry in Canada
History and Heritage

A.B. McCullough

DATE DUE

Studies in Archaeology
Architecture and History

National Historic Sites
Parks Service
Environment Canada

Available in Canada through authorized bookstore agents and other bookstores, or by mail from the Canada Communication Group – Publishing, Supply and Services Canada, Ottawa, Ontario, Canada K1A 0S9.

Published under the authority
of the Minister of the Environment,
Ottawa, 1992.

Editing and design: Jean Brathwaite
Production: Suzanne H. Rochette, Lucie Forget, and Rod Won

Parks publishes the results of its research in archaeology, architecture and history. A list of publications is available from National Historic Sites Publications, Parks Service, Environment Canada, 1600 Liverpool Court, Ottawa, Ontario, K1A 0H3.

Canadian Cataloguing in Publication Data

McCullough, A. B. (Alan Bruce), 1945-

The primary textile industry in Canada: history and heritage

(Studies in archaeology, architecture and history,
ISSN 0821-1027)
Issued also in French under title: L'industrie textile primaire au Canada.
Includes bibliographical references.
ISBN 0-660-14398-4
DSS cat. no. R61-2/9-57E

1. Textile industry — Canada, Eastern — History. 2. Textile factories — Canada, Eastern — History. I. Canadian Parks Service. National Historic Sites. II. Title. III. Series.

HD9864.C32M32 1992   338.4'7677'00971   C92-099580-2

Cover: The weave shed, Canada Cottons Limited, Cornwall, Ontario, ca. 1948. National Archives of Canada, PA 179681, Malak Collection, 959-11245

Contents

Preface

As one of the first industries to introduce mechanized production in a factory setting, the textile industry came to symbolize Canada's development as an industrial nation and, equally important, the harsh conditions under which workers — men, women, and children — laboured. But if the industry has left an indelible imprint on many aspects of Canadian history, its once-prominent imprint on the physical landscape is far less certain. The brick, stone, and concrete legacy — so much a part of the fabric of towns and cities in many parts of the country — is today under increasing threat. Many of the industrial "monuments" associated with the history of Canadian textile manufacturing have disappeared; most of the others face an uncertain future.

This historical overview of the Canadian textile industry is a by-product of a research project initiated by the Parks Service of Environment Canada in response to direction from the minister, who was asked during the mid-1980s to designate certain textile mills as national historic sites. Under the Historic Sites and Monuments Act, the minister of the Environment is the federal minister responsible for commemorating places of national historic interest or significance. Two things became apparent at the beginning of the research. While a number of excellent historical treatments had been done or were in progress on various aspects of the textile industry, no overview existed that would provide a historical context for assessing surviving (but not necessarily operational) textile mills. Of equal importance, it quickly became apparent that the preservation of textile mills was a major heritage issue. Significant initiatives were underway in places such as Marysville, New Brunswick, Sherbrooke, Quebec, and Almonte, Ontario, to conserve individual mills or mill complexes, partly because the preservation of such places — combined with their adaptation to other purposes — seemed preferable on aesthetic, social, and economic grounds to alternative land uses, and partly because such places were finally being recognized as significant landmarks in the history of their communities. There was considerable irony in the fact that structures that would once have been demolished in the interests of urban beautification were now seen as bulwarks against the "blight" of urban redevelopment.

In the spirit of the World Heritage Convention, which Canada signed in 1976, the present work is intended to contribute toward the "identification, protection, conservation, presentation and transmission" of an important part of the nation's cultural heritage. It is an attempt to blend heritage and historiography, an admixture that is not nearly as common as one might think. The historiographical emphasis is on providing a sound, succinct history of the primary textile industry rather than a detailed account. It is hoped that the history will provide a useful source for the many historians, curators, and heritage activists who are working on various aspects of the Canadian textile industry, as well as for the interested general public. The 21 thumbnail sketches of individual textile mills are intended to give a sense of the richness and diversity of the built heritage associated with the industry. These sketches record some of the significant losses to this heritage as well as what survives and may yet be saved.

A number of individuals have contributed to the development of this book. Gordon Bennett of the Canadian Park Service, Ben Forster of the University of Western Ontario, Adrienne Hood of the Royal Ontario Museum, Kris Inwood of the University of Guelph, and Larry McNally of the National Archives read and commented on the manuscript. Jim Quantrell, archivist of the City of Cambridge, Ann Gillespie of the City of Hamilton's LACAC office, and J.E. Warnock of Tiger Brand Knitting provided information on specific textile mills. Alec Barbour of the Architectural and Engineering Services for Environment Canada, Public Works Canada, assisted me in identifying and describing the technological processes and structural techniques illustrated in Figures 1 to 21, 31 to 35, and 38 to 55. My colleagues Felicity Leung, David McConnell, and Jean-Claude Parent have always been generous in sharing information gathered in their study of Canadian manufacturing centres. In addition, Felicity's "Catalogue of Significant Extant Textile Mills Built in Canada Before 1940" provided the basis for most of the site histories in Part II of this book. Jean Brathwaite, my editor, helped me to avoid many errors of commission and omission. Those that remain are, of course, my responsibility.

Part I
The History
of the
Primary Textile Industry

Introduction

For over a century the manufacture of clothing and cloth has been a major component in Canada's manufacturing sector. In 1880, 13 per cent of all Canadians employed in manufacturing were in the clothing industry and 5 per cent were employed in the manufacture of cloth. Taking the two together, only wood products, with 24 per cent of all manufacturing employment, was more important. The manufacture of cloth and clothing ranked third in gross value of production. By the late 1950s, textile manufacturing's relative importance had declined slightly, but the textile industry still ranked third as an employer and fifth in terms of value of production.

The importance of the textile industry lies not only in the numbers it employed, but also in the role it played in the growth of Canadian manufacturing. The textile mills that flourished in the 1880s were one of the first and most visible fruits of the protective tariff, or National Policy, introduced in 1879. The difficulties that the same mills experienced in later years provided an education for Canadians in the problems of nurturing domestic industry. The financing of the industry, which was largely Canadian owned, provided an outlet for Canadian capital as well as salutary lessons for a generation of Canadian financiers. The industry also provided experience for Canadian labour. Textile mills were among the earliest large employers of Canadian labour in a factory setting; this was especially the case for female labour, which formed a large part of the textile industry's labour force. Finally, for the student of architectural history, the rich collection of textile mills that survive from all periods of the industry's history provides a resource for the study of the evolution of industrial architecture.

Broadly defined, a textile is any kind of cloth. The Latin root is the verb "texere," to weave, and traditionally textiles have been woven, but they may also be knitted, crocheted, braided, or felted. The term is also applied to the fibrous raw materials from which cloth is made. Traditionally the raw materials most commonly used in Europe and North America have been wool, flax, silk, and cotton; today synthetic fibres are produced from wood and from petroleum or coal derivatives.

An industry is a trade or manufacture. In popular usage the term, when applied to manufactures, is often linked with the factory system as it developed during the Industrial Revolution. The factory system was characterized by the grouping of large numbers of workers and machines under a single roof and by the use of mechanical power to drive the machinery.

In its narrowest sense the textile industry may be defined as the manufacture of woven cloth under factory conditions. In a broader sense it may be defined as the processing of textile fibres in a domestic, shop, or factory setting, and the manufacture of any type of thread, yarn, string, rope, carpet, fabric, cloth, or clothing that has textile fibres as a raw material.

In its first comprehensive statistical report on the textile industry in Canada (published in 1929) the Dominion Bureau of Statistics used a broad definition of textile based on the use of a common raw material, textile fibres. The report identified 23 subgroups or sectors within the textile group of industries:[1]

Cotton textiles, comprising:
1. Cotton yarn and cloth
2. Cotton thread
3. Cotton and wool waste
4. Batting and wadding
5. Cotton textiles not elsewhere specified

Woollen textiles, comprising:
6. Woollen yarn
7. Woollen cloth
8. Carpets
9. Woollen goods not elsewhere specified

Other:
10. Hosiery and knit goods
11. Fabric gloves and mittens
12. Silk goods
13. Hats and caps, including factory millinery
14. Men's factory clothing
15. Women's factory clothing, including laces and embroidery
16. Corsets
17. Men's furnishing goods
18. Oiled and waterproof clothing
19. Awnings, tents and sails
20. Cordage, rope and twine
21. Cotton and jute bags
22. Linen goods
23. Dyeing, cleaning and laundry work

The list made no mention of synthetic textiles nor did it mention the home production of textiles and clothing. Synthetics were not manufactured in Canada until after 1924 although they had been imported for 20 years; since the Second World War the synthetic-textile subgroup has become one of the most important sectors within the textile industry. During the nineteenth century the home production of cloth was a significant factor in total textile production; by 1929, when the Dominion Bureau of Statistics survey was prepared, home production of cloth had become statistically insignificant although home production of clothing was probably still important.

A popular definition of the textile industry would probably exclude the various branches of the clothing industry or would describe them as secondary industries within the textile group. In general the clothing sub-groups use cloth rather than textile fibres as a raw material. In contrast the primary industries in the textile group convert raw materials, such as wool or cotton, to thread and cloth. The secondary textile industries also use different technologies from those used in the primary textile industries. The hosiery and knit-goods and the fabric gloves and mittens sectors form a special category in which the process of making cloth and making clothing is accomplished by the same or closely related operations. Traditionally they have been treated as part of the primary textile industry.

This paper will not attempt to present a detailed history of the entire textile industry. Instead it will concentrate on four major sectors (identified on the basis of employment and value of production) in the primary industry — woollens, cottons, knit goods/hosiery, and silk/synthetics — and on the major themes mentioned earlier — tariffs, finance and ownership, labour, and industrial architecture. The major emphasis will be on the industry as it evolved before World War II.

In general, Canada imported textile technology from abroad; no important technological developments originated in Canada. Nevertheless, an understanding of textile processes is important to an understanding of the industry; consequently the paper will begin with a brief account of the technology used in the industry.

Technological Developments in the Textile Industry, 1750–1850 and 1850–1950

The transformation of natural fibres such as hemp, wool, flax, cotton, and silk into finished cloth is a complex task involving many discrete processes. These processes can be divided into five major stages: preparation of the fibre for spinning, spinning, preparation of the yarn for weaving, weaving, and finishing. Although the individual processes used in handling different fibres differ somewhat, there is sufficient common ground that a description of the processing of one fibre provides a basic understanding of the processing of all fibres. In this chapter I will use wool, the major textile produced in Canada during the nineteenth century, as the primary example and will refer to the processing of other fibres only when it differs from the processing of wool.[1]

The first stage, preparation for spinning, involves cleaning and combing the fibres so that they are more or less parallel and form a continuous loose strand that may be spun. This stage may be divided into four processes: sorting, scouring, picking, and carding. Wool from different breeds of sheep and from different parts of a sheep's body has different characteristics that will affect its spinning and weaving properties and the quality and texture of the cloth produced from it. In any large-scale cloth-making operation, wool will be sorted into homogeneous lots.

The second process in preparing wool for spinning is scouring. Wool has a natural grease, suint, that is removed by washing the wool in a warm weak alkaline solution; traditionally stale urine (which produces a solvent, ammonium hydroxide) was used. Until about the middle of the nineteenth century, scouring was generally done by hand in large tubs; at that time a mechanical scouring train that automatically moved the wool through a series of tubs was developed.[2] After scouring, wool is rinsed and dried.

Scouring is not required for cotton. Once the seeds are removed from the cotton and it is sorted, processes that normally take place before it is delivered to a mill, it is ready for picking. Flax does not require scouring, but it does require four preparatory processes. The seeds are removed using a comb (rippling), the flax is soaked so as to rot the gum that binds the valuable fibre (bast) to the bark, the bast is loosened from the core of the flax stem (braking) and separated from the core and bark by beating (scutching) with a stick. Once this has been done the fibres (tow) are ready for hackling, a process analogous to carding wool.

Picking is intended to remove dirt, straw, and other impurities that have escaped scouring and to loosen the wool for carding. Originally picking involved beating the wool with sticks to loosen the fibres and remove dirt. In the late eighteenth century a mechanical picker was developed. It consisted of a rotating drum studded with short spikes onto which scoured wool was fed. Either before or as the picking process is done, oil is added to the wool to make it more pliable and easily worked.

Carding completes the cleaning process and blends the wool into a continuous cohesive strand called a roving, rolag, slubbing, or sliver, which can be spun. Traditionally carding was done by brushing the wool between two wire-studded boards or cards. By the end of the eighteenth century, carding had been mechanized. Essentially carding machines mounted the teeth of the hand-card on cylinders that rotated at different speeds. In order to achieve consistency in the final product, wool was often run through the carding engine two or three times, or two or three carding cylinders were mounted in sequence. When they were first developed, carding engines produced wide mats of carded wool that had to be converted to a roving in a separate operation; by the 1830s, condensers were available that could be attached to the carding engine and produced the roving automatically.[3]

Carding produces a roving that is suitable for the production of woollen yarn, but if worsted yarn is to be produced, the carded wool has to be combed. Basically combing is a carding refinement that arranges the individual fibres so that they are more nearly parallel to one another and to the yarn of which they form a part than are the fibres in woollen yarn. In addition, combing removes shorter fibres from the carding so that the average length of fibres in worsted yarn is longer than in woollen yarn.[4] Combing is also necessary in the production of some finer types of cotton thread and cloth.

Worsted manufacture, which did not emerge in Canada until the 1880s, is considered to be a distinct branch of the woollen sector. In some ways its technical processes are more akin to those of the cotton sector than to those of the woollen sector. Worsteds are made from wool fibres that are longer than those used to produce woollens. The fibres are combed so that they are more nearly parallel than the fibres in woollen cloth. Worsteds tend to be woven more tightly than woollens, to be less likely to shrink or felt, to have a harder feel, and to be less bulky than woollens. Tweeds are typical woollen cloths; serges and gabardines are more likely to be worsted.

In spinning, the roving — a loose strand of untwisted fibres — is simultaneously elongated and twisted to form yarn. Until the eighteenth century, yarn was produced using spinning wheels similar to those used by handicraft workers today. They consisted of a drivewheel that drove a spindle. Rovings were attached to the rotating spindle, twisted into yarn at the same time as they were drawn out to make them longer, and then wound upon the spindle.

In the early forms of the spinning wheel, spinning stopped while the yarn was wound on the spindle, but during the sixteenth century, rotating flyers were mounted concentrically upon the spindle. The flyer, which rotated at a different speed than the spindle, imparted twist to the thread at the same time as the thread was being wound upon the spindle.[5]

The main limitation of the wheel was that only one yarn could be produced at a time, and during the eighteenth century several efforts were made to develop a machine that could spin more than one thread at a time. In 1769 Richard Arkwright patented a powered throstle, or "water frame," that was capable of spinning many threads on the continuous system. It simultaneously drafted (elongated) the roving using a system of rollers, twisted it using a flyer, and wound it on a spindle.[6] Ultimately his system was developed into the cap and the ring spinning systems that became popular in the United States in the late nineteenth century.

In 1770 James Hargreave patented the spinning jenny, a hand-powered machine that could spin 16 threads simultaneously. During the 1770s Samuel Crompton modified the jenny so that it could be powered. He also incorporated the concept of roller drafting from Arkwright's throstle into his machine, which in recognition of its mixed parentage was known as the mule. Crompton's mule was versatile, could spin lower quality cotton than the throstle, and was capable of spinning very fine thread. Its major disadvantage was that it spun discontinuously; that is, it spun the thread and then stopped spinning and wound the thread on the spindle; consequently it was slower than the throstle or ring spinner. It also required more skilled, and expensive, labour than did the throstle. It was widely used for spinning wool both in Britain and North America and was the most popular means of spinning cotton in Britain until after the Second World War. Cap or ring spinning was more popular in the United States;[7] both methods were used in Canada.

In the 1820s the Sharp Roberts Company developed a mule that was almost automatic. Self-acting mules required less attention than the hand-operated mules. One spinner-minder with two assistants could operate two self-acting mules of about 600 spindles each. Despite its apparent advantage the self-acting mule was only adopted gradually. It became common in Yorkshire after 1850 and in the United States in the 1870s.[8]

The equipment used in picking, carding, and spinning cotton was much the same as that used for wool; in fact most of the textile machinery developed during the eighteenth and nineteenth centuries was first used in the cotton industry and then introduced into the woollen industry. In addition the cotton industry introduced two processes — drawing and roving — between carding and spinning, processes that were not used in the production of woollens although they were used in worsted manufacture. Drawing involves combining several rovings and drafting them with rollers.

Drawing straightens the fibres, produces a more even sliver, and reduces its diameter. In roving the sliver, or roving, is elongated further, its diameter is reduced, and it is given a slight twist as it is wound on a spindle by a flyer. The roving process is often repeated three or four times on separate machines to produce progressively finer rovings.

Mechanization came much later in the linen industry than in the cotton and woollen industries. Powered braking and scutching equipment was available at the beginning of the nineteenth century, but a satisfactory spinning system was not developed until the 1820s, and hackling (carding) remained a handicraft operation even later. The failure to mechanize in the face of growing competition from cottons was a major cause of the relative decline in the importance of linen in Canada and elsewhere.[9]

The steps involved in preparing the thread for weaving are straightforward and few. If the thread is intended to serve as the weft (woof or filling) of the cloth, it is rewound from the spindle or bobbin onto quills that will fit into a shuttle. After the spinning mule was developed, bobbins were designed to fit into shuttles and quilling of mule-spun yarn was eliminated. If thread is intended for use as the warp, thread from a number of bobbins is transferred to a large spool and then the thread from many large spools is wound on a warp beam that can be mounted in a loom. Sometimes before warp threads are wound on the warp beams they are strengthened by being passed through a starch solution. The process, known as sizing or slashing, is more common in the cotton industry than it is in woollens. It strengthens the thread and protects it against chaffing. Drawing-in is the final process in preparation for weaving; in drawing-in the individual threads on the warp beam are drawn through the heddles and beater on the loom. The preparatory processes for weaving cotton and linen are much the same as those for wool.

Weaving consists of interlacing a continuous weft thread with a large number of warp threads in a repeating pattern so as to form cloth. The horizontal hand loom that is used by home weavers today, and that was the common loom among hand-loom weavers in the eighteenth and nineteenth centuries, was developed in the Middle Ages. In weaving, the weaver performs a regular series of actions. First, by means of foot peddles the weaver lowers one heddle (or series of heddles) and raises another. This opens a diamond-shaped space (the shed) formed by alternately raised or lowered warp yarn. The weaver then passes the shuttle, which carries the weft yarn, through the shed. Finally, the weaver pulls a frame, the batten or beater, against the weft yarn that has been passed through the shed, thereby driving it home against the other weft yarn. This completes the sequence and the weaver raises and lowers the heddles, thus changing the conformation of the shed before passing the shuttle back through the shed. The process may be repeated 50 or 60 times to produce an inch of cloth. Each pass of the shuttle is called a pick, and cloth is described as having so many picks per inch. Periodically the weaver also has to wind the cloth produced onto the take-up beam, reload the shuttle with a new stock of yarn, and repair broken warp or weft yarn.

In order to develop a power-driven loom that did not require the continuous attention of a weaver, all these actions had to be automated and carefully synchronized. The first power looms were introduced in Britain about the end of the eighteenth century. The early ones were crude and could only be used for coarse cloth made with strong thread, but by 1810, power looms were common in the most advanced British cotton mills; by the 1850s they were well established in British worsted mills, but power looms did not completely replace hand looms in the British woollen industry until the 1890s.[10] Some Canadian woollen mills were reported to have power looms in the 1840s and 1850s.[11]

Yarn may also be made into cloth by knitting. In knitting, cloth is formed by interlooping a thread or threads using knitting needles. Knitting may be used to form cloth or it may be used to transform yarn directly into clothing such as sweaters, undergarments, and hosiery. A hand-powered knitting machine was developed in the sixteenth century; it produced flat pieces of knitted fabric that were sewn into stockings. Although the knitting frame was used to produce knitted material on a commercial basis, it was usually employed in a cottage-industry setting. Factories with large numbers of powered knitting machines did not become common until the latter half of the nineteenth century.[12]

When cloth comes from the loom it is inspected for faults and if minor faults are found they are repaired, or burled.

For some purposes the cloth that comes from the loom is ready for use, but in many instances it must go through a number of finishing processes that develop special characteristics. Only the most important of these processes — fulling, napping, shearing, bleaching, dyeing, and printing — need be discussed here.

Fulling is only used for woollen and occasionally worsted cloths. Essentially it involves working the finished cloth vigorously when it is wet, thus causing it to shrink and begin to felt. As a result the weave becomes tighter and warmer. Originally fulling was done by walking on the cloth or pulling it by hand. Fulling was time consuming, and as early as the twelfth century, water-driven trip hammers, or fulling stocks, were used to full cloth in England. During the nineteenth century, rotary fulling mills, which used rollers instead of hammers, were developed and they gradually replaced fulling stocks.[13]

Once woollen cloth is fulled the surface fibres may be napped or raised slightly to give the cloth a better feel. Traditionally napping was done with hand-held combs in which large burrs or teasels were mounted. By the nineteenth century, rotary teasel gigs had been developed and by the 1830s they had largely replaced hand napping.[14] Although napping is most commonly used on woollens, it can also be used on cottons to produce material such as flannelette.

After the nap was raised, stray fibres were trimmed off so that the cloth had an even texture. This shearing was done using a set of heavy shears similar to, but much larger than, the hand shears used for shearing sheep. Shearing was a skilled operation and not all cloth was sheared. The invention of a rotary shearing machine largely replaced hand shearing in the United States after 1800.[15]

Bleaching was not usual in the production of woollens in the nineteenth century, but it was common in the production of linen and cotton. Linen is brownish in its natural state and cotton is grey; traditionally they were bleached by steeping in an alkaline solution, washing, spreading in fields to be bleached by the sun, steeping in an acid solution (sour milk), washing, and spreading in the sun again. The process had to be repeated several times. In the 1780s, chlorine was introduced as a bleaching agent and reduced bleaching time from months to days or hours. By the 1830s, bleaching in large mills was almost entirely mechanized.[16]

After cotton has been bleached it may be sold as white cotton or printed or dyed. Originally printing was done by hand using wooden blocks. In the 1780s a method of printing using rotating engraved copper cylinders was developed in Lancashire.[17] The method provided an immense saving in labour and quickly replaced block printing in ordinary work. Ultimately large printing machines with many cylinders were able to print many colours simultaneously.

Although dyeing is listed as one of the finishing processes, it could be done at several stages in cloth production. Both wool and cotton can be dyed as raw material after they have been cleaned, as yarn, or as finished cloth. Both wool and cotton were dyed by immersion in vats of boiling water to which dyes had been added. The process was relatively simple and has changed little although much of the procedure has been mechanized. The technically challenging part of dyeing was in the choice of dyes and matching of dyes with materials since not all dyes were suitable for all materials. Until the 1860s all dyes were extracts from natural products; since then synthetic dyes have replaced many natural dyes.

The period 1750–1850 was one of immense change in the textile industry. At the beginning of the period most processes were carried out using handicraft methods; at the end of the period large mechanically powered machines performed almost all processes in modern factories although handicraft methods survived. Equally important, at the beginning of the period the great British woollen industry was primarily a cottage industry and the cotton industry was only beginning; by the end of the period, production in large factories was the norm and cotton had replaced woollen cloth as Britain's main export product. A thriving cotton industry had developed in the United States. When Canada began to develop a significant textile industry in the second half of the nineteenth century it was able to import mature industrial processes from both Britain and the United States. No major technological developments in the industry originated in Canada, and most machinery used in Canadian mills was imported.

In general, technological developments in the century after 1850 were less dramatic than those in the previous century; most were incremental improvements on existing technology. The improvements tended to improve productivity by running machinery faster or by reducing labour costs.

For example, in 1850 a cotton weaver might have tended four 36-inch looms, each operating at 112 picks per minute; by 1925 the same weaver would have tended 20 or more looms operating at 170 picks per minute. Assuming an equal amount of downtime, the weaver's productivity was increased 750 per cent. There were similar although perhaps not so spectacular increases in other processes. In 1850, spinning mules in New England mills operated at 2.75 "stretches" per minute and produced 0.93 pounds of yarn per spindle per 100 hours; in 1925 they operated at 5 stretches per minute and produced 1.94 pounds of yarn per spindle per 100 hours. Over the same period spindle speed on a ring spinning frame increased from 5000 rpm to 9000 or 10 000 rpm and production increased from 1.26 to 2.5 pounds per spindle per 100 hours.[18]

Three developments over the period 1850–1950 were particularly important: the replacement of mule spinning by ring spinning, the development of the automatic loom, and the introduction of long-draft spinning and roving. A fourth development, the growth of the synthetic-fibre sector, should also be classed as a major, indeed a revolutionary, development; however, as it is outside of the general tradition of the textile industry it will be considered separately.

Spinning mules were intricate and flexible machines. They were capable of spinning a variety of fibres and of producing a wide range of yarn. They were capable of much finer spinning than rings and they produced a softer yarn; moreover, they could do this using a lower grade of cotton than rings. The initial cost of mules was less per spindle than the cost of rings, and mule spindles required less power than rings. These characteristics made mules popular in Britain, where they remained the dominant form of spinning until after World War II.

Ring spinning had a number of advantages over the mule. Because a ring frame spun continuously and at higher speeds than the mule, it produced more yarn per spindle than a mule did. Ring-spun yarn was harder and stronger than mule-spun yarn of the same count (weight), and in many weaving mills ring-spun yarn was used for warps and mule-spun for wefts. Ring spindles occupied about one-third less space than mule spindles. Ring

19

spinning mills were less susceptible to fire than mule spinning mills and could be insured for less. Perhaps the most important advantage of ring frames was that they could be operated by less-skilled labour, low-wage women and children, rather than by skilled, highly paid, adult males.[19] This last advantage was probably decisive in a decision by American cotton-mill owners to shift most of their production to rings after 1870. In 1870, 48 per cent of American cotton spindles were on mules; by 1905 only 23 per cent were and the percentage continued to decline.[20]

Mules survived several decades longer in the Canadian cotton sector than they did in the American industry. As late as 1920 over 30 per cent of Canadian cotton spindles were on mules; however, they were being replaced, and by 1935 only 4 per cent of cotton spindles were on mules.[21] Although the mule was obsolete in the North American cotton industry by the 1930s, it remained the principal spinning machine in the British industry until after World War II. It also continued to be the common means of spinning wool in Canada until after the war; in 1945, 93 per cent of the spindles in the woollen branch of the industry and 34 per cent of the spindles in the worsted branch were on mules. In addition, 45 per cent of the spindles in the hosiery and knit-goods sector in 1940 were on mules.[22] Stanfield's Limited at Truro, Nova Scotia, was probably the last major Canadian firm to use mules; they were replaced by ring frames about 1970.

The development of the automatic loom in the 1890s was a second major technological development in the century after 1850. The power looms used throughout the nineteenth century were not automatic. They required the regular attendance of a weaver to replenish the yarn in the shuttle, about 100 times in a ten-hour day, and to repair broken warp and weft threads, perhaps 40 or 50 times per day. To refill shuttles or repair broken threads the loom had to be stopped; as a result looms were stopped at least 12.5 per cent of the working day.[23] The looms also had to be stopped to change the beam, usually once a day or less frequently. Depending on management practice, a weaver might also be required to oil and clean machines and tend to a number of other minor tasks. As a result weavers could seldom tend more than four to six power looms.

Between 1889 and 1893 George W. Draper and Sons of Hopedale, Massachusetts, developed the Northrop loom. Because it contained a hopper, or magazine, from which empty shuttles were automatically replaced with full ones without stopping the loom, it came to be known as the automatic loom. In addition to this shuttle-loading mechanism the Northrop loom incorporated other mechanisms that did jobs formerly done by the weaver. It threaded the shuttle automatically; previously this had been done by the weaver sucking the yarn through an eye in the shuttle. It also had a warp-stop mechanism that stopped the machine if one of the warp threads broke. Previously detection of broken threads had depended on the weaver's vigilance. If she failed to see a broken thread, the cloth developed a run that had to be repaired. The loom also included a weft-stop motion, but this had been available before the introduction of the Northrop loom.[24]

One advantage of the Northrop and subsequent automatic looms was that they eliminated the stop required to reload the shuttle. This change had the potential to increase output per loom by 5 to 10 per cent. It also freed some of the weaver's time for other tasks or for watching an increased number of looms. The warp-stop motion also increased the number of looms that a weaver could tend at the same time as it reduced the incidence of faults in the cloth produced. Cotton weavers commonly moved from tending 4, 6, or at most 8 common looms to 16 to 20 automatic looms. The effect was to cut labour costs in the weave room by as much as 50 per cent.[25]

Under the influence of "scientific management" theories, Canadian cotton mills increased the number of looms per weaver even more in the late 1920s and early 1930s. "Battery hands," often youths, were assigned to refill the shuttle magazines and clean and oil the machines. Others were assigned to perform repair work and change beams. The weaver's responsibility was reduced to watching for breaks, repairing them, restarting the machine, and general supervision. Depending on circumstances, the battery- or multiple-loom system made it possible for a weaver to tend 50 to 70 looms.[26] The introduction of the battery system did not necessarily reduce the number of employees in the weave room, but it did replace relatively well-paid weavers with lower paid labour. When Montreal Cotton introduced the battery system in 1929–30 the number of weavers employed was reduced from 514 to 331 at the same time as the number of weave-room employees rose from 687 to 725. In spite of the increased employment, the wage cost per 1000 yards of cloth produced fell from $14.89 to $13.80.[27]

In spite of the advantages of the automatic loom, it was several decades before it replaced the common loom in North America and even longer in Britain. The first automatic looms required a stronger yarn than common looms and could only weave plain cloth. They cost three times as much as a common loom, were more expensive to maintain, and occupied more space.[28] Looms had long working lives and mill owners were reluctant to replace them until it was necessary. Many common looms were upgraded by installing warp-stop motions on them so that a weaver could tend more looms.[29]

The Canadian cotton industry adopted automatic looms more rapidly than most. A syndicate headed by A.F. Gault, the leading Canadian cotton manufacturer, acquired the rights to manufacture Northrop looms in Canada[30] and began production in 1898. By 1914, 47 per cent of all Canadian cotton looms were automatic compared to 44.5 per cent in the United States; by 1935, 96 per cent of Canadian cotton looms were automatic.[31]

21

Automatic looms were adopted more slowly in the woollen sector. Woollen yarn is weaker than cotton. As a result there were more breaks and even by the 1920s, weavers could only tend 6 or 8 automatic woollen looms compared to 25 or more cotton looms. Consequently there was less incentive to install the new looms.[32] By 1945 only 33 per cent of looms in the woollen cloth sector were automatic.[33]

Long-draft spinning and roving were the third major developments of the period 1850–1950. Both spinning and roving involved drafting, that is, the lengthening of the sliver or roving as it passed through the machine. In the cotton and worsted industries drafting was done by passing the sliver through two or more pairs of rollers on the roving or spinning frame. Succeeding pairs of rollers rotated more rapidly than the preceding sets; as a result the sliver was lengthened and its circumference reduced. The sliver could not be drafted too much at a single pass through the machine or it would bunch or break. To achieve the amount of drafting required for fine spinning, it was necessary to repeat the drafting on four separate roving machines; coarse yarn required only two roving frames.[34]

In 1913 Fernando Casablanca developed a device that, when attached to a standard spinning frame, allowed the draft to be increased several times at one pass. As a result it was possible to eliminate one of the preparatory roving operations. Subsequent application of the principle of long drafting to roving frames made it possible to eliminate another of the roving operations.[35] Long-draft spinning and roving ultimately resulted in important labour savings in the textile industry. However, their introduction into general use in North America was delayed by World War I and then by developmental problems until the 1930s.

The substitution of ring spinning for mule spinning and the development of the automated loom and long-draft spinning and roving were the major technical innovations of the textile industry in the years 1850–1950. Other significant but lesser developments were the introduction of the flat roller card in the 1880s, the perfection of one-process picking in the 1920s, and the development of high-speed spooling and warping in the 1930s. These advances, plus a host of minor improvements, resulted in approximately a tenfold increase in productivity, measured as value added in constant dollars per employee in the cotton, woollen, and knit-goods sectors combined between 1871 and 1940 (see Table 19).

The century 1851–1950 was one of major technical progress in the knit-goods and hosiery sector. As noted earlier, a hand-operated knitting frame had been developed in the sixteenth century. With minor modifications it was used until the mid-nineteenth century to produce flat pieces of knitted fabric that were then sewn into stockings. Power was not applied successfully to the knitting process until about 1850, when Matthew Townsend patented a machine that knitted fabric in a ribbed tube. In 1864

William Cotton developed a powered flat knitting frame capable of producing a dozen stockings at once.[36] Over the next 40 years a variety of knitting machines were developed to produce specific items such as cuffs, leggings, and ribbed stocking tops. The sector also benefited from the development of numerous specialized sewing machines used in sewing together pieces of knit fabric to form underwear and stockings. Until power was applied to knitting machines, knitting had been largely a cottage-based industry both in Britain and the United States, but after 1850 (or the 1880s in Canada) it evolved rapidly into the factory system.

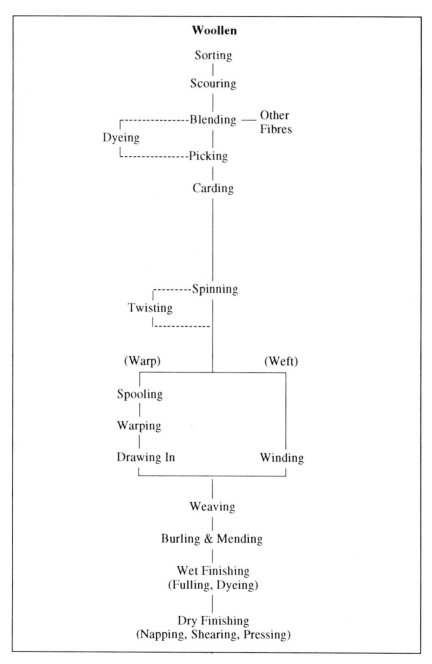

1   Production processes in woollen manufacture.

Adapted from G.E. Largy, "Textiles: Wool," in K.C. Livingston and T.C. Graham, *Manufacturing Processes in Canada* (Toronto: University of Toronto Press, 1960), p. 257

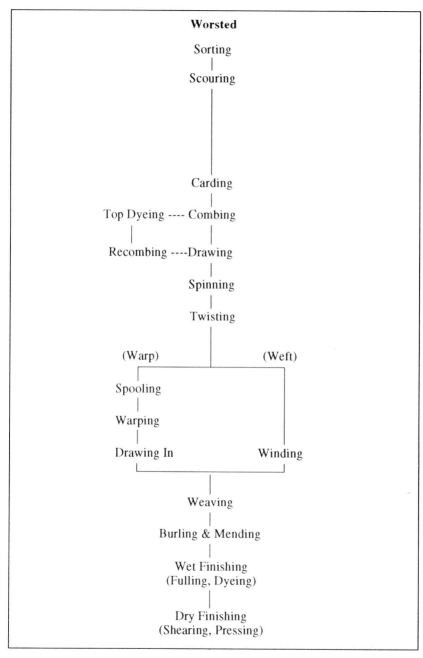

2 Production processes in worsted manufacture.

Adapted from G.E. Largy, "Textiles: Wool," in K.C. Livingston and T.C. Graham, *Manufacturing Processes in Canada* (Toronto: University of Toronto Press, 1960), p. 261

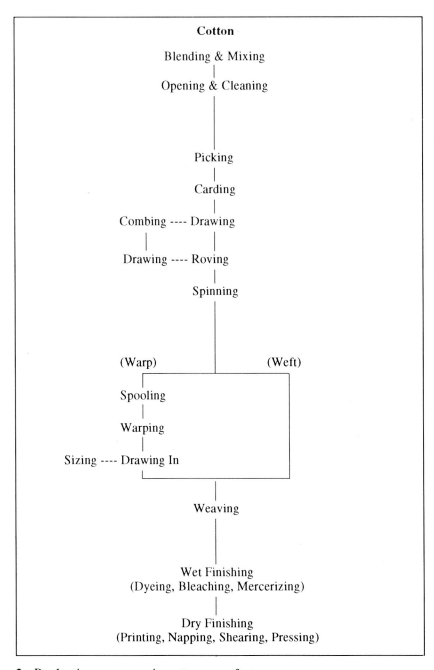

3 Production processes in cotton manufacture.
Adapted from J.R. Dunkerley, "Textiles: Cotton," in K.C. Livingston and T.C. Graham, *Manufacturing Processes in Canada* (Toronto: University of Toronto Press, 1960), p. 252

4 Raw cotton in bales in a Dominion Textile warehouse at Montmorency, Quebec.
Notman Photographic Archives, McCord Museum of Canadian History, MP 2091 (8)

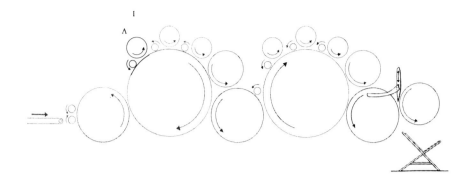

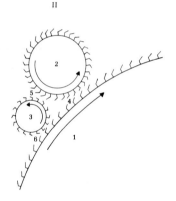

5 The carding process.

I: A carding engine with two main cylinders. The carding takes place at section A and is repeated another five times as the wool passes through the machine.

II: An enlargement of section A. The wool is carried by the main cylinder, 1, until it reaches point 4, where the action of the worker cylinder, 2, against the main cylinder, 1, cards the wool. Wool picked up by the worker cylinder is removed at 5 by the action of the stripper cylinder, 3, which is in turn stripped of its wool at 6 by the main cylinder.

Merrimack Valley Textile Museum, *Homespun to Factory Made: Woolen Textiles in America, 1776–1876* (North Andover, Mass.: 1977), p. 67, illustration by J.S. Dugger, AIA

6 Carding room at Penmans Limited, 1930. Roller cards of this type were more common in woollen manufacturing than in cotton mills. These are secondary cards; the sliver or roving being fed into the machine from the right has already been carded once. The cards are driven by belts from pulleys below the floor.
National Film Board, B-9; National Archives of Canada, PA 800605

7   Card room, Mount Royal Spinning mill, Montréal, 1929. These are revolving flat cards that were used in carding cotton. Carded cotton emerges from them in the form of a single strip of sliver that is fed into the tall, narrow, sliver cans. The cards are equipped with a dust-extraction system and are driven by overhead shafting. This mill was built in 1907 using steel beams and wooden flooring.
National Film Board, B-44; National Archives of Canada, PA 800636

8 The operation of a spinning jack (mule)

1. The cycle is about to begin as the operator engages the machine to the mill's power source.

2. The feed rollers are paying out roving from the jack spools. The spindles are turning and the carriage has begun to move away from the stationary frame.

3. The feed rollers have stopped rotating and no more roving is being paid out. The carriage continues to the rear as the spindles turn and impart twist to the roving.

4. The roving has been spun and drafted. The operator turns the hand wheel and reverses the direction of the spindles in order to back the yarn off the spindle tips.

5. The operator twists the spindles by turning the wheel at the same time as he pushes the carriage forward. He depresses the faller bar to wind the yarn onto the spindle.

Merrimack Valley Textile Museum, *Homespun to Factory Made: Woolen Textiles in America, 1776–1876* (North Andover, Mass.: 1977), p. 77; illustration by J.S. Dugger, AIA

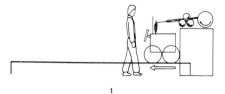

1

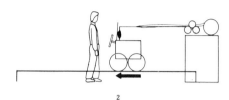

2

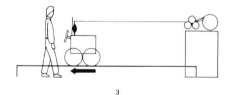

3

4

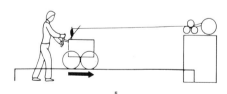

5

9 Spinning mule with the carriage rolled in, Toronto Carpet Manufacturing Company, 1928. This appears to be a 480-spindle mule. Parts of the fire protection system, fire buckets, and an overhead sprinkler system are clearly visible. This is a heavy timber mill-construction building.
National Film Board, B-66; National Archives of Canada, PA 800652

10   Mules with the carriage extended, Penmans Limited, 1930.
National Film Board, B-8; National Archives of Canada, PA 800604

11 Spools of carded roving that will be mounted on mules and spun, Renfrew Woollen Mills, Ontario, ca. 1947.
National Archives of Canada, PA 179685, Malak Collection, 926-9667

12 A worker at a spinning mule. Empty bobbins, ready to replace full ones, hang upside down at the front of the mule. Renfrew Woollen Mills, ca. 1947.
National Archives of Canada, PA 179684, Malak Collection, 926-9671

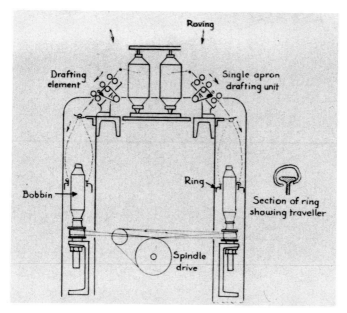

13 A ring spinning frame, ca. 1950. The roving passes through the drafting rollers, which draft (lengthen) the roving. The roving is then guided around the traveller by the ring at speeds of up to 10 000 rpm; this spins the roving into yarn. As the yarn passes through the ring it is wound onto the bobbin, which moves up and down through the ring so as to distribute the yarn evenly.

Adapted from J.R. Dunkerley, "Textiles: Cotton," in K.C. Livingston and T.C. Graham, *Manufacturing Processes in Canada* (Toronto: University of Toronto Press, 1960), p. 240; National Library of Canada, NL 16979

14 Ring spinning machines built by Platt Brothers of Oldham, Great Britain. These were designed to spin warp thread. Mount Royal mill, 1929.
National Film Board, B-42; National Archives of Canada, PA 800634

15 Warping machines at the Verdun, Quebec, mill of Dominion Textile, 1929.
Yarn from about 450 spools was wound onto the warp beam (foreground), which
was then mounted in a loom.
National Film Board, B-20; National Archives of Canada, PA 800616

16 Two drawers-in are threading the warp threads from the beam behind the operator in the foreground through the heddles of a loom prior to beginning weaving, ca. 1940.
National Film Board, WRM 1595; National Archives of Canada, PA 160566

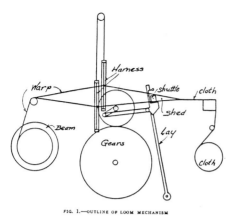

FIG. 1.—OUTLINE OF LOOM MECHANISM

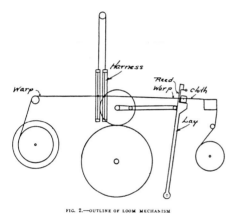

FIG. 2.—OUTLINE OF LOOM MECHANISM

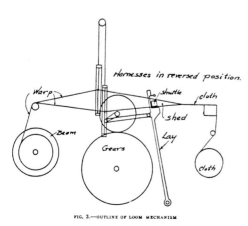

FIG. 3.—OUTLINE OF LOOM MECHANISM

17 Schematic diagram of the operation of a loom.

Fig. 1: "Shuttle at near end of lay in position for 'pick,' which sends it through 'shed' formed by warp threads above and below. Shuttle-throwing device not shown. Note position of harnesses. Every alternate warp thread passes through one harness, the remainder through the other harness. Thus each harness lifts half the warp."

Fig. 2: "Lay in forward position, forcing the thread left by the shuttle into position as one of the crosswise threads of the cloth. This is done by the 'reed,' which is a fine comb on the lay. One thread of the warp passes through each space of the reed. Harnesses are just passing each other in their exchange of position."

Fig. 3: "Shuttle at far end of lay in position for return trip through shed. Note that threads which were above in first position are now below, and vice versa. This is accomplished by reversal of harnesses."

Albert Walton, "Electric Drive for Weaving Machinery," *Cassier's Magazine*, July 1909, pp. 252–53

18   Weave room at Montreal Cotton, Valleyfield, Quebec, ca. 1940. These are Draper automatic looms with circular magazines holding bobbins of yarn that are automatically loaded into the shuttles. The looms are driven by individual electric motors.
National Film Board, WRM 1596; National Archives of Canada, PA 160558

19 Burling. After cloth was woven it was inspected and minor faults were repaired. Renfrew Woollen Mills, Ontario, ca. 1947.
National Archives of Canada, PA 179683, Malak Collection, 926-9728

20 Circular knitting machines in Mercury Mills Limited, Hamilton, Ontario, 1929. The Mercury mill, built in 1916–17, was a reinforced-concrete mill; this allowed the walls to be entirely devoted to window space. Although the mill used electric power, the profusion of belts indicate that it had not yet adopted individual drive.
National Film Board, B-56; National Archives of Canada, PA 800644

43

21 Printing machines at Dominion Textile's Magog, Quebec, mill, 1929.
National Film Board, B-32; National Archives of Canada, PA 800625

Homespun Cloth Production

The production of textiles in Canada predates European contact. West Coast native cultures have produced woven textiles for use as clothing for several millennia using the inner bark of the cedar as their principal fibre. Mountain-goat wool and dog hair were also used as raw material. Spinning was done using a spindle and weaving was done on a vertical loom. Particular individuals or families specialized in cloth production. There is little evidence that other native cultures made extensive use of textiles although blankets made from strips of woven fur were common.[1]

European immigrants produced cloth from the earliest years of settlement. A Quebec inventory of 1657 mentions both coarse and fine hemp cloth of local manufacture. Talon, the intendant, from 1665 to 1672 encouraged both weaving and spinning, and when he left the colony he boasted that "l'habitant pouvait se vêtir des pieds à la tête avec les productions du pays."[2] About 1700 Mme. Legardeur de Repentigny established a workshop in Montréal where she employed a number of weavers who produced linen, woollen, and hemp cloth.[3]

The earliest cloth produced in New France was made from hemp or flax. Although woollen cloth might have been more suitable for the climate, there were few sheep in New France until the 1720s and most woollen cloth was imported. Homespun woollen or linen-wool combinations became more common in the late eighteenth century and hemp cloth became rarer. During the nineteenth century, Quebec home weavers produced about two yards of woollen cloth for every yard of linen.[4]

In spite of the evidence of cloth manufacturing in Canada from the early years of New France, home spinning and weaving were probably not as common in the seventeenth and early eighteenth centuries as tradition (which is based mostly on nineteenth-century experience) suggests.[5] No solid evidence of the extent of domestic production of cloth is available prior to the 1827 census of Lower Canada, but there is evidence in estate inventories that by the beginning of the nineteenth century most urban families dressed in clothes made from imported cloth. Most rural families in the Québec City area owned spinning wheels and about 40 per cent had looms, but even these families produced only about half of the cloth they used; the remainder was imported.[6]

Even less is known of early home spinning and weaving in Ontario and the Maritime provinces. In both areas domestic textile production probably dates from the last half of the eighteenth century and was well established by the early nineteenth century. By 1851 Nova Scotia and New Brunswick produced more cloth per capita, 4.08 and 3.21 yards, than Quebec, 2.82

yards.[7] Ontario produced only 1.83 yards of homespun cloth per capita in 1851 and its production was declining. Presumably Ontario homespinners and weavers found it increasingly unrewarding to compete with mass-produced goods from Canadian and foreign factories. Although there was a revival of home spinning and weaving in Québec in the 1860s and 1870s, it was short lived and by 1900, homespun cloth production was so insignificant that the census ceased to report it.

The popular image of homespun cloth production is of a farmer shearing his sheep and his wife and daughters carding, spinning, and finally weaving wool into cloth. The entire operation was carried out on the farm by members of the farm family. For the eighteenth century it is probable that this image is accurate, but by the early nineteenth century some of the more labour-intensive stages of woollen and linen production were being done commercially outside the home. Carding and fulling were the first processes to be done commercially. In 1827 there were 91 carding and 79 fulling mills in operation in Lower Canada; by 1842 there were 186 carding mills and 144 fulling mills in Canada West. The 1851 census showed similar establishments in Nova Scotia and New Brunswick. By 1871 the Canadian census listed scutching mills (35) and dyeing and scouring mills (35) as well as 650 carding and fulling mills.[8] When these mills were first established is not known, but it is probable that a few were in existence at the end of the eighteenth century; there was a fulling and carding mill at Sherbrooke, Lower Canada, in 1805, and the earl of Selkirk noted three fulling mills in the Kingston-Napanee area in 1803.[9] The mills served local markets and were generally small; in 1851 the average mill employed less than two persons.[10] Some of the early mills operated in conjunction with grist or saw mills; others expanded from simple carding operations to become fully integrated mills with spinning, weaving, and finishing capabilities.

The Rosamond Woollen Company of Almonte, Ontario, is an example of such an evolution. James Rosamond established a grist and saw mill at Carleton Place during the 1830s. He soon added carding and fulling facilities to his mill, and in 1846 he established an integrated woollen mill. Subsequently he moved his main operation to Almonte, where his sons expanded it.[11] By the 1870s the Rosamond Woollen Company had become one of the leading Canadian woollen mills.

As home spinning and weaving declined, the small carding and fulling mills expanded their services and became woollen mills, converted to other purposes, or closed down. The decline of the custom carding and fulling industry was gradual. The 1911 census listed 38 wool carding and fulling establishments that employed five or more hands; it did not list the smaller mills, nor would it have listed grist mills and sawmills that did custom carding as sidelines. Some small carding mills continued to operate until quite recently. The Wile carding mill in Bridgewater, Nova Scotia, was built in 1860, was busiest in the 1880s, and did not close until 1968 although for many years it had been operating on a part-time basis.[12] It is now a part of the Nova Scotia Provincial Museum system.

Weaving could also be contracted out of the home to professional weavers. The weavers worked in their own homes or shops and produced cloth and blankets to order. They used both wool and linen; in some cases they used yarn supplied by their customers, in others they purchased yarn. The 1851 census reported that there were 1738 professional weavers in Ontario and 166 in Quebec; some of these, perhaps 15 per cent, may have been employed as weavers in woollen factories, but most worked in their own homes or shops. (In 1851, 786 hands were employed in woollen factories; of these about one-third might have been weavers.) Detailed information on the number of home weavers in the Maritime provinces in 1851 is not available, but there were 5475 hand looms in New Brunswick and 11 096 in Nova Scotia in 1851. As late as 1891, when competition from both woollen and cotton mills might have been expected to have thinned the ranks of the independent hand-weavers, the census still listed 2445 weavers working in 2085 establishments in Canada. Given the average size of the establishments, it is clear that these were home or cottage weavers. In rural areas, cottage weavers continued to work well into the twentieth century, producing specialized traditional items such as coverlets.

Although it is clear that home weavers performed valuable service in their communities, it is difficult to evaluate this service during most of the nineteenth century because of omissions and inconsistencies in the census record. However, recent studies of manuscript schedules of the 1871 census suggest that at that time, 78 per cent (by monetary value) of the woollen and cotton cloth produced in Nova Scotia was produced by home weavers; in New Brunswick the figure was 60 per cent, in Quebec it was 58 per cent, and in Ontario it was only 16 per cent. Clearly home production was important in some areas; nationally, it is probable that about 53 per cent of all cloth produced in Canada in 1870 was produced in factories.[13]

Early Growth

The evolution of the woollen industry from small-scale domestic production to large-scale factory production was gradual and incremental. Traditionally it has been accepted that the first integrated woollen mill in Canada was built by Mahlon Willette at L'Acadie, Lower Canada, in 1826. It was moved to Chambly in 1830, and Willette's son operated a mill there until the end of the century.[1] However, there is evidence that Joseph Atwood converted a carding mill at Magog to a woollen mill in 1825–26; whether this was an integrated mill with spinning and weaving is not clear. Charles Goodhue built a combined sawmill, grist mill, and woollen mill at Sherbrooke in 1827; the Goodhue mill was either on or adjacent to the site of the Paton Manufacturing Company mill, which was the largest woollen mill in Canada in the later nineteenth century.[2] The first woollen mill in Upper Canada was thought to have been the Barber brothers' mill built at Georgetown in 1837 and moved to Streetsville in 1844, but a cursory survey of newspaper advertisements has produced at least two earlier mills: at Earnestown in 1828 and at Gananoque in 1832.[3] There is also evidence that James Crooks had a woollen mill at Crook's Hollow in West Flamborough as early as 1822, and there may have been a mill in the Village of St. John in the Short Hills in 1827. George Ball built a carding and fulling mill at Glen Elgin on Twenty Mile Creek (about eight miles west of St. Catharines, Ontario) in 1824. In 1827 he expanded the mill to include the manufacture of woollen cloth.[4] Very little is known of early mills in the Maritime provinces. An article in the *Canadian Journal of Fabrics* in 1887 stated that there was a woollen mill at Kingston, New Brunswick, in 1830.[5] The 1826 Nova Scotia *Blue Book* reported that coarse woollens were manufactured in the colony, but it did not say whether they were produced in factories or by home weavers.[6]

It is unclear when non-human power was introduced into the woollen mills. It is probable that in the early mills, carding and fulling equipment were powered, while spinning and weaving equipment were hand operated. The equipment in the Willette mill consisted of one small carding machine, a slubbing billy (which converted strips of carded wool to rovings), a 75-spindle spinning jenny, and two hand looms.[7] Of these only the carding engine was adaptable to power driving. The Barber brothers installed power looms at their Georgetown mill in 1840. The Lomas or Sherbrooke woollen mill, which began operation in 1843 and was rebuilt in 1846, was completely powered in 1851. Whether the equipment in the 1843 mill was powered is not certain although one source identifies the Lomas mill as the first water-powered mill in the Eastern Townships.[8]

22 A woollen mill at Sherbrooke, Quebec, owned by the British American Land Company, 1836. This is probably the mill established by Charles Goodhue in 1827.
"Woollen Factory, Sherbrooke...," hand-coloured lithograph from *British American Land Company Views in Lower Canada, 1836*; National Archives of Canada, C 6339

By mid-century the woollen industry was well established. The 1851 census reported 74 woollen factories and 147 carding and fulling mills in Canada West. For Canada East the comparable figures were 18 and 193. For the Maritime colonies information on weaving and carding mills was combined; there were 81 in Nova Scotia and 52 in New Brunswick. Some of the important firms that would become leaders in the industry had made a start by the 1850s. The Lomas mill at Sherbrooke, the Barber brothers' mill at Streetsville, and the Rosamond mills in Carleton Place and Almonte have already been mentioned. The woollen industry grew slowly through the 1850s; the number of woollen mills increased, but the number of carding and fulling mills declined. Growth was more rapid in the 1860s, and by 1871 there were 270 woollen factories employing 4453 hands and 650 carding

23 The Barber brothers' woollen mill at Streetsville, Ontario, 1873. The mill was established in 1843, burned in 1862, and was immediately rebuilt.
Canadian Illustrated News, 15 March 1873, p. 165; National Archives of Canada, C 59055

and fulling mills with 1215 hands. The carding and fulling industry peaked in the 1870s and declined through the 1880s and 1890s, but woollen manufacturing continued to grow until the 1890s, when there were more than seven thousand Canadians employed in 377 woollen mills.

Although the woollen sector continued to grow during the 1870s and 1880s, it was losing its market share to the cotton sector, and during the 1890s both employment and value of production in the cotton group of industries surpassed figures in the woollen group. Equally important, foreign suppliers, primarily British, increased their share of the woollen market from 52 per cent in 1870 to 55 per cent in 1900 (*see* Table 9). The introduction of British preference in 1897 was a devastating blow to an already weakened woollen industry, and during the first decade of the twentieth century, employment in the sector fell by 17 per cent (*see* Table 1).

Because cotton could not be grown in Canada there was no tradition of domestic production of cotton cloth although home weavers sometimes used imported cotton warp thread. With this minor exception the history of cotton manufacture in Canada begins with the construction of two small mills at Chambly and Sherbrooke, Lower Canada, in 1844. Initially the Chambly mill only produced cotton bats, but by 1846 it was producing 800 yards of cloth per day. The Sherbrooke mill, with 1000 or 1200 spindles, produced about 1000 yards of cloth per day. It also had a number of knitting machines and produced hosiery and underclothing.[9] Nothing is known of the subsequent history of the Chambly mill, but the Sherbrooke mill operated successfully until it burned about 1854.[10]

A mill was established at Thorold on the Welland Canal in 1847. The mill operated for several years, but suffered from a lack of skilled labour, experience, and capital. It closed in the early 1850s and burned in 1864.[11] (The site has been marked by the Ontario government with a plaque identifying it as the first cotton mill in Ontario.)

In 1853 Frederick Warren Harris, an American textile manufacturer from Middlebury, Vermont, built a cotton mill below the Saint-Gabriel locks on the Lachine Canal. In 1856 he added a wadding and batting mill. By 1861 he employed 68 hands and produced over $174 000 worth of goods. Although Harris died in 1863, the mill continued to operate as Wood, Dunlop and Company until 1875.[12]

There was a small boom in mill construction during the early years of the American Civil War. The Lybster Cotton Company built a mill at Merritton, Ontario, in 1860; two mills were built in 1861, one at Dundas, Ontario, and one at Saint John, New Brunswick. The Saint John mill, built by William Parks, was the first cotton mill to be built in the Maritimes. A fourth mill was built at Hastings, Ontario, but it was closed about 1872 and the business moved to Cornwall. In addition to these mills and the Harris mill in Montréal, there were four small mills operating in central Canada at the time of the 1861 census. Nothing is known of these smaller mills; they may have only produced yarn or batting.

The period between the American Civil War and the introduction of the National Policy in 1879 was one of retrenchment and then slow growth; two mills were built in Cornwall, one in Montréal, and one in Salaberry-de-Valleyfield during the early 1870s. The period of slow growth ended in 1879 when the tariff on imported cottons (and woollens) was raised substantially. Between 1879 and 1885 a total of 18 mills was built, 5 in Quebec, 6 in Ontario, 4 in New Brunswick, and 3 in Nova Scotia.

This great burst of building activity created much of the physical plant in which the cotton sector was to operate until after the Second World War. Of the 18 mills built between 1879 and 1885, at least 10 were still in use in 1950, as were 3 of the mills built in the early 1870s and William Parks's Saint John mill built in 1861. The mills had been extended and renovated, and new mills had been built, but the basic framework of the cotton sector was established between 1879 and 1885.

The growth of the cotton sector in the 1880s had a dramatic effect on the textile industry in Canada. In 1870 Canada had imported cotton goods valued at $9 208 000 and had manufactured cotton goods valued at $782 000; by 1890, cotton imports had risen to $4 236 000 and domestic production had climbed to $9 127 000 (*see* Table 9). Employment in the cotton textile sector rose from 745 (3 per cent of all employees in the textile group) in 1871 to 8734 (12 per cent of the textile group) in 1891. Over the decade of the 1890s, cotton replaced woollens as the most important sector within the primary textile industry, a position it held until after the Second World War.

Hand-powered knitting machines were invented in the sixteenth century and were widely used in cottage industries. The first known use of them in Canada is at Montréal's Hôtel Dieu, where a number of knitting machines were installed about 1720.[13] Nothing further is known about knitting in an industrial setting until the middle of the nineteenth century. As has already been noted, the cotton mill built at Sherbrooke in 1844 had several knitting machines. There were also a number of knitting machines in the Lomas mill at Sherbrooke in the 1840s,[14] but there is no mention of knitting mills in the 1851 census. The 1861 census reported two mills in Ontario with a combined annual production of $20 500; there were none in Quebec. Although it is not reported in the 1861 census, there was, at Ancaster, Ontario, a mill that used powered knitting machines and spun its own yarn. W.E. Adams was associated with the mill; he had begun the manufacture of drawers and hosiery in Belleville in 1857 and in 1867 he moved to Paris, Ontario, where he formed a partnership with John Penman.[15] The firm ultimately became the Penman Manufacturing Company, the largest knitting firm in Canada. Stanfield's Limited of Truro, Nova Scotia, is another knitting firm with roots in the mid-nineteenth century. C.E. Stanfield had a textile mill in Prince Edward Island in the 1850s. In 1882 he built a weaving and knitting mill at Truro, Nova Scotia; in 1906 his sons incorporated the firm as Stanfield's Limited.[16]

In 1871 the knitting sector was still very small, with only 245 employees, all but one of whom were in Ontario. In the 1870s it grew rapidly and although it continued to grow in the 1880s and 1890s, it remained a small industry in comparison to both the cotton and woollen sectors. Its most dramatic growth occurred during the years 1900–1930 when employment and production figures in knitting doubled those in woollens and rivalled those in cottons.

The silk and synthetic sector in Canada is largely a twentieth-century phenomenon. Belding Brothers of New York established a small plant in Montréal in 1876, and in 1884, as Belding Paul and Company, the firm built a large mill on the Lachine Canal. At about the same time it absorbed the short-lived Corriveau Silk Mills, which had operated in both Montréal and Saint-Jean, Quebec. In 1889 the Corticelli Silk Mills, a branch of the Nonotuck Silk Company of New York, built a mill in Saint-Jean, Quebec. The Belding and Corticelli firms, which merged in 1911, constituted almost the entire Canadian silk sector until the First World War. Although Belding Paul produced some silk cloth in the 1880s and 1890s, the Canadian sector concentrated on the production of braids, laces, ribbons, and sewing thread until the 1920s.[17]

The homespun production of linen cloth dates from the seventeenth century in Canada, but there was no known attempt to industrialize the process before 1850. In 1851 M.B. Perine established a flax scutching mill at Doon in Waterloo County. During the 1850s he exported flax straw and tow to mills in the United States. In 1862 Perine began to spin linen twine and cordage; later in the decade he installed looms and manufactured sacking.[18] The expansion may have been in response to the cotton famine and consequent rise in prices caused by the American Civil War. Other entrepreneurs were also attracted to the linen industry. George Stephen of Montréal and a group of associates invested in a linen mill at Preston, Ontario, and the distillers Gooderham and Worts backed Perine in establishing a mill at Streetsville. The Preston mill produced linen duck, bags, sheeting, towelling, rope, and twine; the Streetsville mill concentrated on bagging. Neither mill survived the fall in prices after the the war.[19] Shortly after the turn of the century there was another attempt to establish a linen industry in Canada, but although some of the firms established in this second wave were modest successes, linen manufacture failed to become a major factor in the Canadian textile industry. Linen production was a labour-intensive industry: until after World War I the flax used in linen production had to be pulled by hand, and Canadian agricultural labour was too expensive to allow Canadian manufacturers to compete with low-wage producers.[20]

The flax industry, as opposed to the linen industry, survived the slump at the end of the civil war. Perine's firm, the Doon Twine and Cordage Company, and a number of competitors produced tow for sale to American and Canadian upholstery firms and manufactured twine and cordage. The industry was concentrated in central and western Ontario; in 1891, 1406 of the 1409 employees in Canadian flax mills worked between Toronto and Windsor. The flax industry seems to have peaked in the 1890s; employment declined by about 16 per cent over the next decade and remained stagnant for a decade after that.[21]

Important as the secondary branches of the textile industry were during the nineteenth century, the garment trades continued to employ more than 50 per cent of all labour in the textile industry until at least 1911. A large part of this labour was employed in tailor shops in the production of custom-made clothes, but in the last half of the nineteenth century the increasing popularity of ready-made clothing resulted in more and more garment workers being employed in factories or in their own homes, as part of a putting-out system.

Crisis and Consolidation

The boom in the years 1879–85 resulted in a cotton-sector crisis that was not resolved until the 1890s. The first years of the boom were profitable, especially for established companies, but as the production from the new mills appeared, the market was glutted.[1] The capacity of the Canadian industry increased from approximately 30 million yards of cotton in 1877 to 135 million yards in 1883. Over the same period imports declined from about 73 million yards to 65 million yards. As a result of the expansion there was a potential for 200 million yards of cotton, or 45 yards per capita, being put on the market at a time when experts estimated the normal Canadian consumption was about 30 yards per capita.[2]

The surplus was about equal to imports, but Canadian mills were in no position to drive imports out of the market. In general, Canadian mills were only equipped to produce basic cotton or grey cloth. They did not have the equipment to produce more-finished cloth, and it was this area that was dominated by imports. In addition, the large English and American mills were both willing and able to dump goods on the Canadian market if such action was necessary to preserve their market share.[3]

The position of the cotton mills was further complicated by the fact that, just as most of the mills came into production in 1883–84, the economy was moving from a period of growth to a recession.

During 1882–83 the trade journals were replete with notices of mills operating on short time, closing down completely for weeks or months, or in some cases, failing. Publicly traded cotton companies' stocks, which had been at a premium, fell to less than 50 cents on the dollar in 1884 and 1885.[4] The most dramatic development was the near-failure of D. Morrice, Sons and Company of Montréal. Morrice was the agent for 36 cotton, woollen, and knitting mills including some of the most important in each field. In order to keep the mills operating as the recession deepened in 1882–85, Morrice continued to advance money to the mills against their deliveries of cloth. By November 1883 he had advanced $1 million to cotton mills and $500 000 to woollen mills, but was unable to continue and was forced into receivership. He was only saved from bankruptcy when the Bank of Montreal agreed to further advances on condition that the mills he represented be run at one-third capacity.[5]

Even before Morrice's suspension the need to reduce production and to diversify had been realized. In September Morrice, in company with Andrew Gault of Gault Brothers, organized the Canadian Cotton Manufacturers' Association. The members of the association agreed to reduce production by shutting their mills for two days each week and to diversify their production.[6] The agreement was weakened by Morrice's failure and had collapsed by May of 1884, when grey cotton manufacturers were reported to have reached a new agreement. The 1884 agreement failed in March 1885 and another combination was formed in the summer of 1886. The 1886 combination was more successful and lasted, with some defections, until 1888–89.[7]

The sector also managed to diversify its product. In 1884 the Magog Textile and Print Company began operation of the first cotton-printing factory in Canada. The mill converted low-value grey cottons into high-value prints. It was expected to produce 15 million yards of print annually, thereby taking roughly 10 to 15 per cent of the grey cotton produced in Canada out of the market.[8] Much of this advantage was lost when the Magog mill began weaving its own cloth in 1888.[9]

In 1887 the sector opened new markets by shipping cloth to China via the new railway. Between 1887 and 1898 Canada shipped about 2.3 million pounds of cottons annually to China. Much of the cloth was produced at the Montmorency Cotton Company mill that was built in 1889 specifically to produce for the China market, but a proportion was supplied by other mills.[10]

All of these measures restored some profitability to the stronger cotton mills. The Hochelaga Cotton Manufacturing Company paid a six-per-cent dividend in 1885 and ten-per-cent dividends from 1886 to 1888. The Montreal Cotton Company resumed dividends in 1887.[11] Some of the weaker companies only survived — William Parks's Saint John mills closed for two years in the mid-1880s and were never far from bankruptcy.[12] From 1883 the St. Croix Cotton Manufacturing Company operated under the direction of a creditor's committee and was eventually sold at a loss.[13] The Ontario Cotton Mills Company in Hamilton and the Magog Textile and Print Company in Quebec failed in 1889, and the Coaticook Cotton Company mill closed in 1890.[14]

By 1890 the Canadian Cotton Manufacturers' Association had failed again as an instrument to control prices and production. Its principal organizers, Gault and Morrice, decided to achieve the same end through takeovers. In 1889 the Hochelaga Cotton Manufacturing Company, of which Gault was president, bought the Magog Textile and Print Company for about half of its original cost.[15] In 1890 the Hochelaga Cotton Manufacturing Company was sold to the Dominion Cotton Mills Company, which had been organized by Gault and Morrice. At the same time Dominion Cotton bought seven grey-cloth mills in Halifax, Coaticook, Brantford, Chambly, Moncton, Windsor, Nova Scotia, and Kingston, Ontario. Because of the weakness of the mills outside the Montréal area, Dominion Cotton was able to acquire them for about half of their original cost.[16]

24 Andrew Frederic Gault, 1833–1903. Born in Ireland, Gault emigrated to Canada with his family and formed the wholesale dry-goods firm of Gault Brothers and Company. He was involved in the formation of the Stormont Cotton Company (1870), the Hudon Cotton Mills Company (1873), the Montreal Cotton Company (1874), and the St. Ann Spinning Company (1882). By 1885 he was president of all four. In 1890 and 1892 he and David Morrice merged 15 cotton mills to form two companies, Dominion Cotton Mills and Canadian Coloured Cotton Mills. During the 1890s he was known as the "Cotton King"; at his death in 1903 he was working on the merger that became Dominion Textile.
E.J. Chambers, *The Book of Montreal* (Montréal: n.p., 1903), p. 8; National Library of Canada, NL 17007

25 David Morrice, ca. 1831–1914. Morrice emigrated from Scotland to Canada in 1855 and established D. Morrice and Company of Montréal, manufacturers' agents and general merchants. By 1883 the firm represented 36 Canadian cotton, woollen, and knitting mills. In the recession it nearly failed but was rescued. Over the next decade Morrice worked with Andrew Gault to limit production and competition in the textile industry. He and Gault organized Dominion Cotton Mills and Canadian Coloured Cotton Mills; after 1897 Morrice became president of Canadian Coloured Cotton. From 1882 he was a director of Penman Manufacturing; in 1906 he became president.
Notman Photographic Archives, McCord Museum of Canadian History, 17,738-I

In 1892 Gault and Morrice completed their consolidation of the cotton sector by forming the Canadian Coloured Cotton Mills Company and buying the St. Croix mill in Milltown, New Brunswick, the Merritton and Lybster mills in Merritton, the Canada and Stormont mills in Cornwall, the Ontario mill in Hamilton, and the Dundas mill in Dundas. These mills were also purchased for about half of their original value.[17]

The formation of Canadian Coloured Cotton gave Gault and Morrice control of about 86 per cent of the capacity of the Canadian cotton industry.[18] In addition to the mills controlled by Dominion Cotton and Canadian Coloured Cotton, Gault controlled the huge Montreal Cotton Company mills at Valleyfield and the Montmorency Cotton Company. As well, Canadian Coloured Cotton had a marketing agreement by which it controlled the output of the Hamilton Cotton Company and the Gibson mill at Marysville.[19] The only large mills that remained outside Gault and Morrice's control were the Merchants mill in Montréal, the Yarmouth Duck and Yarn Company mill, and the two mills controlled by William Parks and Son in Saint John.

The first years of the 1890s were prosperous for the combine. It was able to have mills specialize in certain lines, to re-equip some of the older mills, and to close down the least efficient. About 1894, profits began to decline partly as a result of over-expansion and partly as a result of foreign competition. There was also increased domestic competition after 1897, when Morrice and Gault split; Gault kept control of Dominion Cotton, Morrice took over Canadian Coloured Cotton. In 1899 Canada lost its Chinese export market and the Montmorency mill, which had been export oriented, began to compete directly in the Canadian market. The introduction of British preference in 1897 further increased competition, and in 1901 Dominion Cotton missed a dividend for the first time since its formation. In 1902 the company had to go to its directors for operating expenses.[20]

In 1903 Gault died and was replaced as president of Dominion Cotton by L.J. Forget, a Montréal stockbroker and a major figure in the Canadian merger movement in the years 1905–10.[21] Before his death Gault and others had been working on plans for further mergers in the sector; Forget developed these plans and in 1905 organized the Dominion Textile Company. The new firm included all of the holdings of Dominion Cotton, the Merchants Cotton Company and the Montmorency Cotton Company, and the Colonial Bleaching and Printing Company; this was equivalent to about 43 per cent of the total capacity of the cotton sector.[22] In addition Dominion Textile maintained a close relationship with Montreal Cotton. Together the two firms continued to account for about 50 per cent of sales until the Second World War. Canadian Coloured Cotton (reorganized in 1910 as Canadian Cottons Limited) accounted for about 17 per cent, Wabasso for about 9 per cent, and the remaining production was distributed among five smaller firms.[23]

During the late 1870s and 1880s the cotton industry had been the most dynamic sector in Canadian manufacturing; the consolidations of 1890 and 1892 marked the passing of the dynamism. They also marked the weakening of independent regional branches of the cotton industry. The formation of Dominion Textile further weakened the regional branches of the cotton industry as Dominion Textile gradually concentrated its operations in Quebec. By the early 1930s its mills in Halifax and Windsor, Nova Scotia, Moncton, New Brunwick, and Kingston, Ontario, had all been sold or closed.

The consolidation movement also accentuated a tendency for the technical management of mills to be separated from the financial/policy management and for management to be separated from ownership. This split was evident as early as 1888 when A.F. Gault, president of the Hochelaga Cotton Manufacturing Company, testified before the Royal Commission on the Relations of Labour and Capital that he would never interfere in matters of discipline, which were the responsibility of the manager.[24] Chief executive officers such as Gault, David Morrice, and Charles Gordon, vice-president, president, and chairman of Dominion Textile from 1905 to 1939, had most of their experience in the dry-goods business and had little first-hand experience in operating textile mills. Perhaps the split between technical and financial management in the large cotton companies was result of their large capital requirements. The tendency towards separation of financial and technical management seems to have been less marked in the woollen and knit-goods sectors, where capital requirements were less. Several important firms — Stanfield's of Truro, Nova Scotia, Rosamond of Almonte, and Galt Knitting of Galt, Ontario — survived for three or more generations under the active management of the same family, and one may assume that management had working knowledge of the industry even if it did not actively manage at a technical level.

Although a full record of share ownership is not available, it is probable that financial management of the larger firms was also separated from legal ownership during the period of corporate concentration. It seems unlikely, for example, that A.F. Gault was ever a majority shareholder in the firms he directed. In 1897, just before he gave up the presidency of Canadian Coloured Cotton, Gault and his relatives controlled about 3000 shares out of about 27 000 shares outstanding; D. Morrice, who succeeded him as president, controlled 2100.[25] In 1901, when Gault was president of the Montreal Cotton Company, his family controlled slightly over 11 per cent of the outstanding shares.[26] After its early years, ownership of Dominion Textile was quite widely dispersed: of 69 406 shares outstanding in 1919, Sir Charles Gordon, the president, held 200; Sir Herbert Holt, vice-president, held 1233; F.G. Daniels, general manager, had 470. The largest single block, 2750 shares, was held by a director, W.A. Black.[27]

Both the woollen and knitting sectors in the later nineteenth century have attracted less attention from historians than has the cotton sector. In part the interest in the cotton sector may be traced to its apparent positive relationship with the National Policy. Equally the neglect of both the woollen and knitting sectors may be a result of the diversity of the sectors and the lack of a strong centralizing movement in them; both of these factors make the history of the woollen and knitting sectors difficult to research and write. Whatever the reason, the detailed history of the woollen and knitting sectors in the later nineteenth century remains to be written. What follows is necessarily tentative.

Although there was some growth in the woollen sector following the introduction of the National Policy in 1879, growth during the 1880s appears to have been slower than it was during the 1870s. (It is difficult to be certain of growth rates because the 1881 census apparently included home weavers in the woollen-sector statistics whereas the 1871 and 1891 censuses did not.) The industry as it emerged in the 1880s consisted of a few large companies such as the Rosamond, Paton, Cobourg, and Cornwall companies, which produced for the national market, and many smaller firms, which produced for local markets. All of the firms, but especially the small ones, faced problems that grew more serious towards the end of the century. Many of the small mills produced coarse, heavy, strong cloth similar to the homespun that it was displacing. When tastes changed and the market demanded finer woollen cloth and worsteds, the smaller mills were unable to adapt to the changes both because they lacked the capital and because locally produced wool was not suited to finer woollens. Successful mills imported more and more of their raw material and as a result came into competition with British and American producers. In spite of the tariff protection, these foreign producers often sold cloth on the Canadian market at prices that Canadian producers with shorter production runs could not match. In addition to competing in the Canadian market for high-quality goods, British manufacturers produced a very cheap cloth, called shoddy, from recycled wool. Canadian manufacturers lacked both the technology and the large-scale operations that made shoddy production possible and economic. Finally, woollen manufacturers faced a shift from heavy woollens to lighter, finer woollens, to worsteds, and ultimately, to cottons. Between 1870 and 1900 the apparent annual per capita consumption of woollens declined from $4.76 to $3.35 (in constant dollars) compared with an increase in apparent consumption of cottons from $1.36 to $3.48 annually.[28]

In 1882–83 and 1888–89 the woollen sector suffered sharp recessions during which many mills closed temporarily or went on short hours. Some failed. The response to the recessions was the same as it had been in the cotton sector. In October 1883, representatives of the woollen and knit-goods sectors met in Toronto and agreed to restrict production; neither agreement lasted for more than a few months.[29] Over the next decade there were many other attempts to restrict production, but none were successful; the number of small independent firms in the industry made enforcement of agreements impossible. They also made diversification such as took place in the cotton industry difficult. Although the larger firms were able to convert some of their production to worsteds and fine woollens, the smaller firms lacked the capital, the expertise, and in some cases the initiative to convert their mills.[30] The great number of mills also made the takeover option, which had been successful in the cotton industry, difficult.

The only major attempt at combination in the woollen sector occurred in 1900 when six mills in Carleton Place, Lambton, Markham, Hespeler, and Waterloo were organized as the Canada Woollen Company. The firm was essentially Toronto based; W.R. Brock, a Toronto dry-goods wholesaler was president; the board included Timothy Eaton; Reuben Millchamp, a Toronto mill agent and president of the Maple Leaf Woollen Mills at Markham; A.W. Brodie, proprietor of the Brodie Mills at Hespeler; George Benson, a Montréal wool importer and president of the Hawthorne Woollen Manufacturing Company at Carleton Place; and John Morley, manager of the Waterloo Woollen Company.[31] With an authorized capital of $2 million and 46 sets of cards, the company was more than twice as large as its nearest competitors; it was not, however, large enough to dominate the industry and thereby restrict production. Initially it was planned to rationalize production among various plants, but this plan was never implemented and the firm failed in 1904.[32]

During the 1880s the woollen sector sought improved tariff protection and to a certain extent received it. In 1880 the average tariff on woollens was 26.8 per cent; by 1890 it had been increased to 28.7 per cent and by 1895 was 31.8 per cent (*see* Table 11). The election in 1896 of a government generally favourable to lower tariffs was a setback. Between 1897 and 1900 the government introduced a series of tariff measures, referred to as British or imperial preference, which reduced the tariff on British and some other goods by one-third.[33] By 1900–1901 the average tariff on woollens was down to 25.7 per cent; over the decade 1901–10, imports of woollens increased from $9.8 to $19.5 million (in constant dollars) while domestic manufactures declined from $8.2 to $7.7 million.[34] Although the government began to increase protection again in 1903–04, it was too late for many mills. Over the census period 1901–11, employment fell from 6795 to 4512 and 67 of 157 mills closed; significantly, this period of failure in the woollen sector occurred during a period of marked growth in the Canadian economy. The knit-goods sector surpassed the woollen sector both in terms of employment and value of production. Although the woollen industry recovered somewhat during World War I, employment in the industry did not regain 1890s levels until the Second World War. The introduction of British preference was not the sole cause of the decline of the industry, but it was a blow that crippled an already weak industry.

The knitting industry began on a very small scale in the 1840s and 1850s, and although it grew rapidly in absolute terms, it remained much smaller than either the woollen or the cotton sector. In 1901 hosiery and knitting employed 3687, woollens employed 7037, and cottons employed 11 954. The knitting sector's period of most rapid growth was between 1901 and 1930; by 1930 it employed 18 570 compared with 18 590 in cottons and 7710 in woollens.

In the nineteenth century the woollen and knitting sectors were closely linked. Many woollen mills operated knitting machines as well as looms. It also seems likely that wool was the major material used in producing hosiery and underwear in the nineteenth century. There is, however, no statistical record of raw materials used in the knitting industry until 1925, when wool and cotton were of about equal importance by weight; by value, wool was twice as important as cotton.[35] The close linkage made the transition from a woollen mill to a knitting mill relatively easy, and when woollen mills failed they were sometimes converted to knitting mills. For example, the two mills that the Canada Woollen Company owned in Carleton Place were reopened as knitting mills four years after the company failed.[36] Similarly, Penman Manufacturing, a major knitting firm, acquired the Saint-Hyacinthe plants of the Canadian Woollen Mills Company in 1903.[37]

The knit-goods sector experienced the same problems as the woollen and cotton sectors in the late nineteenth century and reacted much as the larger sectors did. When overcapacity in 1883 and 1884 threatened the industry, agreements to restrict production were made and broken.[38] When voluntary attempts to limit production failed, many weaker firms closed or were absorbed by stronger firms.

The Penman Manufacturing Company of Paris, Ontario, was a leader in this takeover movement. John Penman and W.E. Adams began the manufacture of knitted goods at Paris, Ontario, in 1868. In 1882 the Penman Manufacturing Company Limited was incorporated with a capital of $250 000. John Penman was the president and managing director. The board included investors from Hamilton and David Morrice of Montréal; W.E. Adams had retired from the firm and formed a new knitting company in Paris. In 1887 Penmans made its first acquisition, the Grand River Knitting Mills of Paris. In the next 20 years the firm purchased the Coaticook Knitting Company of Coaticook, the Peninsular Knitting Company of Thorold, the Norfolk Knitting Company of Port Dover, the Watson Manufacturing Company of St. Catharines, and the Canadian Woollen Mills Company of Saint-Hyacinthe.[39] In 1906 a Montréal syndicate, headed by members of Dominion Textile's board, David Yuile, Charles Gordon, and J.P. Black, bought control of Penman Manufacturing and reorganized it as Penmans Limited. The company was not absorbed by Dominion Textile, but it remained closely linked to the cotton sector through interlocking directorships for the next 60 years. David Morrice, who had been one of the incorporators in 1882 and whose firm had been Penman Manufacturing's selling agent, became president of Penmans Limited; at the same time he was president of Canadian Coloured Cotton and a director of Dominion Textile. On his death in 1914 he was succeeded by Charles Gordon, president of Dominion Textile, who in turn was succeeded by F.G. Daniels, also president of Dominion Textile. On Daniels's death in 1933 R.B. Morrice, the son of David, became president. In 1965 Penmans became a wholly owned subsidiary of Dominion Textile.[40]

At the time it was taken over by the Montréal syndicate, Penmans was the largest knitting firm in Canada. It was not the only example of corporate concentration in the knit-goods and hosiery sector. For example, in 1906 Puritan Knitting Mills was organized in Toronto. In 1911 it was reorganized as York Knitting Mills and by 1928 it owned the former Zimmerknit plant in Hamilton and Harvey Knitting Company and Hosiers Limited, both of Woodstock, Ontario.[41] In spite of a trend towards concentration, ownership in the sector remained more dispersed than it did in the cotton sector. In 1938, 11 firms accounted for 70.2 per cent of sales in the knit-goods branch; Penmans alone accounted for 17.8 per cent of sales, but this was not a sufficient share to allow it to control the market. In the hosiery branch of the industry one firm, Julius Kayser and Company of Sherbrooke, accounted for 20.2 per cent of sales; eight other firms accounted for 52.7 per cent of sales.[42]

Although the woollen and knit-goods sectors had a number of characteristics in common, the former was near collapse by the end of the nineteenth century while the latter was entering its period of greatest growth. Precisely why the knitting industry flourished while the woollen industry languished is not clear. It seems likely that the reasons were not specific to the Canadian industry; a similar decline in the American woollen industry took place over the same period.[43] Changing styles favoured knitting. In the 1860s the knitting industry was largely confined to the production of hosiery, but by the 1890s, knitted undergarments began to replace woven flannels. After the turn of the century there was an increased market for knitted outerwear, sweaters, sports clothes, and similar items.[44] Per capita consumption of woollens, in constant dollars, declined between 1870 and 1910 at the same time as consumption of all textiles doubled (*see* Table 9). The rapid developments in knitting machinery, particularly after 1900, may also have contributed to the knitting sector's growth. Tariff treatment may also be important; a 1903 tariff revision that placed a surtax on imports of knitted goods from Germany has been described as "the first real impetus to the expansion and prosperity of the domestic knitting industry."[45]

The customs returns are not sufficiently detailed to permit careful comparison of the levels of protection given knit goods, woollens, and cottons; however, the general impression from the returns is that knit goods, especially after 1900, received at least the average level of protection of other woollens and cottons. Estimates of the apparent consumption of knit goods in Canada also indicate that imports formed a much smaller proportion of total consumption than they did for either woollens or cottons. (Estimates for 1889–1911 run about 22 per cent for knit goods compared to 35 per cent for all textiles.)[46] Knitting may also have benefited in competition with imports from being a low-wage industry; wages were about 86 per cent of wages in woollens.[47]

Causes of Growth:
Tariffs and Finances

Traditionally the rapid growth of the Canadian textile industry in the last half of the nineteenth century has been attributed to the protective tariff introduced by the Macdonald government in 1879. While the influence of the tariff was certainly important, at least two other major factors, the growth of the Canadian market and the availability of financing, aided the growth of the industry. In addition if one is to explain the growth of the textile industry, one must recognize that not all sectors of the industry performed equally. The cotton sector experienced extraordinary growth, but the woollen sector, which received virtually the same tariff treatment, grew slowly until the 1890s and then went into a period of decline. The knitting sector's period of most dramatic growth came after 1900.

Between 1870 and 1910 the Canadian population doubled. The apparent consumption of textile products increased fourfold. The value of production of the entire textile industry in Canada increased from $23 million to $112 million; the value of textile imports increased from $18 million to $64 million. (All figures are in constant dollars; *see* Table 9). The increase in consumption, with or without tariff protection, would have given the Canadian textile industry an opportunity for growth.

With the notable exception of the woollen sector, the domestic textile industry was able to increase its share of the growing market. Apparent consumption of all textile products increased from $41 million in 1870 to $174 million in 1910; imports declined from 45 per cent to 37 per cent of this total. The value of cotton manufactures increased six times between 1880, when the sector may be considered to have been fully established, and 1910. During the same period, imports of cotton manufactures increased 130 per cent but shrank from 68 to 43 per cent of apparent consumption. In the hosiery and knit-goods sector, production increased 866 per cent between 1880 and 1910 (*see* Table 3); most of this increase was in the last decade of the period when knit goods surpassed woollens in importance. The domestic knit-goods sector also increased its share of the market; imports declined from 32 to 20 per cent of apparent consumption between 1891 and 1911.[1] In contrast to the cotton and knit-goods sectors, the woollen sector performed very poorly. In constant (1900) dollars its production declined by 8 per cent between 1870 and 1910; during the same period, imports of woollen manufactures increased by 215 per cent. The woollen sector was a more mature industry in 1871 than was the cotton sector in 1881 and could not be expected to make the same relative progress; nevertheless, its failure to maintain its market share against foreign competitors, even though it received virtually the same protection as the cotton sector, suggests that factors other than tariff protection were important in the growth of the textile industry.

Discussion of the tariff in relation to the textile industry has focussed on the series of changes introduced by the Macdonald government between 1879 and 1887. There was, however, an earlier period of tariff adjustment. In the early 1850s the Province of Canada's tariff on manufactured woollens and cottons was 12.5 per cent; in 1856 it was increased to 15 per cent and in 1859 to 20 per cent, where it remained until 1866 (see Table 11). There was no specific rate for hosiery or knitted goods; they were treated as woollen or cotton manufactures. One woollen manufacturer credited the increased protection with increasing the demand and steadying the market for domestic woollen manufactures.[2] The increase may well have been a factor in the establishment of cotton mills at Saint John, New Brunswick, Dundas, Merritton, and Hastings in the 1860s. It has also been suggested that the mills were a result of the dislocations in the cotton industry caused by the American Civil War.[3]

American tariff policy also affected Canadian industry. Under reciprocity, raw wool had been admitted duty free to the United States. When the reciprocity treaty was abrogated in 1866, Canadian wool faced a high tariff and as a result the Canadian price of wool fell. This change, while harmful to Canadian wool producers, was a boon to Canadian woollen manufacturers.[4]

In 1866 the Province of Canada reduced the tariff on woollens and cottons to 15 per cent, at which level it remained until 1874, when the MacKenzie government raised it to 17.5 per cent. In spite of the lower tariff, four large cotton mills were built between 1870 and 1875. The woollen sector also experienced more rapid growth during the 1870s than in any subsequent decade.

The tariff changes that formed part of the National Policy were introduced between 1879 and 1887. The changes raised the average tariff on both cotton and woollen manufactures from 17.5 per cent in 1878 to 28.7 per cent on woollens and 29.6 per cent on cottons in 1890. Selected categories received a higher level of protection, often through a combination of fixed and ad valorem rates. In 1890 the higher rates were on finished clothing including most of the products of the knitting sector. Cotton clothing was generally charged 35 per cent; cotton shirts, 49.5 per cent; and cotton socks and stockings, 37.8 per cent. Ready-made woollen clothing was charged between 32 and 34 per cent, and woollen or worsted socks and stockings, 40 per cent. Knitted shirts, drawers, and hosiery were charged 27.9 per cent, slightly less than the average for all woollens.[5] Raw wool and cotton were admitted free, as were most cotton yarns; woollen yarn paid 29.3 per cent.

In addition, from 1879 to 1881 the tariff on textile machinery that was not manufactured in Canada was eliminated.[6] The increase in the tariff on manufactured textiles coincided with the great burst of cotton-mill construction and certainly contributed to it. The increases did not, however, promote a similar construction boom in the woollen or knit-goods sector; woollen production stagnated and, in constant dollars, declined slightly. Knit-goods production increased a modest 38 per cent over the decade.

It has also been argued that although the introduction of the National Policy coincided with a massive increase in the cotton sector's capacity, the increase in actual production was much more modest.[7] Annual production figures are not available, but annual raw cotton imports, which provide good substitutes for production figures, show that there had been a rather erratic increase in production averaging 20 per cent annually in the years 1871–79; in the years 1879–87 the rate of annual growth was 17 per cent (*see* Table 10). The sustained rate of growth after 1879 was impressive, but it was not a revolutionary change. The interpretation that the burst of construction after 1879 involved a massive increase in capacity with a more modest increase in production is supported by contemporary accounts of an initial period of overproduction that ended about 1883 and was followed by almost a decade of attempts to limit and diversify production.

A third factor that contributed to the growth of the Canadian textile industry in the last half of the nineteenth century was the availability of capital to finance large-scale development. It is evidence of the growing maturity of the Canadian economy that most of the capital to finance the growth in the textile industry was available domestically.

In 1871 the average woollen mill employed about 16 hands and had a capital of about $10 000; the average cotton mill employed 93 hands and had a capital of $79 000. Twenty years later the scale of operation had increased at least fourfold in the cotton sector, but had hardly changed in the woollen sector (*see* Table 12). In the hosiery/knit-goods industry the evidence of growth in the scale of operations is less clear; one suspects there is an anomaly in the 1891 census figures, which show a sharp drop in the scale of knitting mills. However, by 1901 and 1911, knitting mills had roughly twice as many employees as woollen mills; they were much smaller than cotton mills.

The woollen sector evolved over a period of 50 years from small custom carding and fulling mills to small but integrated mills. To a considerable extent woollen mills were able to finance this growth internally, but to advance to the front rank, the larger mills often had to recruit outside capital. James Rosamond was able to build a substantial woollen mill at Almonte in 1857, but when his sons planned a much larger mill in 1866 they organized a company with George Stephen of Montréal.[8] The Rosamond family retained control of their firm, but some mill owners lost control of their firms as they expanded. Andrew Paton organized Andrew Paton and Company in 1866 and built the Paton mill in Sherbrooke. When the firm was incorporated as the Paton Manufacturing Company in 1868, control passed from his hands to a group of Montréal capitalists who included George Stephen.[9]

The knitting sector seems to have been financed in much the same way as the woollen sector. Mills were begun by individuals or partners and grew gradually. Although there were notable cases of consolidation, such as Penman Manufacturing, ownership remained family dominated. In many cases, for example Joseph Simpson and Sons of Toronto (established 1865), J.R. Moodie and Sons of Hamilton (established 1888), C. Turnbull Company of Galt (established 1859), and R. Forbes Company of Hespeler (established ca. 1874), major mills remained under the management of the founding family into the second and third generations. In the most famous instance, Stanfield's of Truro (established 1880), the current president is the fourth generation of the family to manage the firm.

From its beginning the financing of the cotton industry was different. The first cotton mill in Canada was built by a group of capitalists who organized a limited joint stock company, the Sherbrooke Cotton Company. Most cotton mills were financed by capitalists who had made their fortune in other endeavours and were seeking to diversify their interests. Alexander Gibson, who built the Marysville, New Brunswick, mill in 1883, had already made a fortune in lumbering; the first organizers of the St. Croix Cotton Manufacturing Company in Milltown, New Brunswick, were established lumbermen, shipbuilders, and bankers, and the Craven Cotton Company in Brantford, Ontario, was organized by a group of foundry owners. Montréal capitalists were investors in several mills; Hugh Allan was a major investor in the Montreal Cotton Company at Valleyfield and he, George Stephen, and Donald Smith were involved in the Canada Cotton Manufacturing Company at Cornwall. Stephen and Allan were also the principal figures in the Cornwall Manufacturing Company, which built a large woollen mill at Cornwall in 1868, and from 1866 Stephen was a shareholder in the Rosamond Woollen Company at Almonte and the Paton Manufacturing Company at Sherbrooke.[10]

Of these investors in the cotton industry only Stephen had any knowledge of the textile industry, and his knowledge had been acquired in the dry-goods importing and distributing business. Textile importers were a major source of both fixed and operating capital in the cotton sector. This was true both before the introduction of the National Policy, when they invested in production in order to free themselves from foreign suppliers, and after, when they invested to lessen the impact of the tariff on their importing businesses. The Toronto dry-goods firm of Gordon, Mackay and Company organized the Lybster Cotton Manufacturing Company at

Merritton in 1860; Donald McInnes, a Hamilton dry-goods importer, was associated with Stephen and Smith in both the Canada Manufacturing Company and the Cornwall Manufacturing Company.[11] When Montreal Cotton was organized in 1875 its principal organizers included A.F. Gault and J.-Rosaire Thibodeau, textile importers; Hugh Allan, a shipowner; J.K. Ward, a lumberman; and Samuel Barlow, a British textile-machinery manufacturer.[12] The major shareholders in Victor Hudon's mill, which ultimately formed the core of Dominion Textile, included six members of dry-goods firms, one lumberman, one banker and stockbroker, one wholesale grocer, the treasurer of the Canadian Rubber Company, and C. Gareth, whose occupation is not known. Three of the six major organizers of the Merchants Manufacturing Company were also members of dry-goods firms.[13]

Dry-goods importers and distributors also provided operating capital for many textile mills. Most large mills did not market the goods that they produced. Instead, finished goods were consigned to agents who sold them on commission to wholesalers or to manufacturers who in turn sold to retailers. The agents advised mills on the state of the market and attempted to co-ordinate the production of different mills. Many mills were chronically short of operating capital, and agents frequently advanced funds to the mills against the mills' inventories. Ultimately many of the mills came under the control of their agents.

The two leading figures in the primary textile industry between 1870 and 1910, David Morrice and Andrew Frederick Gault, both came from the tradition of agents. David Morrice was born in Scotland in 1831 and emigrated to Canada in 1855. He established the firm of D. Morrice and Company, general merchants and manufacturers' agents. By the early 1880s he represented some 36 mills and had an interest in many of them. After the near-failure of his firm in 1883 he was never as powerful as he had been, but in co-operation with Andrew Gault he continued to be a major figure in the industry. At his death in 1914 he was president of Canadian Cottons Limited and of Penmans Limited.[14] Andrew Gault, born in Ireland in 1833, established a Montréal dry-goods firm in 1853. By the 1870s he was actively investing in and promoting both woollen and cotton mills. With Morrice he was primarily responsible for organizing the Canadian Cotton Manufacturers' Association, Dominion Cotton Mills Company, and Canadian Coloured Cotton Mills Company. At different times he was president of these organizations as well as the Hochelaga Cotton Manufacturing Company, the Montmorency Cotton Company, the Montreal Cotton Company, the Globe Woollen Mills, and the Trent Valley Woollen Manufacturing Company.[15]

Most of the mills were financed within Canada, but there was some foreign investment. Samuel Barlow, a Lancashire textile manufacturer, was an early investor in the Montreal Cotton Company, but he does not seem to have persisted and his investment may simply have been an advance of machinery.[16] The St. Croix Cotton Manufacturing Company in New Brunswick was begun by local capitalists, but they were unable to raise sufficient capital locally and asked two Americans, Amos D. Lockewood, a mill architect, and Lewis Dexter of Providence, Rhode Island, to participate. As a result the majority of St. Croix mill shares was held by Americans. By 1890 control of the mill had passed into the hands of the Owen brothers of Providence, and when the St. Croix mill became part of Canadian Coloured Cotton Mills in 1892, C.D. Owen became vice-president and Theophilus King, a Boston financier, became a director.[17]

It seems probable that American investors controlled Canadian Coloured Cotton into the 20th century. A list of major shareholders in 1897 showed that the president, David Morrice, controlled 2100 shares through his firm D. Morrice and Sons. A.F. Gault and his relatives owned 3080 shares. A.W. Ogilvie, the miller, owned 1000 shares, and C.D. Owen and Theophilus King owned 900 shares each. In addition King held a block of 14 000 shares (equal to about 52 per cent of the shares issued) in trust. If King was the representative of American shareholders on the board, then Canadian Coloured Cotton Mills was American owned. In 1905 it was announced at the company's annual meeting that control, heretofore in American hands, was now in Montréal.[18]

Although both the Yarmouth Duck and Yarn Company in Yarmouth, Nova Scotia, and the Imperial Cotton Company of Hamilton were built by Canadian capitalists, both were acquired by American interests in 1901. They remained under American control until 1926, when Cosmos Imperial Mills Limited was incorporated and purchased both mills. Although Americans apparently continued to hold a considerable interest in Cosmos Imperial, it seems to have been effectively controlled by Hamilton's Young family, which also owned Hamilton Cotton.[19]

Subsidies from municipal governments were another source of financing. Mills provided employment and were viewed as an index of progress. Competition for them was keen, and in the early 1870s local governments began to offer cash grants and tax holidays to firms as incentives to locate in their area. A 20-year tax exemption became a standard item in financing the construction of a mill. Cash grants could be negotiated and in later years companies would demand grants to finance re-equipping plants. On occasion grants were offered to firms to move existing mills from one town to another. Both Ontario and Quebec passed legislation restricting competitive use of bonuses, but the legislation was largely ineffective.[20]

Maturity, 1906–1945

The years between the formation of Dominion Textile in 1905 and the end of World War II may be characterized as a period of maturity in the textile industry; there was growth and change, but the growth was slower and steadier and change less erratic than it had been in the last half of the nineteenth century. The level of corporate concentration achieved in the years 1890–1906 was maintained and in some areas increased. In spite of a growing low-tariff sentiment in Canada, the industry was able to obtain levels of tariff protection that allowed it to survive and in some cases to prosper. Management evolved along the lines that had been established in the years 1890–1906, with a slow widening of the gap between production-oriented plant management and a front-office management that was increasingly finance and sales oriented. Throughout most of the period labour was quiescent, although there was significant labour unrest in the first decade of the century and in the late 1930s.

Between 1900 and 1940 employment in the cotton, woollen, knit-goods/hosiery, and silk/synthetic sectors of the textile industry grew 218 per cent. Growth in the different sectors varied, with woollens much the weakest; there was no significant increase in employment in the woollen sector between 1901 and 1930, but employment doubled during the 1930s. The cotton sector showed steady but not spectacular growth, with employment increasing by 118 per cent between 1901 and 1940. The hosiery and knit-goods sector was much less mature in 1901 than either the cotton or woollen sectors and its growth was proportionately more rapid: from 3687 employees in 1901 to 23 438 in 1940. The case of the silk and synthetic sector is similar to that of the hosiery and knit-goods sector in that the silk industry was insignificant in 1901 and the synthetic industry non-existent. There was substantial growth in the silk industry in the decade 1911–20. In the 1920s, large rayon plants were built at Cornwall and Drummondville; these two plants grew rapidly and by 1940 probably employed over 50 per cent of all employees in the silk and synthetics sector.[1] By 1950 the silk/synthetics sector employed more people than the woollen sector.

The growth in the industry is attributable to population growth, increased per capita consumption, the displacement of imports, and the development of new markets and products. Between 1900 and 1940 the Canadian population grew from 5.3 to 11.5 million and per capita textile consumption increased from $28.07 to $59.79 per annum in constant dollars (*see* Table 9). Apparent consumption of all textiles grew from $151 million to $584 million. Consumption of cottons quadrupled and apparent consumption of woollens increased 3.5 times. Domestic manufacture of knit goods and hosiery increased tenfold in 1935–39 dollars.

During the first decades of the century the textile industry suffered from foreign, principally British, competition, but over the entire period it gradually improved its position. In 1900, 36 per cent of apparent consumption of all textiles was imported; by 1940, imports had been reduced to 21 per cent of apparent consumption. In 1910, woollens suffered most from foreign competition; 72 per cent of woollens consumed in Canada were imported. By 1940, imports had been reduced to 30 per cent of woollens consumed. Hosiery and knit goods seem to have been less affected by imports than most textiles. Based on rough estimates it seems that in 1910, when 37 per cent of all textiles consumed in Canada were imported, only about 20 per cent of the apparent consumption of knit goods was imported.[2]

The textile industry also grew by developing new markets. In the cotton sector the growth of the automobile industry led to increased production of upholstery and tire-cord fabrics. American tire-cord manufacturers established four large branch plants in Canada: Canadian Connecticut Cotton Mills in Sherbrooke (1913), Jenckes Canadian Company in Drummondville (1919), Canadian Manhasset Cotton Company in Saint-Hyacinthe (ca. 1920), and Firestone Cotton Company in Woodstock (1936). The Canadian Manhasset Company was acquired by Goodyear in 1926; the Canadian Connecticut and Jenckes Canadian companies were acquired by Dominion Textile.[3]

There was also expansion in more traditional areas of cotton manufacture. Before 1900 the Yarmouth Duck and Yarn Company in Yarmouth, Nova Scotia, was the principal Canadian producer of cotton duck, which was used for sails and other industrial purposes. Although the market for sailcloth declined rapidly in the early twentieth century, other industrial uses were developed. The papermaking industry became a major user of drying felts, and the Yarmouth mill as well as the Lachute Woollen Mills specialized in producing papermakers' felts. The agricultural implement industry was a major, and expanding, user of industrial canvas. At least two large mills, the Imperial mill in Hamilton (1900) and the Empire mill in Welland (1913), were built to produce industrial textiles.[4]

Before 1905 the Canadian cotton sector had not attempted to produce the finer grades of cotton cloth; these were generally imported from Britain. In 1907 Charles Ross Whitehead organized the Wabasso Cotton Company to fill this gap. Whitehead was the third generation of his family in the textile industry. His grandfather had been a Montréal dry-goods merchant; his father, William James Whitehead, was, successively, manager of the Trent Valley cotton mill at Hastings, Ontario, the Stormont and Canada mills in Cornwall, and the Hudon mill in Montréal. W.J. Whitehead was also a major shareholder in the St. Ann mill in Montréal.[5] C.R. Whitehead's brother,

26 C.R. Whitehead, 1868–1954, the founder of Wabasso.
Canadian Textile Journal, 12 July 1957, p. 25; National Library of Canada, NL 17298

27   The original mill of the Wabasso Cotton Company at Trois-Rivières, Quebec. Built in 1907–08, the mill had a brick and stone exterior but had concrete beams and subfloors with wooden flooring that, on the evidence of an interior view (see Fig. 53), were supported by cast-iron or steel columns.
Canadian Textile Journal, 12 July 1957, p. 22; National Library of Canada, NL 16976

William, was one of the promoters of the Colonial Bleaching and Printing Company and the Mount Royal Spinning Company in Montréal.[6] Charles Whitehead began work as a clerk in the Hochelaga mill and in 1886 went to China to initiate cotton sales there. In 1889 he organized and became the first president of the Montmorency Cotton Company, which was built to produce cotton for the China trade.[7] From 1897 to 1901 he was joint general manager of the Dominion Cotton Mills Company.[8] He was involved in the organization of Dominion Textile, but left it to organize Wabasso.

The Wabasso mill in Trois-Rivières was organized on the lines of an English mill, using English equipment including mules; in 1928 it had 40 000 mule spindles, equal to between one-third and one-quarter of all cotton mule spindles operating in Canada. It was probably the last major Canadian cotton manufacturer using mules when it replaced them with long-draft spinning frames in 1939.[9] The mules were necessary to spin the fine counts of yarn, usually 40s to 45s but as high as 120s, that the company produced. ("Count" indicates the number of hanks of yarn of a definite length per pound of yarn. A "40" yarn has 40 hanks per pound; a "120" yarn was three times as fine as a "40." Most Canadian yarns were less than 40s, and yarns finer than 40s were usually imported.) Most of the fine yarn was used to weave fine cottons, but there was also a growing market for fine yarn in electrical insulation.

The company was a success and built a second plant at Trois-Rivières, St. Maurice Valley Cotton, in 1912 and a third, Shawinigan Cotton, at Shawinigan in 1916. C.R. Whitehead remained president until his death in 1954, when he was succeeded by his son. On his son's death in 1955, control of the company passed to the Woods Manufacturing Company, which owned the Empire mill in Welland.[10] In 1985 the firm was purchased by Dominion Textile.

Although there was little growth in the woollen sector between 1900 and 1940, there was a significant shift from woollen to worsted production. Nineteenth-century statistics do not distinguish between woollen and worsted production, but the 1885 *Canadian Textile Directory* lists several of the larger companies — Rosamond in Almonte, McCrae and Company in Guelph, Harvey and McQuesten in Hespeler, Montreal Woollen Mills in Montréal, and Riverside Worsted in Québec City — as producers of worsteds and serges as well as woollens. The general literature suggests that woollen production was much more important than worsted production in the nineteenth century, but tastes changed and by the mid-1920s, worsted production in Canadian mills was valued at about $7 million compared to $6 million for woollens.[11] Worsteds and serges were important parts of textile imports as well; in 1925 they accounted for about 41 per cent of all imports of manufactured woollens, excluding carpets. Many Canadian mills did not have facilities for combing wool and so imported combed wool from Britain. In 1925 $3.2 million worth of worsted tops (combed wool wound on large cones) was imported compared to $6.5 million worth of raw wool.[12] Because worsted production was somewhat more complex and expensive than woollen production, it tended to favour the larger firms.

The knit-goods and hosiery sector expanded primarily through increased sales of its basic products: underwear and stockings. It also benefited from an increasing demand for knitted outerwear such as sweaters, dresses, and jackets, and after World War I, from the growth in use of full-fashioned silk hosiery. In 1926 the total production of the knit-goods/hosiery sector was worth $52 million; of this, hosiery accounted for about $18 million and underwear for about $16 million. Sweaters, cardigans, jackets, and sweater suits and dresses were valued at $8 million and jersey cloth and stockinette at $1 million. The remaining $9 million worth of production was spread over 21 different categories of products.[13]

Growth in the traditional knit-goods industry, as well as in knitted outerwear, took place within the framework of established firms while growth in the hosiery sector occurred in new firms. In its analysis, based on the year 1935, the Royal Commission on the Textile Industry identified 25 firms whose major activity was the production of silk hosiery. Nine firms were responsible for 73 per cent of all production in the hosiery group; of the 9, at least 7 were organized after 1911. In the knit-goods group, 11 firms accounted for 70 per cent of all production. Of these at least 5 began in the nineteenth century; Ontario Silknit, incorporated in 1922, was the youngest of the firms.[14]

Before World War I the only important silk-producing company in Canada was Belding Paul Corticelli, a 1911 merger of Belding Paul and Company and Corticelli Silk. The firm confined itself to the production of trim, laces, ribbons, and sewing thread; silk cloth was imported. During and after the war several other firms were begun: Riverside Silk Mills of Galt in 1915; Bruck Silk Mills of Cowansville, Quebec, in 1921; Grouts Limited of St. Catharines, Ontario, in 1923; and Associated Textiles of Louiseville, Quebec, in 1929. Grouts and Bruck began weaving silk cloth in 1924 and several other firms followed; by 1933, 2620 looms were devoted to weaving silk and artificial silks.[15] Between 1911 and 1920, employment in the silk sector doubled and production increased from $1 million to $5 million annually. However, this impressive growth was to be completely over-shadowed by the development of the synthetic sector.

The artificial-silk or synthetic industry is the most important and radical example of the development of new products that allowed the textile industry to expand between the wars. The first of the synthetics to be produced in Canada was rayon, a semi-synthetic fibre made by dissolving the cellulose fibres from woody plants and extruding them as a monofilament thread. Although this filament could be used in weaving or knitting, it was usually cut into short lengths and then spun in much the same fashion as natural fibres. Several processes for producing rayon were developed and patented in the 1890s. Commercial production in Europe and the United States began early in the twentieth century. In 1907 a small plant producing artifical silk by the Stearns method was opened in Toronto.[16] It does not seem to have been a success and no major artifical-silk plants were built in Canada until 1925, when Courtaulds, a British firm, built a plant at Cornwall. In 1927 the Canadian Celanese Company, a subsidiary of British and American firms, built a plant at Drummondville. The rayon industry grew steadily through the Depression. Apparent consumption in 1926 was 3.2 million pounds; in 1936 it was 14.8 million pounds. The synthetic-silk industry quickly equalled the real-silk industry in importance; by 1933 Courtaulds (Canada) Limited employed 1370, Canadian Celanese employed 1757, and the 17 natural-silk manufacturers in Canada employed 3407.[17] During the Second World War Canada also began to produce nylon, a synthetic derived from coal or petroleum, at a plant in Kingston. Since the war the diversity and volume of synthetics production has continued to grow.

By 1911, when Belding Paul and Company and Corticelli Silk Mills merged to form Belding Paul Corticelli (after 1920, Belding-Corticelli Limited), the merger movement that characterized Canadian industrial organization in the first decade of the twentieth century had run its course. The cotton sector was dominated by the Dominion Textile–Montreal Cotton nexus with Canadian Cottons and Wabasso in supporting roles. Belding Paul Corticelli dominated the small silk sector and Penmans was much the largest firm in the knit-goods/hosiery sector, although a number of medium and small firms provided it with vigorous competition. The failure of the Canada Woollen Company, with mills in Carleton Place, Lambton, Markham, Hespeler, and Waterloo, in 1904 left the woollen sector with no dominant firm.

Although the growth and diversification of the primary industry between 1911 and 1940 resulted in the appearance of a number of new firms, the degree of corporate concentration achieved during the decade 1901–10 was maintained, and in some areas extended, by interlocking directorships, further takeovers, pricing agreements, and tacit division of markets. Dominion Textile maintained its ties, based on interlocking directorships and common officers, with both Penmans and Montreal Cotton throughout the period. After 1923 Sir Charles Gordon was president concurrently of Dominion Textile, Penmans Limited, and Montreal Cotton; he was succeeded in all of these offices by F.G. Daniels, who had been managing director of Dominion Textile. After World War II both Penmans and Montreal Cottons were absorbed by Dominion Textile.

Dominion Textile also had a close link with the Paton Manufacturing Company. Herbert Holt, vice-president of Dominion Textile from 1911 to 1941, was Andrew Paton's son-in-law and a director of Paton Manufacturing. Senator Robert Mackay, a director of Dominion Textile from 1905 to 1917, was vice-president of Paton Manufacturing in 1913.[18] In 1923 Paton Manufacturing came under Dominion Textile's control and in 1928 F.G. Daniels was elected president.[19] Dominion Textile also maintained its dominant position in the industry through direct acquisition; in 1928 it purchased two American-owned tire-cord plants, Canadian Connecticut Cotton Mills in Sherbrooke and Jenckes Canadian Company in Drummondville, and operated them as subsidiary companies.

Canadian Coloured Cotton Mills Company also expanded through acquisition and interlocking directorships. When the company was re-organized as Canadian Cottons in 1910 it acquired the Gibson mill in Marysville, New Brunswick, and the Mount Royal Spinning mill in Montréal. The Mount Royal mill was leased and later sold to Dominion Textile. Canadian Cottons also acquired a controlling interest in the

28 Arthur O. Dawson, 1864–1940. Born in New Brandon, New Brunswick, he worked with D. Morrice Sons and Company from 1882 until the firm was merged with Canadian Cottons Limited in 1910. He became managing director of Canadian Cottons and, in 1927, president. He was also president of Belding-Corticelli and of Dominion Woollens and Worsteds.
Canadian Textile Journal, 5 Dec. 1922, p. 546; National Library of Canada, NL 16966

Cornwall and York Cotton Mills Company that owned William Parks's two mills in Saint John. The firm had a close, although undefined, link with both Belding-Corticelli and Dominion Woollens and Worsteds; A.O. Dawson, managing director, vice-president, and president of Canadian Cottons from 1910 to 1940, was also president of Belding-Corticelli (1915–40) and of Canadian Woollens and its successor, Dominion Woollens and Worsteds.[20] Prior to the 1930s Canadian Cottons also had corporate links with Dominion Textile; from 1905 to 1927 Canadian Cotton's presidents, David Morrice and Charles Hosmer, were directors of Dominion Textile.[21]

Competition between the major cotton firms, Dominion Textile, Canadian Cottons, Montreal Cotton, and Wabasso, was kept to a minimum. Each specialized in certain types of production. Dominion Textile produced unbleached, bleached, and printed goods; Canadian Cottons produced stock-dyed and yarn-dyed fabrics and Montreal Cotton produced piece-dyed fabrics. Wabasso concentrated on finer fabrics than those produced by the other companies. As a further limit on competition, Dominion Textile, Canadian Cottons, Hamilton Cotton, and Wabasso had an agreement setting cotton yarn prices from about 1906 to 1936.[22]

Control in the synthetic-fibre production sector was even more concentrated than it was in the cotton sector. Both Courtaulds and Canadian Celanese had exclusive Canadian rights to patented processes and were the sole producers of acetate and vicose yarns in Canada. Moreover, they were subsidiaries of British and American firms that until at least 1929 were part of an international cartel controlling rayon production.[23] Canadian Celanese extended the effect of this monopoly by spinning most of its own product and weaving it on its own looms. In 1936 it wove 42 per cent of all rayon cloth shipped in Canada.[24] Courtaulds, by contrast, did not weave or knit. Most of its product was sold as yarn. Dominion Textile began weaving rayon in 1927 and other firms followed suit. By 1936 Dominion Textile, Montreal Cotton, Canadian Cottons, Associated Textiles of Canada, and Bruck Silk Mills each produced between 6 and 8 per cent of the rayon cloth yardage shipped in Canada.[25] By 1939, 7.3 per cent (by value) of the raw material used in the cotton sector was rayon; in the knit-goods/hosiery sector the figure was 8.5 per cent.[26]

In contrast to the cotton and silk/synthetic sectors, ownership in the knit-goods/hosiery and woollen sectors remained diffuse. In 1935, 11 companies controlled 70 per cent of all sales of knit goods; Penmans, with 19 per cent of all sales, was much the most important company. In the hosiery sector Julius Kayser and Company of Sherbrooke controlled 20 per cent of all sales; another 8 firms controlled 52 per cent of production. There were also attempts to control the markets through price fixing, but these arrangements do not seem to have been as successful as those in the cotton sector.[27] In woollens 11 companies had 66 per cent of sales; Dominion Woollens and Worsteds was the largest with 14 per cent of all sales.

There was some tendency towards concentration. Penmans continued to expand, absorbing Ellis Underwear of Hamilton (1911) and building plants in Waterford (1916) and London (1919).[28] The Monarch Knitting Company grew from a single small plant at Dunnville in 1903 to four large plants (one in Buffalo, New York) by 1913. In 1945 Monarch Knitting bought the Joseph Simpson mill in Toronto.[29]

The most spectacular record of concentration in the period was that of Harvey Woods Limited, which, prior to 1966, was known as York Knitting Mills. In 1904 James W. Woods, president of Gordon, Mackay and Company, a Toronto dry-goods firm, organized Puritan Knitting Mills. The company was incorporated as York Knitting Mills in 1911 with his son, J.D. Woods, as president. The company organized a number of subsidiaries — Toronto Hosiery, Dupont Textiles, and Woods Underwear — before taking control of Zimmerknit Limited of Hamilton and its subsidiaries in 1930. Zimmerknit had been organized as the Zimmerman Manufacturing Company in 1907. In 1919 it merged with the Reliance Knitting Company of Toronto and in 1928 purchased Harvey Knitting Company and Hosiers Limited, both of Woodstock. Zimmerknit went into receivership about 1930 and came under the management (and by 1937 the ownership) of York Knitting.[30] The combined firms were important producers in both the woollen and knit-goods/hosiery sectors. York Knitting, primarily a spinning company after 1932, had 6 per cent of sales in the woollen sector in 1935; Zimmerknit and Harvey Knitting had 5.7 per cent of sales in the knit-goods sector, and Hosiers Limited and Toronto Hosiery each had 5.5 per cent of sales in the hosiery sector.[31]

The period saw another attempt at consolidation in the woollen sector. In 1919 the Bonner-Worth Company and the Auburn Woollen Company, both of Peterborough, and Standard Woollen Mills of Toronto were amalgamated as Canadian Woollens. The firm was linked with the cotton and carpet sectors. Its president, A.O. Dawson, was vice-president and, after 1927, president of Canadian Cottons; he was also president of Belding-Corticelli. The vice-president, F. Barry Hayes, was president of the Toronto Carpet Manufacturing Company, the largest carpet-manufacturing firm in Canada. Toronto Carpet also controlled the Barrymore Cloth Company and the Campbellford Cloth Company, important producers of woollens.[32] Canadian Woollens closed the Standard woollen mill and concentrated its production in Peterborough until 1928, when it merged with the R. Forbes Company of Hespeler. The new firm, Dominion Woollens and Worsteds, was the largest producer of woollens in Canada, with 14.4 per cent of all sales in 1935. The Auburn mill was closed in 1938 and the company went out of business in 1958.[33]

29 The Auburn (left) and Bonner-Worth (centre) mills of Peterborough, Ontario, and the Standard mill of Toronto (right) merged to form Canadian Woollens Limited in 1919.
Canadian Textile Journal, 5 Dec. 1922, p. 495; National Library of Canada, NL 16978

The tendency to concentration was balanced by the growth of small- and medium-sized firms; in 1940 there were 172 knit-goods and hosiery mills employing an average of 135 workers each compared to 52 mills employing 75 workers each in 1901. Some of these firms remained small, but others became significant producers and remained independent. Of 20 major firms in the knit-goods/hosiery field in 1935, 12 were begun in the era of World War I or later. In the woollen sector, 4 out of 11 major firms were begun during or after World War I.

A number of these new firms were foreign owned. The four tire-cord plants built between 1913 and 1936 were all subsidiaries of American firms; two of them were acquired by Dominion Textile in 1928. In the hosiery sector Julius Kayser and Company of Sherbrooke with 20 per cent of all hosiery sales in Canada and Holeproof Hosiery of London with 7.3 per cent were both subsidiaries of American firms.[34] In the woollen sector two major British firms, Hield Brothers and Paton and Baldwins, established worsted mills in Kingston and Toronto.[35] Between them they controlled about 12 per cent of Canadian woollen sales. The largest foreign subsidiaries, Courtaulds and Canadian Celanese, completely dominated the synthetic sector. In the natural-silk sector, Grouts of St. Catharines was a subsidiary of a British firm and Associated Textiles of Louiseville was a subsidiary of an American firm.[36]

There are no statistical estimates of the extent of foreign control of the textile industry at the beginning of the twentieth century. Canadian Coloured Cotton Mills and Cosmos Imperial Mills are the only firms known to have been foreign owned and both were bought out by Canadian interests by the 1920s. In 1935 the Royal Commission on the Textile Industry considered the cotton sector and the knit-goods sector to be Canadian owned, but found that about 31 per cent of the silk sector, 16 per cent of the woollen sector, 45 per cent of the hosiery sector, and all of the synthetic sector were foreign owned.[37]

Nineteenth-century mills tended to concentrate on production, with only cursory attention to marketing. Small rural woollen mills dealt directly with the consumer, but larger mills normally consigned their products to mill agents such as David Morrice and Sons or Cantlie, Ewan and Company of Montréal. For a commission of one to three per cent agents arranged all details of the sale and in some cases guaranteed the sale. They also advised mills on products and prices, and using goods consigned to them as security, arranged for advances of operating capital. The central position of a mill agent, particularly one who represented many mills, gave him great influence but also exposed him to great risks. David Morrice's near-failure in 1883 resulted from his continuing to accept cloth from the mills he represented and his continuing to advance money to them at a time when he could not sell the cloth. Seven years later his position as an agent allowed him to play a key role in the formation of Dominion Cotton Mills and Canadian Coloured Cotton Mills.

Mill agents did not sell to retailers or the public; they sold to dry-goods wholesalers, who in most cases were also importers. Andrew Gault, the other principal figure in the formation of Dominion Cotton Mills and Canadian Coloured Cotton Mills, was a wholesaler although his firm, Gault Brothers, probably acted as an agent to a certain extent. Wholesalers sold to retailers, tailors, and manufacturers; they often provided credit for the retailers and smaller manufacturers, handled the complex logistics of importing and distribution, and consolidated numerous small orders into large orders that mills or mill agents would be willing to accept.

In the 1880s and 1890s this selling system began to come under pressure. British exporters began to send out travellers who dealt directly with Canadian retailers and manufacturers.[38] Large Canadian retailers, especially department stores, could send their own buyers abroad and they began to deal directly with mill agents. Backward integration by retailers and manufacturers also reduced the role of wholesalers. The T. Eaton Company established its own knitting mills in Hamilton, and the Woods Manufacturing Company, which manufactured bags, tents, tarpaulins, and waterproof cloth, built its own mill, Empire Cotton Mills, in Welland.

Converters became increasingly important customers who, depending on the scale of their operations, could deal directly with manufacturers. The term converter covered a range of activities, including bleaching, dyeing, printing, and tailoring, in which low-value grey cloth was converted to higher value cloth or clothes. The Magog Textile and Print Company and the Colonial Bleaching and Printing Company were both organized as converters; they did not initially spin or weave. Instead they bleached and printed plain grey cottons produced by other mills. Although both of these firms failed as simple converters, many smaller specialized converters survived.

The development of the ready-made clothing industry led to the growth of large-scale clothing manufacturers who dealt directly with the mills. In some cases the clothing manufacturers were closely linked to textile manufacturers. The Crescent Manufacturing Company, makers of men's shirts and ties, was organized by Andrew Gault's firm, Gault Brothers, in 1898.[39] Charles Gordon, who became president of Dominion Textile in 1909, organized the Standard Shirt Company in 1896; in 1906 it was merged with three other firms to form Canadian Converters Company, manufacturers of shirts, blouses, and white goods. Charles Gordon managed the firm until he became president of Dominion Textile; his family continued to be represented on the board and in the management of Canadian Converters by James R. Gordon. John P. Black, owner of one of the firms that had merged to form Canadian Converters and one of its directors, was also a member of the syndicate that organized Dominion Textile. By 1910 Canadian Converters had over $5 million in annual sales and a paid-up capital of $1.7 million; it was larger than most cotton or woollen mills.[40]

All of these factors had the effect of weakening the role of the wholesaler and forcing those that survived to consolidate. In 1896 the *Canadian Journal of Fabrics* noted that there were only 20-odd dry-goods importers active in Montréal whereas 15 years earlier there had been 68.[41] By 1933 only a fraction of the product of most textile mills was sold to wholesalers and

30 Sir Charles Gordon, 1867–1939. Born in Montréal, Gordon worked in several dry-goods firms before organizing and managing Canadian Converters, a large clothing manufacturer. He was involved in the organization of Dominion Textile and became president in 1909. He continued as president and chairman until his death. He was also president of Penmans, of Montreal Cotton, and of the Bank of Montreal. He was knighted in 1917 for his work with the Imperial Munitions Board.
Notman Photographic Archives, McCord Museum of Canadian History, 292,627-II

jobbers; in the cotton sector, 19 per cent; in the woollen sector, 14 per cent; and in the hosiery sector, 17 per cent. Most of the product of cotton, woollen, and silk mills (67 per cent, 73 per cent, and 58 per cent respectively) was sold to converters. The knit-goods/hosiery sector was different from the other sectors we are considering. To a certain extent it acted as a converter, buying imported or domestic yarn and producing finished goods. Very little of its product required further processing: in the hosiery branch less than 1 per cent, in the knit-goods branch about 8 per cent. Most of the product in both branches was sold directly to chain stores, department stores, and smaller retailers.[42]

Mill agents also came under pressure. Initially their role had been to sell cloth, provide operating capital, and leave the owner/manager of small mills free to manage their mills. As a result of the consolidation of the 1890s and of 1905–06, the technical management of the mills was increasingly divorced from the financial management and ownership. The new class of executive, men such as Andrew Gault and Charles Gordon, had experience in finance, sales, and promotion, and they concentrated on these areas, leaving technical management of the mills to professional managers. They had most of the expertise and contacts that had been provided by mill agents, and when it became necessary to reduce expenses in the 1890s, the larger mills were able to establish their own sales departments and dispense with the agencies.

Dominion Cotton was the first large company to follow this course. As part of a reorganization of Dominion Cotton in 1897, Andrew Gault hired Charles R. Whitehead and Lesley Craig (Gault's nephew) as joint managers of the company and established a sales department within the company. David Morrice and Sons had been the agent for Dominion Cotton, and as a result of the loss of the agency, Morrice and his son resigned from the board. They were replaced by C.R. Whitehead and Gault's brother-in-law, S. Finley. In 1898 Gault resigned as president of Canadian Coloured Cotton and was replaced by David Morrice.[43] Canadian Coloured Cotton came within the sphere of the Morrice family and David Morrice and Sons acted as agent for it until after Morrice's death. Ultimately David Morrice and Sons was absorbed by Canadian Coloured Cotton.[44]

Dominion Cotton was not the only firm to dispense with its mill agent; the Merchants Cotton Company established its own sales department in 1897 when its agent, Alexander Ewan of Cantlie, Ewan and Company, died. By 1907 the Montreal Cotton Company also had its own sales department.[45] The smaller independent mills seem to have been much slower in establishing their own sales departments; in the *Canadian Textile Directory* for 1907–08 most woollen and knitting mills listed selling agents.

Tariffs and tariff policy continued to play important roles in the textile industry. The effect of the introduction of British preference in 1897–98 has already been mentioned. British industry was occupied by production for the Boer War until 1900, but it began to take advantage of the preference after the end of the war. Between 1900 and 1910, imports of woollens, mostly from Great Britain, grew from 55 to 72 per cent of Canadian consumption. Imports of cottons also increased, from 36 to 43 per cent of apparent consumption. The Canadian cotton sector recovered from this setback within a few years, but the woollen sector took much longer; as late as 1930, 53 per cent of Canadian consumption was imported (*see* Table 9).

The primary textile industry's response was to combine so as to be better able to compete and to lobby for a restoration of tariff protection. By 1903 the campaign had had some effect; a revision to the customs act in that year allowed a surtax of 33.3 per cent to be applied to goods from countries that did not give Canadian goods treatment equal to a most-favoured-nation status.[46] In the textile industry this provision seems to have applied primarily to imports of woollen and knit goods from Germany. In 1904 the woollen sector received further assistance through a customs act revision that put a minimum tariff of 30 per cent on a wide range of woollen cloth and ready-made clothing.[47] The act also included an anti-dumping provision. By 1905–06 the average tariff on woollens had climbed to 29.3 per cent from 25.7 per cent in 1900–1901 (*see* Table 11).

Following hearings in 1904–05 in which most textile manufacturers called for increased protection and importers either asked for reductions or adopted a stand-pat policy, the tariff schedule was completely revised. Imports were charged one of three rates according to their country of origin. The lowest tariff scale, the British preferential rate, applied to the United Kingdom and most British colonies; the intermediate tariff applied to goods imported from countries to which Canada chose to extend it (presumably in return for reciprocal arrangements); the general, and highest, tariff applied to all other imports.[48] The net effect of the change was a slight decrease in the tariff on most textiles except silks.

The First World War brought orders and prosperity to the textile industry; even the woollen sector enjoyed moderate prosperity. The prosperity was primarily due to the normal hastening of economic activity that a distant war brings, but it was assisted by a special war tax that increased the British preferential rates by 5 per cent and the intermediate and general rates by 7.5 per cent.[49]

The wartime surcharges on tariffs were retained until 1919–20; their removal coincided with a swelling of low-tariff sentiment as well as a world-wide depression in textiles. In December 1921 a minority Liberal government was elected; it governed with the support of the low-tariff Progressive Party. In 1922 a reduction of ten per cent was made on the British preferential rates. A similar reduction was made in 1923, and a treaty reducing tariffs was negotiated with France. Manufacturers were extremely concerned by the strength and initial success of the low-tariff interest and lobbied hard to defeat it. Their initial goal was the creation of a tariff board that would investigate tariff issues and set tariffs rationally, thereby removing the tariff from the immediate influence of partisan politics and ensuring stability in the tariff structure.

In 1926 the W.L. Mackenzie King government acceded to the manufacturer's appeals and appointed an Advisory Board on Tariffs and Taxation. The board was weaker than the manufacturers had hoped for; it investigated and advised on tariff matters, but did not set tariffs.[50] Nevertheless it provided a forum for manufacturers to put their case.

The woollen, knit-goods, and cotton sectors all applied for increased protection. In each instance consumers' groups, agricultural organizations, and importers opposed the applications. All of the applications were refused. The 1928 budget contained some reductions in tariffs on woollens and cottons although the overall tariff on textiles increased slightly.[51] The net result of tariff revisions during the 1920s was to decrease the rate on woollens by about 4.5 per cent and on cottons by about 2.7 per cent. The effect of these reductions was increased by the fact that many countries exporting to Canada had depreciated currencies.

The silk/synthetic sector was the only area to escape the scaling down of tariff protection. At the beginning of the decade there were no synthetic yarn producers in Canada and synthetic yarn was admitted free. However, when Courtaulds began planning a plant in Canada it asked for, and received, a low protective tariff.[52] The level of protection was gradually increased at the same time as protection for woollens and cottons was decreased.

How seriously the loss of protection affected the woollen and cotton sectors is not clear. Contemporary accounts indicate that the 1920s, particularly the middle years, were unprofitable. However, much of this comment must be taken against the background of the severe deflation that followed the wartime inflationary spiral. In 1920 the wholesale price index for fibres, textiles, and textile products reached 247.6; in 1921 it was 134.6; it did not regain the 1920 level until 1950.[53] The recession seems to have been most serious in the woollen and knitting sectors. In 1924 a bulletin of the Canadian Woollen Manufacturers' Association reported on a survey of 124 woollen and knitting mills. Twenty out of the 124 mills in these sectors were closed; in those that were open, 30 to 40 per cent of the machinery was idle.[54] Over the course of the decade there was no increase in employment in the woollen or cotton sectors although there was substantial growth in the knit-goods/hosiery sector. On the other hand, in spite of lower tariffs the woollen sector, as well as the textile industry generally, managed to increase its share of apparent Canadian consumption at the expense of imports (*see* Tables 1 and 9).

The artificial-silk sector received increased protection over the decade and it flourished. Canadian production of artificial silk grew steadily from less than 1 million pounds in 1925 to more than 13 million in 1936; during the same period imports remained steady at slightly over 1 million pounds.[55] While some of this growth of Canadian production at the apparent expense of imports may be credited to improved tariff protection, it must be viewed in the context that the Canadian manufacturers of artificial silk were subsidiaries of multinational firms that were part of a world-wide cartel; competition from imports was probably restricted by the cartel.

The crash of 1929, the ensuing depression, and the election of a Conservative government brought a sharp reversal of the downward trend in protection for textiles. A series of tariff measures in 1930 and 1931 resulted in the sharpest increase in the tariff since the introduction of the National Policy in 1879 and the highest level of protection in Canadian history. In 1931–32 the average tariff on cottons was 30.9 per cent; on woollens, 41.4 per cent; on synthetics, 53.9 per cent; and on all textiles, 36 per cent. The peak rates were not maintained. The Imperial Economic Conference of 1932 resulted in mutual, but not identical, tariff reductions by Canada and the United Kingdom. As a result of the agreement, tariffs on all textiles fell from 36 to 32.4 per cent between 1931–32 and 1933–34; the reductions on cottons and woollens were even greater; nevertheless, tariff levels remained much higher than they had been in the 1920s. The effect of the agreement was to maintain a high level of protection for most Canadian products while encouraging imports from within the Empire at the expense of those from elsewhere. In 1931 about 44 per cent of all dutiable textile imports entered under the imperial preferential tariff; by 1934, 61 per cent of textile imports entered under imperial preference.[56]

Perhaps as a result of increased tariff protection, the textile industry did better during the Depression than most manufacturing industries. In manufacturing as a whole, employment dropped by 30 per cent from its 1929 levels and did not recover until 1940; in textiles employment fell by 8 per cent and by 1934 it surpassed 1929 levels.[57] The woollen sector was particularly fortunate; between 1930 and 1934, woollen and worsted production tripled,[58] and over the whole decade the domestic woollen sector increased its share of apparent consumption from 47 to 70 per cent. In the knit-goods/hosiery sector the Depression had only a minor effect on employment although the value of production did not regain pre-crash levels until 1939. The cotton sector probably suffered most from the Depression; employment did not regain 1928 levels until World War II.

The silk/synthetic sector, led by the new synthetic plants, enjoyed uninterrupted growth throughout the Depression. In spite of this record, a minor setback in 1934–35 led to the most comprehensive review of the primary textile industry in Canadian history. Through the 1920s and early

1930s Canada had a very favourable balance of trade with Japan based on exports of raw materials and restrictions on imports of manufactured goods. The tariff was the basic device for restricting imports, but its effect was greatly enhanced by the imposition of minimum values for duty and anti-dumping charges. The additional charges were justified as a means of compensating for the devalued Japanese currency. In one example studied by the Royal Commission on the Textile Industry, a silk product that had a real value of $43.60 in Japan was charged $168.66 in duty although the nominal duty was only 40 per cent plus 40¢ per pound.[59] Japan objected to these tariffs and applied sanctions to Canadian goods. After a brief period of countersanctions, Canada agreed to reduce its tariffs substantially; in the example cited above the tariff was reduced to $83.42. The textile industry protested that it could not compete on this basis, and on 17 January 1936 Dominion Textile closed its rayon division in Sherbrooke, throwing 400 employees out of work.[60]

In response the government appointed W.F.A. Turgeon, justice of the Supreme Court of Saskatchewan, a royal commissioner to investigate the entire textile industry. Turgeon's mandate was primarily a fact-finding one intended to give the government the data necessary to evaluate the position of the industry with regard to foreign competition and to determine "the extent to which the employer can reasonably and properly be expected to maintain employment over periods of difficulty."[61]

Turgeon's report, tabled in the House of Commons in March 1938, cannot have been comforting to the textile industry. He found that the industry had been unjustified in its claim for protection from Japanese imports[62] and that the closing of the Sherbrooke rayon mill had been a simple pressure tactic. (The mill re-opened within a few days of the appointment of the commission.) He also found much to criticize in the industry's labour practices including poor working conditions, unusually long hours, hostility towards unions, and low pay. The low level of pay was contrasted with the general prosperity of the industry. In his analysis of corporate finances he found that in some of the major companies, notably Dominion Textile, Penmans, and Dominion Woollens and Worsteds, there had been extensive overcapitalization. He concluded that overcapitalization, secret inventory reserves, and improper charges to operations had been used to disguise high profits and to argue for increased tariff protection. In the case of Dominion Textile he argued that an actual investment of $1 million in 1905, capitalized as $5 million in common stock and $5 million in preferred stock, had yielded 98 per cent annually. Some of the subterfuges he considered sufficiently serious that he referred them to the income tax office.[63]

Turgeon also found that tariffs had kept Canadian prices of textile products substantially higher than they would have been and higher than was necessary for the financial health of the firms. Many firms, he stated, "could, on a proper capitalization, have prospered with less tariff protection than they have received, and ... the consumer has been called upon to pay more than ought fairly to have been asked of him."[64] In conclusion, Turgeon found that a company that had received tariff protection on the implicit understanding that the protection would create jobs had a moral obligation to maintain employment during temporary economic downturns. He recommended that manufacturers who breached this understanding should lose the benefit of the tariff.

The report was a moral blow to the textile industry and must have made it more difficult to make the case for tariff protection, but it is difficult to discover any immediate concrete results arising from the report. Eight companies were prosecuted and convicted of evading taxes totalling slightly over $1 million; however, on appeal to the Exchequer Court the conviction was overturned.[65] A private member's bill that would have prevented the paying of dividends by companies considered to pay unacceptably low wages was introduced in Parliament but was never passed. Although the government expressed sympathy for the intent of the bill, it did not introduce anything similar on its own account.[66] Perhaps the commission's most important result was an intangible one. The years 1936–37 were marked by massive strikes against the major textile firms; the publicity generated by the commission's hearings may have helped to create a climate favourable to these strikes.

Labour and Working Conditions

Two factors characterized the labour force in the textile industry: a large number of employees per plant and extensive employment of both women and children. The average cotton mill in 1871 employed 93 hands; only a few other manufacturing industries — engine building, smelting, and straw works — employed comparable numbers per plant. In 1911 the average number of employees on wages per cotton mill was 443; the average for all textile plants was 50, and the average for all manufacturing plants was 24.5.[1] The typical woollen or knitting mill was much smaller than the typical cotton mill; in 1871, woollen mills employed an average of 16 hands and knitting mills employed an average of 22. However, the more prominent woollen mills were comparable in size to smaller cotton mills. In the late 1880s the Paton Manufacturing Company employed 543 hands, the Cornwall Manufacturing Company employed 225 hands, and the Kingston Hosiery Company employed 130 to 140 hands.[2] During the 1920s and 1930s the average size of textile plants continued to grow, albeit slowly; cotton mills remained several times larger than the average knitting or woollen mill. Cotton mills were also about twice the size of the average silk/synthetic plant. However, this average is misleading; the 2 synthetic mills employed about 1100 each in the early 1930s; the 12 major silk mills that were active at the time employed about 200 each.[3]

Women and children supplied a large part of the labour employed in the textile industry. Between 1871 and 1911 from 38 to 46 per cent of employees in the cotton yarn and cloth, the woollen yarn and cloth, and the hosiery and knit-goods sectors were women over 16 years of age. In the same sectors, between 21 and 10 per cent of employees were under the age of 16 (*see* Table 14). Employment of women and children peaked in the 1880s, when women accounted for 45 per cent of all employees in the three main sectors of the textile industry and those under 16 years of age accounted for 18 per cent of all employees. In manufacturing generally the comparable percentages were 16 and 8. Over the period 1871–1911 the woollen sector had the lowest percentage of female and youthful workers. The cotton sector was a major employer of women and children in the nineteenth century, but it gradually reduced its reliance on women and children before World War I. During the war, women returned to work in the cotton mills; in the 1920s and 1930s the number of women employed in the cotton sector declined until by 1940 only 34 per cent of employees were female. The silk industry also began as a major employer of women, but the commencement of the synthetics industry in the 1920s resulted in the employment of a larger proportion of males. Over the entire period, 1871–1940, the hosiery/knit-goods sector remained a major employer of female labour; generally about two-thirds of the employees in that sector were female. Except for the 1880s and 1890s, the hosiery/knit-goods sector was not a major employer of child labour. In spite of a gradual decline in the use of female and child labour after 1880–90, the textile industry continued to employ an unusually large proportion of women. In 1940, 46 per cent of all wage earners in the four major sectors were women; in the manufacturing and mechanical industry as a whole the comparable figure was 21 per cent.[4]

Women and children filled the lower paying job categories. At the Paton Manufacturing Company in 1887, women and girls provided 76 per cent of the labour in the lowest paid categories (see Table 15). Forty years later at the Empire cotton mill in Welland, women constituted 59 per cent of the entire labour force and 69 per cent in the lower paid job categories. Even when women or girls were employed in higher paying departments they usually served as assistants. In the weave room most of the weavers would be women, but all of the loom fixers and supervisors would be men. Mule spinners were always men and during the decade 1911–20 were paid about 28 cents per hour compared to 17 cents per hour for female ring spinners.[5]

There is ample evidence that in addition to occupying lower paying job categories, women were paid less for doing the same job. The secretary-treasurer of a Hamilton cotton mill stated that a man operating four looms would make $8–10 per week and a woman would make $6–8 per week. In 1884 the Ontario Bureau of Industries conducted an extensive survey of wage rates and hours of work in manufacturing. It found that in the cotton industry male spinners earned $7.69 for 59.45 hours of work; female spinners earned $4.95 for 59.85 hours. Male weavers earned $6.72 per week; female weavers earned $5.93. Much the same differential was found in every job category where men and women worked; the same was true of the knitting and woollen mills surveyed.[6] Data assembled by the Royal Commission on the Textile Industry in 1936–37 indicates that women were still paid substantially less than men in the same job categories. At the Hespeler plant of Dominion Woollens and Worsteds "male mule-spinners who were earning from $18.00 to $22.00 per week for a fifty-hour week" were "replaced by girls at half the wage."[7]

Traditionally it was argued that jobs occupied by men required more skill or strength; this was said to be the case with mule spinning as opposed to ring spinning.[8] Initially this was probably true, but strength was not an important factor after the self-acting mule came into widespread use in the later nineteenth century. In England it seems probable that mule spinning remained a male occupation because the powerful Amalgamated Association of Cotton-Spinners and Twiners refused to accept female spinners.[9] J. Parr's studies of the hosiery/knit-goods sector in Ontario and in Britain strongly suggest that male/female jobs were determined primarily on the basis of labour availability and management strategies and preconceptions rather than on the inherent skill levels required by the job.[10]

In the early years of the cotton industry there were no legal restrictions on the use of child labour in mills. Although most child employees were between the ages of 14 and 16, some were as young as 9 or 10.[11] In 1884 and 1885 Ontario and Quebec passed factory acts that prevented the employment of girls under 14 and boys under 12 years of age. In 1895 and 1907 the minimum age was raised to 14 in Ontario and Quebec respectively.[12] Although the enforcement of these acts was lax, they may have contributed to a decline in child labour in textile mills from 21 per cent of the total in 1871 to 10 per cent in 1911 and 2 per cent in 1931.[13] Legal restrictions may also have restricted adult female employment. For example, in Quebec women were not permitted to work night shifts, and after 1925 they were covered by minimum-wage legislation while men were not. This legislation led to the replacement of women by men at Sherbrooke, Trois-Rivières, and Magog.[14]

Technological change also contributed to the decline in child and female labour in the textile industry. The introduction of heavier machinery that operated at higher speeds and required greater strength to operate made the employment of children and women less advantageous. Many technological developments that were introduced between 1900 and 1940 — the automatic loom, warp-tying machines, and long-draft spinning — eliminated jobs in areas where female employment had been concentrated.[15] Changing social attitudes also seem to have contributed to a decline in the employment of women in some sectors of the industry. In her study of the cotton sector in Quebec, Gail Cuthbert Brandt found that prior to World War I there was a general acceptance of women working outside the home under certain economic circumstances; after the war, attitudes changed and there was considerable opposition to women working. This attitude was not confined to elites and the managerial classes; in 1939 the Confédération des travailleurs catholiques du Canada, with which the Fédération catholique nationale du textile was affiliated, passed a resolution against the employment of female labour.[16]

Children were employed at various light tasks: taking full spindles off spinning machines, carrying supplies from one machine to another, and working as apprentices. Quite often children were taken on as apprentice weavers and spinners and expected to work for several weeks or months without pay while they learned the work. Even after they became proficient, children were paid at lower rates than adults. The *Canadian Journal of Fabrics* noted in 1886 "Now-a-days, they [children] can quickly be taught, to do what ten years ago would have been called men's work. They do this at boy's wages and as efficiently as men."[17] The practice of substituting children for adults was resented, and in one instance the Montreal Cotton

Company mill was struck for two weeks in protest against the use of learners (unpaid apprentices).[18] In 1935 the Wabasso mill at Trois-Rivières was struck to protest the replacement of men by young women. The collective agreement negotiated by the Fédération catholique nationale du textile with Dominion Textile and Montreal Cotton in 1937 limited the number of learners in any mill to five per cent of the total number of employees.[19]

Initially most workers were recruited locally; indeed, the availability of labour was one consideration in locating a mill. The presence of large numbers of immigrant Scots weavers has been put forward as one of the reasons for the growth of the woollen sector in Lanark County. Equally the availability of abundant, cheap, and docile labour is sometimes given as a reason for the growth of the cotton sector in Montréal and the Eastern Townships. Although assumptions about the docility and cheapness of the Quebec labour force have been challenged,[20] there is little doubt as to the abundance of the labour force. For a generation before the development of the cotton industry in Quebec, thousands of French Canadians had been migrating to the mill towns of New England. French Canadian mill workers also moved to Cornwall and Hamilton to work in mills there.[21] When Quebec mills exhausted their supplies of local labour, they recruited from more distant areas, particularly the Saguenay. Often entire families were brought to work in the mills.[22]

Large mills also recruited workers in Great Britain. Penmans Limited, for example, recruited about 700 workers in Britain for its Paris plants between 1907 and 1928.[23] Wages were higher in Canada than in Britain and experienced workers were easily recruited. In several cases British workers were recruited as strikebreakers or were hired in the aftermath of a strike to keep wages down. As a result they were often resented. After a strike at the St. Croix mill in Milltown, New Brunswick, in 1886, 116 Scottish mill workers were imported to replace those who had been most active in the strike; they were ostracized and most left within a few months.[24] At the Kingston, Ontario, mill there was a near-riot between Canadian and English women as a result of resentment over the low wages that the English employees were willing to accept.[25]

British workers were also recruited for their experience and, in the case of lower level management, for the formal training that many had received in British trade schools. Some experienced workers and supervisors were recruited in the United States. As a result of recruiting abroad there was often strong British, and to a lesser extent American, influence from the level of the section hand (foreman) up. The split between shop floor and management was particularly noticeable in Quebec, where the workers were usually French speaking and management was English speaking; in the Montreal Cotton Company plant at Valleyfield a French Canadian did not rise above the level of assistant overseer until 1900.[26]

Mill managers and owners were primarily English speaking. One exception was Victor Hudon, who organized both the V. Hudon Cotton Mills Company and the St. Ann Spinning Company. Apparently both mills had substantial inputs of French Canadian capital; the Hudon mill is the only major mill known to have kept its early minute books in French. However, by 1884 Hudon had lost control of both mills to A.F. Gault, who amalgamated them as the Hochelaga Cotton Company.[27] Jacques Grenier, a Montréal merchant, also had extensive textile interests; he served as a director of the Hudon mill and of Montreal Cotton and vice-president of the Dominion Cotton Mills Company.[28] The stockbroker Senator L.J. Forget replaced him as vice-president of Dominion Cotton Mills in 1902 and became president on the death of A.F. Gault in 1903. As president Forget was a member of the syndicate that organized Dominion Textile in 1905.[29]

Working conditions in the large textile mills were characterized by long hours, low pay, strict discipline, and comparatively unhealthy and unsafe working conditions. During the nineteenth century a 60-hour week was universal in the textile industry; equally long weeks were common in most other industries. Often Saturday was a half day, but this was achieved by working 11 hours on weekdays. When business was good and the mill was running behind on orders, the workday could be extended by 3 or 4 hours. As late as 1935 the industry made no distinction in wage rates between regular and overtime work. The 1937 contract signed by Dominion Textile and Montreal Cotton was apparently the first major contract to place a premium (of five per cent) on overtime work.[30] Although work in the textile mills was not seasonal in the way that work in sawmills often was, it could be irregular. Water-powered mills often had to close down because of abnormally high or low water. During recessions mills often ran on short time or closed entirely for weeks or months. A. Gault, secretary of the Stormont Cotton Manufacturing Company in Cornwall, Ontario, a relatively successful and stable mill, estimated that the mill provided between nine and ten months of work annually.[31]

The 60-hour week remained a standard in the industry until the first decade of the twentieth century when some mills began to operate on 55- or 57-hour weeks.[32] By the mid-1930s most mills in Quebec had moved to a 55-hour week while most mills in Ontario and the Maritimes had adopted a 50-hour week. A majority of workers in the cotton sector worked 55 or more hours per week; most workers in the woollen and silk/synthetics sectors worked between 48 and 54 hours per week. Hours were shorter in the knit-goods and hosiery sector; 71 per cent of employees in the sector worked 50 hours or less per week.[33] Throughout the period of this study, shift work was unusual but not unknown; one large cotton mill in Quebec adopted a three-shift system in 1935.[34] Penmans in Paris in the 1930s operated a two-shift system; the night shift was staffed by men, the day shift was staffed by women and youths.[35]

In 1881 the average worker in the cotton sector received an annual wage of $202; workers in the woollen and knit-goods sectors received about the same amount (see Table 13). Assuming that mills worked an average of 259 days (ten months) each year, this works out to an average of 78 cents per day, or $4.70 per week, compared to about $7.10 per week for a labourer and $10.00 per week for a carpenter.[36] The low rate is largely attributable to the number of women and children employed. The superintendent of a Nova Scotia mill testified in 1888 that in his mill with about 300 employees, 45 men earned an average of $7.50 per week, 110 women earned an average of $3.90 per week, and 145 children earned an average of $1.25 per week for an overall average of $3.16 per week.[37]

The average rate of $4.70 per week covered a broad range. At the Stormont cotton mill in 1888, boys received 35 cents per day and the fabric designer received $4.25 per day. A 15-year-old cotton spinner with one year's experience in a Nova Scotia mill earned $1.25 to $1.50 per week on piecework. Weavers were generally paid by the "cut" or piece of cloth completed. Experienced male weavers could earn $8 to $10 per week operating four looms; women could earn $6 to $8.[38]

By 1911, wages had increased. The average annual wage for a cotton worker was $370; for a woollen worker, $359; and for a knit-goods worker, $336 (see Table 13). Adult males in the cotton sector earned $450 annually, adult females earned $311, and children earned $192.[39] In spite of the increase, wages in the textile industry lagged behind those in manufacturing generally; the average annual wage in manufacturing in 1910 was $417.[40]

Although the textile industry was, and remains, a low-wage industry in comparison to manufacturing generally, it was relatively more attractive for women than it was for men. In 1934 the average weekly earnings for a male in the textile industry were $17.32 compared to $21.28 for all males employed in the principal manufacturing industries. In contrast the average woman employed in the textile industry earned slightly more, $12.41 per week, than the average, $11.82, for women employed in manufacturing.[41]

Wages were generally higher in the woollen sector than in other branches. In 1881, wages in the woollen sector were about $216 per year compared to $202 in the cotton sector and $201 in the knit-goods sector. Over the entire period 1871–1940, wages in the woollen sector averaged 111 per cent of wages in the cotton sector and 116 per cent of wages in the knit-goods sector. Until at least 1911 the higher wages in the woollen sector can probably be explained by the higher proportion of adult males employed in woollens; after 1911 the cotton sector employed proportionately more men than did the woollen sector. Knit goods, by contrast with the woollen industry, consistently employed a high proportion of women and paid the lowest wages in the textile industry. The silk/synthetic sector provides the clearest illustration of the inverse relationship between wage levels and the proportion of women employed. In 1920 it had the highest level of female employment, 77 per cent, and the lowest annual wages, $702, of the four major textile sectors. Between 1925 and 1940, the synthetic sector (which employed a high proportion of men) grew from nothing to be the employer of roughly half of the hands in the silk/synthetic sector. As a result, by 1940, women constituted only 35 per cent of the labour force in the sector. Annual wages had increased to $1030 per employee, only slightly less than the level paid in the woollen sector and well ahead of the levels in cottons and knit goods (*see* Tables 13 and 14).

Why the woollen sector employed proportionately more adult males than other branches of the textile industry is not clear. It was the oldest and most conservative branch of the textile industry, and many small mills were located in small centres where there may have been cultural restraints on the employment of women and children outside the home. It is noteworthy that in the late 1880s the Paton mill in Sherbrooke, the largest and one of the most progressive mills in the country, employed an unusually high proportion of women and children, 73 per cent compared to 56 per cent in the woollen sector at large. Technological conservatism may have contributed to a high proportion of adult male employees. The woollen sector was slow to introduce labour-saving devices, which often permitted the substitution of female for male labour; most noticeably the woollen sector continued to use the mule, a male-operated machine, long after it had been abandoned by the cotton sector. On the other hand, the knit-goods sector, which employed the highest proportion of women, also continued to use the mule after it had been abandoned by the cotton sector.

In addition to wages, many companies offered a variety of minor benefits, often referred to as "welfare work," that were designed to secure and hold a contented labour force. Many of the larger firms provided some company housing: in 1888 the Hochelaga Cotton Manufacturing Company in Montréal owned 50 to 60 houses that it rented for about $60 per annum. Imperial Cotton in Hamilton built 50 houses for its employees in 1901, and the St. Croix mill operated a 42-room boarding house. It is unclear whether or not the companies subsidized rents in their lodgings. No statistics are available that are directly comparable to the rental rates of $60 per year charged by the Hochelaga mill. However, Jacques Rouillard has estimated that in 1900 a skilled worker with a family of five paid $108 annually in rent in Montréal. General wholesale and retail price indices for the period 1888–1900 either remained stable or declined; if the same were true of housing costs, then the Hochelaga tenement rate of $60 per year was relatively low. It was also low in comparison to housing costs in comparable Ontario textile centres. An Ontario Bureau of Industries survey for the year

1884–85 reported annual rental rates of $58 in Almonte, $70 in Galt, $86 in Hamilton, $51 in Hespeler, $70 in Kingston, $71 in Peterborough, and $110 in Toronto.[42]

The concept of profit sharing was widely discussed during the 1890s and early twentieth century, but few plans seem to have been organized. In 1919 Canadian Cottons introduced an incentive program based on productivity increases, but little is known about how effective it was.[43] Dominion Textile, Montreal Cotton, and Canadian Cottons all had employee pension plans; Dominion Textile's non-contributory plan was begun in 1923.[44]

Most companies made some contribution towards employees' recreation in the form of company picnics, Christmas parties, and sports teams. In Valleyfield Andrew Gault and the Montreal Cotton Company established and endowed a combined Protestant kindergarten, primary school, and academy. The company also organized the Gault Institute, which provided recreational facilities including a billiard room, library, baths, skating rink, bowling green, and tennis courts. Membership was confined to company employees but was not automatic. In 1897 when the company employed about 1500, the institute had only 140 members;[45] one wonders if membership was drawn primarily from management.

Textile mills were noisy, hot, dusty workplaces; to a certain extent they were also unhealthy and dangerous. In the weaving room the clatter from the looms made conversation impossible and hearing impairment an occupational hazard. Because textiles could be worked best in a hot, humid atmosphere, weave and spinning rooms were often heated and humidified by releasing live steam into them; in 1924 an article in the *Canadian Textile Journal* suggested a temperature of 75–80 degrees Fahrenheit and a relative humidity of 65–70 per cent was desirable for spinning wool.[46] Many nineteenth-century authorities suggested higher temperatures and humidities. The air was full of fly (loose fibres), which resulted in a high rate of respiratory disease among mill workers.[47] In the rayon plants, fumes from the acids used in producing rayon fibres caused so much eye irritation that workers sometimes could not complete their shifts.[48]

The work was seldom either mentally or physically demanding, but it required close attention over long hours. The long hours were damaging to the health of the younger workers and, through fatigue, contributed to accidents. Textile mills were not as dangerous as many other industries (particularly heavy industry),[49] but the combination of young, often-tired workers with vast numbers of unprotected shafts, gears, and belts led to numerous accidents. Picking and carding rooms were particularly dangerous, and many workers lost fingers, hands, and arms in the gearing and in the cards themselves. Belt drives, shafts, and elevators were also frequent sources of accidents, many of which were fatal.

During the 1880s, factory inspectors were appointed in both Ontario and Quebec to control child labour and to enforce safety regulations; labour groups complained that the inspectors were ineffectual. In 1891 the Hamilton Trades and Labour Council accused the local factory inspector of neglecting his duties. It charged that he regularly made his inspection in the company of foremen and that whereas the inspector had reported 20 accidents in Hamilton in 1890, the local newspapers had reported twice that number.[50] The continuing litany of accidents in the *Canadian Journal of Fabrics* (a trade publication, and not necessarily a friend of labour) reinforces the impression that the factory inspectors were not as effective as one would have hoped.

The *Journal* also makes frequent reference to employees, or the parents or spouses of employees, suing for damages suffered in accidents. Under workmen's compensation acts passed in Quebec and Ontario in the 1880s and under common law,[51] employees had to prove negligence on the part of employers to obtain compensation under the law. In 1910 Quebec passed a workers' compensation act that largely removed the question of responsibility from the award of damages. In 1914 Ontario passed a similar act; Nova Scotia and New Brunswick passed acts modelled on Ontario's in 1915 and 1918.

In the absence of effective legal protection against the consequences of accidents or sickness, some employee groups (or employers) organized protective associations that provided rudimentary accident, life, and sickness insurance. The 1888 constitution of the Relief Society of the Star Woollen Mills (the R. Forbes Company of Hespeler) provided up to ten weeks of sick benefits, accident insurance, and death benefits.[52] The society may have been organized by the company and was certainly approved of by the company. Membership was compulsory except for learners (apprentices). It was financed by wage deductions and managed by the overseers of the various departments, and its funds were held by the company's treasurer, who paid interest on them. Plans such as this were comparatively rare according to a report made in 1882.[53]

The testimony given before the Royal Commission on the Relations of Labour and Capital gives a good view of factory discipline in the 1880s. Discipline, including hiring and firing, was in the hands of overseers of the various divisions such as weaving or spinning and ultimately in the hands of the mill manager.[54] Discipline was usually enforced by fines and its rigour varied from mill to mill. In the Cornwall Manufacturing Company, fines were imposed for bad work, destroying property, neglect of work, quitting without due notice, and being absent.[55] Faults in weaving had to be repaired, an expensive process, or the cloth discarded; consequently most mills levied fines for poor work in the weave room. Fines for being late were also common. Fines for destroying property apparently were related to horseplay that resulted in broken windows or minor damage to equipment. Deliberate damage to equipment probably led to dismissal and legal action.[56] Almost all mills held back a week to two weeks' pay, which could be used as a disciplinary lever. In particular, if employees failed to give the customary two weeks' notice when leaving work, they usually forfeited their pay. Mills did not give notice when they discharged employees. How common fines were is unclear. In the Parks mills in Saint John, fines totalling $23.58 were collected over a six-month period in 1887–88 when the total wage bill was $49,920; at the Paton mill at about the same time, fines equalled two per cent of the weavers' earnings.[57]

There was occasional verbal and physical abuse of employees, but it does not seem to have been an accepted norm. A St. Ann mill overseer who struck an employee was taken to court, and a Stormont mill overseer who swore at his female employees because "they talked and laughed and made some noise" during their lunch hour later apologized to them.[58] Two employees in a Nova Scotia mill reported to the Royal Commission on the Relations of Labour and Capital that they had seen overseers slap and kick child employees.[59] The questions asked by the commissioners indicate that there was concern about discipline in the mills, but the answers the commissioners received leave the extent and harshness of discipline unclear.

In some mule-spinning and weave rooms discipline was delegated to workers through subcontracting. At the Paton mill in 1888, mule spinners were paid by the pound of wool spun. Master spinners were responsible for more than one mule and hired assistants to run them. In one case a spinner was responsible for five mules and employed five assistants who were responsible for repairing broken ends on the machines.[60] It is not known how common the system was in Canada, but a similar system was universal in Britain. Similar subcontracting systems existed in some weave rooms. Experienced weavers were usually paid by the piece or cut of cloth produced. In the 1880s a good weaver could tend four looms at a time, each of which would produce one cut per day. Some weavers increased their production by employing assistants or tenders to help with minor tasks so that the weaver could tend six looms. The tender was usually a child learning to weave and was paid a minimal salary of $1.00 per week.[61] The weaver was responsible for paying, disciplining, and training the tender.

Most textile workers received their training on the job under the eyes of experienced workers. More-formal training was unusual but not unknown: the Barrymore Cloth Company maintained a weaving school in its Toronto mill in 1927, and the Rosamond Woollen Company offered evening courses to its employees (1920).[62] The need for formal training was recognized from early in the century, but it was not until 1945–47 that textile trade schools were established in Saint-Hyacinthe and Hamilton.[63] To a considerable extent the industry bypassed the need for more extensive training in Canada

31 Tieing ends on a loom at the Collie woollen mill in Appleton, Ontario, 1947. The dark row across the warp threads (below the man's elbow) is a warp-stop mechanism that stopped the loom if a warp thread broke.
National Archives of Canada, PA 180950, Malak Collection, 725-124

by importing skilled workers and managers from Britain and the United States. In some cases Canadian-born managers went abroad to study the industry; for example, Alexander Rosamond, the heir apparent to the Rosamond business, took a four-year course at the Yorkshire Textile College in Leeds.[64]

Low pay, long hours, and unpleasant working conditions combined with large numbers of workers in a single location could have provided fertile ground for labour unions, but organization proved difficult. In Hamilton in the 1880s the Knights of Labour organized two local assemblies that consisted primarily of cotton workers. Knights of Labour were also active in Cornwall and at Milltown, New Brunswick.[65] None of these locals are known to have survived for very long, and it is difficult to measure their influence. Knights of Labour organizers may have been involved in the St. Croix strike in 1886, and Knights of Labour assemblies were involved in the strikes at the Canada and Stormont mills in Cornwall in 1886–87.[66] The

32 Inspecting a Howard and Bullough flat card, ca. 1940.
National Film Board, WRM 1600; National Archives of Canada, PA 160565

Trades and Labour Council supported strikes at the two cotton mills in Hamilton in 1890, but whether or not the Knights of Labour were involved is not known.[67] Labour relations were unusually bad at the Stormont and Canada mills, which had at least ten strikes between them between 1883 and 1899. The St. Croix and Moncton companies were each struck at least three times in the same period, and ten other cotton mills were struck at least once. Strikes seem to have been less common in woollen mills, but they were not unknown. Most of the strikes in the nineteenth century were in reaction to pay cuts; a few related to working conditions and discipline.[68]

In 1900 and in 1906–08 there were a series of bitter and violent strikes in Quebec. Four strikes at Valleyfield in 1900 apparently centred on the employment of apprentices, discipline, sympathy for construction workers building extensions to the mill at Valleyfield, and rivalry between French- and English-speaking workers.[69] Very little was gained by the strikes and by 1903 the Union ouvrière fédérale, which had represented the strikers, collapsed.[70]

106

33 Workers leaving the Collie woollen mill, Appleton, ca. 1948.
National Archives of Canada, PA 179686, Malak Collection, 725-182

A series of strikes at Montreal Cotton's Valleyfield mill, Dominion Textile's Quebec mills, and Penmans' Saint-Hyacinthe plant between 1906 and 1908 began with demands for pay increases and recognition of the Fédération des ouvriers textiles du Canada (FOTC) and the United Textile Workers of America (UTWA). Initially the strikes were successful, but when a recession in the textile industry developed in 1907, the employers' attitude hardened. In 1908 the group of managers and owners who jointly controlled Penmans, Montreal Cotton, and Dominion Textile instituted wage cuts of ten per cent and the ensuing strikes broke the FOTC.[71] Although unions continued to exist in the textile industry, they were relatively ineffective until the 1930s.[72]

Despite a sustained organizing effort and a series of major strikes (strikes in the textile industry accounted for ten per cent of all time lost to strikes in Canada between 1901 and 1915),[73] labour's attempt to organize the textile industry was a failure. This failure has been attributed to a number of factors: the number of young women and children with few skills who were employed in the industry, a tradition of acceptance of authority, and no

34 Workers in front of the main drivewheel of the Gibson mill in Marysville, New Brunswick. The photograph appears to have been taken at the time the wheel was installed, ca. 1884. The mill contained eight miles of belting and was powered by two Harris-Corliss steam engines of 650 horsepower each.
Public Archives of New Brunswick, P61/66

tradition of union activity. It is significant that many of the strikes in the years 1906–08 began among the mule spinners, who were male, skilled, and often had experience in English mills, where mule spinners formed one of the strongest unions. The location of many mills in small towns where the mills provided the only employment contributed to union weakness. Finally, the concentration of ownership, with the resulting ability to shift production from a struck mill, was a great advantage for management.[74] This advantage did not apply to the woollen sector; however, the continuing decline of the woollen sector left labour unable to make any gains except in some of the larger mills.

35 Workers in the Gibson mill, Marysville. The beams in the foreground and the extraction hoods to the left indicate that this may have been the sizing department, where warp threads were passed through a starch solution to strengthen them for weaving.
Public Archives of New Brunswick, P5/416

Much of this explanation of the failure of unions in the textile industry has been challenged by Jacques Ferland. He argues that most of the strikes in the Province of Quebec and in Cornwall in the years 1900–1908 were begun by weave-room employees who were predominantly young French Canadian women. The skilled adult male workers were comparatively conservative until 1906–08, when the mule spinners led several strikes.[75] Ferland suggests that the weavers' militancy was one reason why Canadian mills were so quick to introduce automatic looms, which reduced weave-room staff by over 50 per cent. On the other hand, he suggests that the survival of mule spinning in Canada after it had been abandoned in the United States can be attributed, in part, to the conservatism of the mule spinners. Without accepting Ferland's case in its entirety, the frequency of strikes in the years 1900–1908 strongly suggests that it was not the passivity of the workers but the strength of the textile companies that led to the failure of the unions in this period.

The labour unrest of the years 1900–1908 was followed by a quarter century of relative peace. There was a major strike at Dominion Textile's Montréal and Montmorency mills in 1919, but it seems to have arisen from the general postwar labour unrest rather than from causes that were specific to the textile industry. Union activity was unimportant during the 1920s. A few UTWA locals survived through the decade, and in 1926 the Confédération des travailleurs catholiques du Canada (CTCC) organized the Fédération catholique nationale du textile (FCNT) as an umbrella group for a number of locals. The FCNT became dormant after 1930.[76]

The long period of labour quiescence came to an end in 1936–37 when a series of strikes cost the industry over 400 000 working days, equal to 49 per cent of all time lost to strikes in manufacturing. The major strikes were at Wabasso in Trois-Rivières (17 500 days lost), Courtaulds (37 000 days) and Canadian Cottons (44 000 days) in Cornwall, Dominion Woollens and Worsteds in Peterborough (29 000 days), Empire Cotton in Welland (29 000 days), and Dominion Textile, Montreal Cotton, and Drummondville Cotton plants in Quebec (200 000 days).[77]

The principal issues in these strikes were wage increases, working conditions, and union recognition. In many respects union recognition was the key element in the strikes as the companies wished to avoid recognition at all costs and the workers found the united voice and continuity provided by a union essential to enforce agreements. In 1935 the workers at Wabasso struck in protest against a company policy of replacing adult male workers with girls. Following intervention by the mayor of Trois-Rivières, the workers returned to work on the promise of Wabasso to give preference to married employees and those supporting families. The company also accepted a plant committee. Dissatisfaction with Wabasso's implementation of the contract arose within months, and the plant was organized by the

UTWA and was struck again in February 1936. The strikers' demands included union recognition and wage increases. After a ten-day strike and intervention by the mayor and federal government mediators, the strikers agreed to return to work on the promise of a later wage increase but no union recognition.[78]

In 1936–37 both Courtaulds and Canadian Cottons in Cornwall were shut down by major strikes. At Courtaulds in 1936 two UTWA organizers began to organize an independent local, the Rayon Textile Workers Industrial Union. Several workers were dismissed for union activity; this led to a brief wildcat strike and then to a three-week general strike. The major demands were increased wages, improved working conditions (particularly better ventilation of the fumes produced in the rayon process), and union recognition. After mediation by a federal conciliation officer, the company granted most of the workers' pay and working-conditions demands, but refused to recognize the union. The workers returned to work on these terms, but over the next year resorted to a number of job actions to enforce the agreement and reinstate dismissed union members. Because of the continuous nature of rayon production, Courtaulds was particularly vulnerable to irregular work stoppages, and in order to secure labour peace it recognized the union in 1937. Recognition was made easier when the workers disaffiliated from the American-dominated UTWA and received a charter from the Trades and Labour Council of Canada.[79]

The Courtaulds strike gave an example to the workers at Canadian Cottons in Cornwall (and the Rayon Textile Workers Union provided organizational support), and in 1937 the company's mills in Cornwall were struck for 24 days. The strikers' principal demands were the recognition of the union (the UTWA), increased wages, and improved working conditions. The Cornwall strike coincided with a strike at Dominion Woollens and Worsteds in Peterborough. Initially the Peterborough workers were unorganized, but during the strike they affiliated with the UTWA. In both strikes company officials refused to meet with UTWA officials, but did meet with workers' representatives. Ultimately both strikes were settled through the mediation of the Ontario Department of Labour. Some improvements in working conditions were granted, and the question of hours and wages was referred to the Industry and Labour Board of Ontario. Both companies agreed to accept workers' committees, but refused to recognize the union. After the strike, workers in both locations disaffiliated from the UTWA and joined the Canadian Textile Workers Union; in 1938 Canadian Cottons recognized the union in order to guarantee labour peace. Dominion Woollens and Worsteds refused to recognize the new union and transferred much of its operations from the Auburn mill in Peterborough, where the strike had begun, to its Hespeler plant, which had refused to join the strike. In 1939 the Auburn mill was closed.[80]

The UTWA was also involved in a strike by 865 workers at Empire Cotton Mills in Welland. The workers' demands included a 20-per-cent wage increase and changes in working conditions that affected the productivity of pieceworkers.[81] Demands of this nature were not uncommon; the Peterborough settlment included clauses guaranteeing equitable distribution of piecework and payment for pieceworkers kept idle more than eight minutes.[82] After a 35-day strike and intervention by both the federal and provincial departments of labour, the Empire mill workers returned to work with a promise of improved working conditions, pay increases for some workers if efficiency warranted, and acceptance of shop committees, but no recognition of the union.[83]

In 1935–36 the CTCC revived the FCNT and began organizing Dominion Textile, Montreal Cotton, and Drummondville Cotton, a Dominion Textile subsidiary, as well as a number of smaller Quebec firms. In 1937 the FCNT asked Dominion Textile to negotiate a collective agreement and when the company refused, the union called a strike against all three firms in Montréal, Magog, Valleyfield, Drummondville, and Sherbrooke. The strike affected 9000 workers and lasted 24 days. In the end the union was forced by economic weakness and the return to work of some operatives in Montréal to accept a mediation proposal by Premier Duplessis.[84] A committee composed of both unionized and non-unionized employees negotiated a contract that provided for a reduction in hours, wage increases, recognition of overtime work, partial union recognition (but no closed shop), slightly improved working conditions, and control of the number and duration of apprenticeships.[85]

Although the contract was favourable to the workers in many respects, it could be abrogated after only six months. Dominion Textile took advantage of this clause and renounced the contract in May of 1938. The FCNT did not feel strong enough to strike again and appealed to the Quebec Fair Wages Board for mediation. The Fair Wages Board continued most of the provisions of the 1937 contract, but the union lost the degree of recognition it had gained. In 1938 and 1939 the FCNT locals in Montréal and Valleyfield collapsed. Although locals continued to exist in Drummondville, Sherbrooke, and Magog, they were moribund; only the Montmorency local was active.[86]

In general the textile firms were much more willing to grant improvements in working conditions and minor increases in wages than they were to concede union recognition. Only the Cornwall mills granted full union recognition; the partial recognition granted by Dominion Textile was lost in 1938. From the union perspective the strikes of 1936–37 must be considered failures, but they were only the first round in a continuing struggle that lasted into the mid-1950s. During World War II there were numerous minor strikes throughout the industry. Kent Rowley and Madeleine Parent successfully organized Dominion Textile workers in Montréal and Montreal Cotton workers in Valleyfield for the UTWA and in 1946 led a long and bitter strike that forced both companies to recognize the union as well as grant certain other benefits.[87] In 1947 the UTWA lost a bitter strike at Lachute, but the FCNT fought successful strikes in Louiseville, Drummond-ville, Magog, Montmorency, and Sherbrooke.[88]

There were major strikes (93 500 working days lost) in Saint-Jean, Drummondville, Sherbrooke, and Saint-Georges-de-Beauce in 1948 and another strike at Dominion Textile's Montréal and Valleyfield mills in 1952. Although not all of these strikes were successful, they did serve to make unions an accepted presence in the textile industry. By 1950 about 40 per cent of workers in the primary textile industry belonged to the three major unions: the UTWA (15 000 members), the FCNT (10 000), and the Textile Workers Union of America (15 500);[89] the Textile Workers Union of America had absorbed many Canadian Textile Workers Union locals that had originally been organized by the UTWA.

The strikes of 1936–37 and 1946–52 were qualified successes when compared to those of 1900 and 1906–08. In general the workers were organized prior to the strikes or quickly joined recognized unions. Consequently they had the benefit of experienced organizers although they garnered little financial support from their affiliations. Public attitudes were probably more favourable to unions in the latter period than they had been in the former. Some of the strikes garnered important local support.[90] Although neither the Ontario nor Quebec government could be considered pro-labour, both provinces had labour legislation that provided for arbitration and union recognition. The Depression had undermined the confidence of industry and had weakened the public's acceptance of the unfettered rights of capital. The Royal Commission on the Textile Industry had publicized the industry's shortcomings and emphasized its responsibilities. Even industry leaders such as A.O. Dawson, president of Canadian Cottons, Dominion Woollens and Worsteds, and Belding-Corticelli, admitted (in 1934) that workers had a right to bargain collectively.[91] Ultimately Dawson recognized a union at Canadian Cottons in Cornwall although not at Dominion Woollens and Worsteds.

Geographical Distribution[1]

The early carding and fulling mills and woollen factories were water powered and the location of suitable water power determined their specific location. Because communications were poor and because the mills served local markets, mills were widely distributed; in 1851 there were carding mills in 37 of the 42 rural census districts in Upper Canada and woollen factories in 28 districts. In Lower Canada 34 out of 36 rural districts had carding mills and 13 had woollen factories. Twenty years later 75 per cent of census districts in Canada had carding mills and 45 per cent had woollen factories. By 1891 there were carding mills in 61 per cent of the census districts in Ontario, Quebec, Nova Scotia, and New Brunswick, and woollen factories in 54 per cent of the districts. In addition 68 per cent of all census districts had, on average, 17 local weaving shops (*see* Table 16).

Although woollen mills were widely distributed there were nevertheless regional concentrations. In 1871, 73 per cent of the woollen mills and 83 per cent of employment in the mills were in Ontario. The woollen cloth industry remained Ontario based until after the Second World War, and it was not until the 1950s that employment in the Quebec branch of the sector exceeded that in the Ontario branch. Not only was absolute employment in the woollen sector in Ontario greater than in any other province, the per capita employment in Ontario was double that in any other province from 1871 to 1911 (*see* Table 8).

Within Ontario certain regions specialized in woollen production. In 1871 the two most important areas, each of which produced about 15 per cent of all woollen cloth produced in Canada, were the Upper Grand River Valley in Waterloo and Brant counties and the Mississippi Valley in Lanark County. There were lesser but still important concentrations of mills around, but not in, Hamilton and Toronto and in Cornwall. Outside Ontario the only important centres of woollen production were Sherbrooke, Quebec, and Saint John, New Brunswick. Twenty years later the distribution of the sector was much the same except that the Mississippi Valley had declined slightly in relative importance and Sherbrooke and the Eastern Townships had increased in relative importance. There were also important mills in Toronto and Montréal.

The distribution of carding and fulling mills was different from the distribution of woollen mills. Carding and fulling mills existed primarily to serve the homespun industry and because homespinning was more common in Quebec than in Ontario, carding mills were more common in Quebec than in Ontario. In proportion to population they were also more common in Nova Scotia and New Brunswick than in Ontario.

Perhaps because of its early origin as an adjunct to domestic textile production, the woollen sector had a tendency to locate in smaller centres. In 1933 about 40 per cent of all employees in the woollen sector were in towns with populations of less than 5000.[2] Some quite small towns supported large mills: the Rosamond mill in Almonte (population in 1931, 2415) employed 204 in 1933 and the Dominion Woollens and Worsted plant in Hespeler (population 2752) employed 619.

Like the woollen sector, the knitting sector was primarily Ontario based. In 1881, 66 out of 83 knitting mills in Canada were in Ontario, and from 1881 until after World War I from 70 to 85 per cent of employment in the sector was in Ontario mills. It was not until the 1950s that the majority of employees in the sector worked in Quebec, and even today almost one-third of the employees in knitting mills work in Ontario. The Maritime provinces have never had a very large knitting industry. The knitting sector developed much later than the woollen sector and, perhaps because mills were designed to serve more than local markets, it was never as geographically dispersed as was the woollen sector. In the 1891 census Toronto was the single most important centre of the industry, with important production in the Eastern Townships, in Kingston, in the Grand River Valley, in the Mississippi River Valley, and in Middlesex and Welland counties. The industry operated in both large and small centres: in 1933 about 17 per cent of its employees were in towns of less than 5000; at the other extreme, about 17 per cent were employed in Toronto. Toronto remained the single most important centre for the hosiery/knit-goods sector in the 1930s; its importance was the result of the presence of a large number of medium-sized firms. The largest firms in the sector, Penmans and Julius Kayser, operated in medium-sized centres such as Paris, Saint-Hyacinthe, and Sherbrooke.[3]

The geographic distribution of the cotton sector was very different from that of the woollen or knit-goods/hosiery sector. Because production was concentrated in 20 to 30 large mills, it could not be as dispersed as the woollen sector. Moreover, after beginning as an industry with a substantial base in each of the four provinces, it became, by 1900, a Quebec-dominated (56 per cent of total employment) industry with substantial segments in Ontario (20 per cent) and New Brunswick (18 per cent). The concentration of the sector in Quebec has continued to the present day with roughly two-thirds of all jobs in the cotton yarn and cloth sector being in Quebec. In spite of the absolute importance of the sector in Quebec, it is worth noting that on the basis of employment per capita, the industry was substantially more important in New Brunswick between 1881, and 1911 than it was in Quebec. For example, in 1891, 55 out of every 10 000 New Brunswick residents were employed in cotton mills; in Quebec the figure was 25 per 10 000 (*see* Table 8).

The cotton sector was primarily an industry of the larger industrial towns and cities. Three small towns — Montmorency, Quebec (population in 1931, 4638); Milltown, New Brunswick (population 1735); and Marysville, New Brunswick (population 1512) — had large mills, but they were essentially industrial suburbs of larger centres. The Montréal area had the largest and most important concentration of mills in Canada. In 1891 there were three large mills in Montréal and its suburb, Hochelaga, a small mill at Chambly, and a very large mill at Valleyfield. Their total production was valued at about $2.7 million. In addition, by 1892 Montréal was the headquarters of the Dominion Cotton Mills Company and the Canadian Coloured Cotton Company, which together owned 64 per cent of all the spindles in the Canadian cotton industry. After Montréal, Cornwall was the most important centre with production valued at $1.3 million. The Cornwall industry was very much a subsidiary of the Montréal industry. Most of the mills outside the Montréal area had originally been built by local entrepreneurs and had remained independent until 1890, but the Cornwall mills were built and operated by Montréal interests. After Cornwall there were a number of areas of about equal importance with the annual value of production ranging from about one-half to three-quarters of a million dollars in 1891. They were Stanstead County in Quebec, Hamilton in Ontario, and Milltown, Marysville, and Saint John in New Brunswick. All other areas may be considered minor.

Montréal remained much the most important cotton centre until after World War II. In 1933 roughly 20 per cent of all employees in the cotton sector were in Dominion Textile's six Montréal mills, another 12 per cent were in Montreal Cotton's Valleyfield mill, about 14 per cent were at six plants in the Eastern Townships, and 9.5 per cent were in Montmorency. Cornwall and Hamilton accounted for about 8 per cent each. The only major change from the 1890s was the importance of the Trois-Rivières–Shawinigan area, where Wabasso employed about 12.5 per cent of all workers.[4]

Why the woollen and knitting sectors became so closely identified with Ontario while the cotton sector became primarily a Quebec industry is unclear. The early development of the Ontario woollen industry may have been encouraged by the large quantity of wool produced in Ontario compared to Quebec (*see* Table 7). Equally the early decline of home-spinning in Ontario may have opened a market for Ontario mills. It is, of course, possible that once mills were established, they encouraged wool production and discouraged home weaving. The availability of financing and of labour may also have been a factor in the different development of the woollen and cotton sectors. Many of the weavers in the small Ontario woollen mills and in the cottage industry were British immigrants with experience in British mills. Many French Canadians had experience in the cotton mills of New England.

The average investment in a cotton mill in the nineteenth century was from 8 to 24 times larger than the investment in a woollen mill (*see* Table 12). During the period when the cotton mills were built, Montréal was the undisputed financial capital of Canada, and it may be that Montréal capitalists, with the support of Montréal banks, were more able to finance and operate large mills. Many of the mills in New Brunswick and Ontario (except for the Cornwall mills, which were owned in Montréal) failed during the 1880s because, after financing the construction of the mills, local capitalists could not supply operating capital.[5] The average cotton mill also employed many more hands than the average woollen mill; a typical cotton mill in 1891 had almost 400 hands. The need for a large labour force limited cotton-mill sites to the larger towns and cities, and Montréal, as the largest city in Canada, had an advantage in having a large labour force. It has also been suggested that cotton mills were built in Quebec to take advantage of the low-priced labour that was available there; however, the evidence about comparative wage scales in Quebec and Ontario mills is not conclusive.[6] Moreover, although wage scales in the knitting sector were lower than they were in the cotton sector, the knitting sector was overwhelmingly an Ontario-based industry.

Prior to the 1930s the silk/synthetic sector was so small that it is difficult to discuss its geographical distribution in a meaningful way. Until World War I the industry was completely dominated by the Montréal-area firms of Belding Paul and Company and Corticelli. After the war the industry expanded in the Eastern Townships and in central Ontario. In the 1920s two large synthetic plants were built at Cornwall and Drummondville.

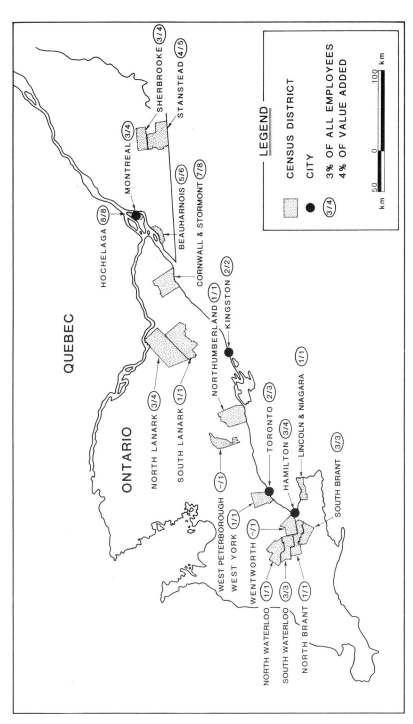

36 Ontario and Quebec census districts with 1% or more of the total employees in Canada (21 349) or value added in Canada ($10 298 794) in selected textile categories (carding, fulling, woollens, cottons, hosiery, knitting, silk, and weaving), 1891.

Drawing by M. Benoit, adapted by D. Kappler

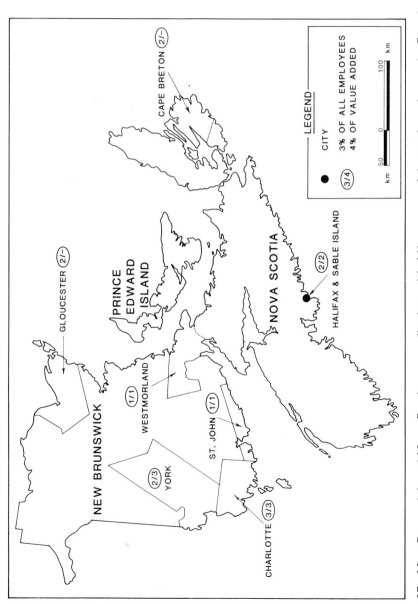

37 New Brunswick and Nova Scotia census districts with 1% or more of the total employees in Canada (21 349) or value added in Canada ($10 298 794) in selected textile categories (carding, fulling, woollens, cottons, hosiery, knitting, silk, and weaving), 1891.

Drawing by M. Benoit, adapted by D. Kappler

Structures

The early woollen mills were built by local craftsmen according to local styles using local materials. Some, probably many, of the early carding and fulling mills and woollen factories were of frame construction. A few have survived. One of these is the Asselstine mill. Built at Earnestown, Upper Canada, between 1828 and 1855, it is now at Upper Canada Village. The Asselstine mill is a small post-and-beam two-storey building with a pitched roof. Stone was also used in early mill construction, and as mills became larger, stone and then brick superseded wood in mill architecture although some smaller mills were built of wood in the later nineteenth century. The Barrington woollen mill, in Barrington, Nova Scotia, and the Stanfield mill at Truro, Nova Scotia, were built of wood in 1882.[1]

By the last half of the nineteenth century when the major Canadian textile mills were built, mill design had become formalized and standardized, although there were important structural differences between British and American mills. Textile mills were long, comparatively narrow three- to six-storey buildings with numerous regularly spaced windows and low gable roofs. The shape was determined by cost and function. Three- to six-storey buildings were marginally cheaper to build than either lower or higher buildings.[2] They were also more compact than lower buildings; this was important because motive power had to be transmitted from a central source to the machines by shafts, belts, and pulleys. Taller buildings suffered from excessive vibration and problems with fire protection. The windows provided natural light, which in the era before electricity was preferred on grounds of quality and safety; narrow buildings ensured that no machines would be too far from a window. High buildings provided more wall space for windows than did lower buildings of comparable areas. Overhead lighting, from skylights, was introduced in Britain about 1830 and made single-storey mills feasible; it was not introduced in North America until about 1880 and was never as popular as it was in Britain.

Mills were very susceptible to fire and both British and American mill architects worked to reduce the risk of fire. The British solution was to eliminate flammable materials in the structure. Wooden frames were replaced by load-bearing brick walls, and wooden columns and beams were replaced by cast-iron beams and columns. Wooden flooring was replaced by concrete supported by shallow brick arches. Where wood could not be eliminated it was enclosed in non-flammable materials. The solution was broadly successful except that if a fire in a building's contents were sufficiently hot, the cast-iron supports would buckle and the entire building collapse.[3]

American mill architects developed the "slow burning" or "mill construction" building. Like the British they adopted load-bearing brick or stone walls, but they did not use cast iron or brick in the internal framing. Instead they employed massive wooden columns and beams and heavy plank flooring. By eliminating joists they reduced the amount of surface exposed to flames and so reduced the speed with which a fire could spread; they also eliminated areas where sprinklers or fire hoses would not reach. It is probable that the differing British and American approaches to mill construction reflected the relative costs of building with iron and brick in Britain and building with wood and brick in the United States.[4]

Most of the large Canadian mills built in the 1870s and 1880s were built on the slow-burning principle. The most probable reasons why Canadians followed the American example were the proximity of American mills, the availability of American mill architects, and the cheapness of wood and the availability of skills necessary for working with wood in Canada.

The typical large Canadian textile mill of the later nineteenth century was a brick or, less frequently, stone rectangular building of three to five storeys with a flat or slightly pitched roof. Mills were large buildings for their time; the main building in the Marysville mill measured 418 feet by 100 feet and was four storeys high (see Fig. 113). Aside from its size, rows of large windows on each floor were a mill's most distinctive exterior feature. A mill usually also had an external staircase tower, often centred on one side of the mill. The upper storey of the tower often contained a water tank connected to a sprinkler system in the mill. The inside of the mill consisted of large open spaces divided into aisles by rows of supporting columns.[5]

In large integrated mills, carding, spinning, weaving, and some of the finishing processes were located in the main mill building; other processes were often located in adjacent buildings. Spinning, particularly mule spinning, was often done on the upper floor because the light was better. It was possible to reduce the number of supporting columns on the upper floors and to provide room for the spinning mules, which were very large, although relatively light, machines. Weaving and carding were generally done on the lower floors, where the weight of the machines and the vibration they caused could be most easily accommodated.[6]

Fear of fire resulted in the relegation of a number of activities to separate buildings. Raw materials and finished goods were kept in separate warehouses. Because fires often occurred in the picker, which opened wool and cotton prior to carding, the picker was located in a separate building. Scouring and dyeing departments were located in separate buildings or on lower floors partly because they had to be close to steam and hot water and partly because of the fumes they produced. Because of the need for steam and hot water in the scouring, dyeing, bleaching, and other finishing processes, mills had boiler rooms even if the mill equipment was water powered. Mill yards also contained large coal or wood sheds; the need for transportation to deliver fuel was one reason for locating the mills on navigable waterways.

Although the weaving room was usually in the main mill building, some mills, when they expanded their weaving capacity, built separate weave sheds. The weave sheds were usually one storey high and were often very large; the one built beside the Canada Cotton Company mill in Cornwall in 1882 and added to in 1916 is 550 feet by 184 feet.[7] It has a low basement, which housed machine shops and shafting for the looms on the ground floor. Most of these broad buildings had some form of skylights to light the centre aisles. Although the sawtooth roof provided excellent light, it was prone to leakage, condensation, and dry rot in Canada's harsh climate; as a result monitors were often used in Canada where sawtooth roofs would have been used in Britain.

Most of the early carding, fulling, and woollen mills were located on rivers. Abundant supplies of water were essential for washing wool and for washing, dyeing, and fulling cloth. Water provided the cheapest form of transportation for raw materials, fuel, and finished products. Most important, water provided cheap power and most of the early mills were water powered. Although water power was cheap compared to steam,[8] Canadian winters and the seasonal variations in flow of the smaller rivers meant that many water-powered mills could not operate year round. While seasonal operation was an acceptable limitation on small mills that served local markets, it became less acceptable as the size of mills increased. The large investment in a big mill could not be allowed to lie idle during a part of the year, particularly when competition was fierce and profit margins were narrow, as they were in the 1880s. As a result many mills added auxiliary steam power or relied exclusively on steam.

Of 24 major cotton mills listed in the 1892 edition of the *Canadian Textile Directory*, 13 were powered by steam, 6 by water, and 5 by a combination of steam and water. Small carding and woollen mills were generally water powered, but most of the larger woollen mills were steam powered or had a combination of steam and water power. Where water power was well located and reliable it remained competitive with steam. The Montreal Cotton Company mill at Valleyfield used a combination of water and electric power as late as 1908.[9]

Electricity was a third alternative in powering mills. It was first used to light mills. Early mills were lit with oil or gas lamps. Both types of light were fire hazards and when electric light became available it was adopted quickly. The Canada Cotton Manufacturing Company at Cornwall installed an incandescent lighting system in its new weave shed in 1883; the installation ranks among the first large inside installations of incandescent lighting in Canada. Montreal Cotton installed electric light in September 1883 and other mills followed throughout the decade.[10]

Electric motors were not used to drive equipment until the late 1890s. The Montreal Cotton Company at Valleyfield installed generators and motors in 1897; electric drive was installed at the Hochelaga mills of Dominion Cotton Mills in 1898.[11] The use of electric power spread rapidly. In 1901, of 31 489 horsepower used in Canadian cotton mills, 22 per cent was electric, 39 per cent was direct drive from water power, and 35 per cent came from steam. By 1930, 86 per cent of the horsepower employed in cotton yarn and cloth mills was supplied by electric motors; the remaining 14 per cent was supplied by direct-drive steam and water power. Knitting and woollen mills were much slower to adopt electric power (*see* Table 18). In the case of the woollen mills the slowness to adopt the new technology may be explained by the severe depression that struck the sector in the early 1900s.

Electricity not only provided a new source of power, it also provided a new means of transmitting power. In both water- and steam-powered mills, power was transmitted from the water wheels or steam engines to the machines by systems of shafts, gears, belts, and pulleys. Overhead shafting and belts were dirty, interfered with lighting, and were safety hazards. The power transmission system often weighed many tons and consumed as much as 25 per cent of the power produced. Moreover the shaft speed in even a well-adjusted mechanical transmission system fluctuated by ±10 per cent; this affected the quality of the yarn and cloth produced.[12] In the early applications of electric drive, most of the mechanical-power transmission system was left intact and large electric motors were installed to drive entire mills or sections of mills using the existing power transmission system. By the 1920s, small motors were available to drive individual machines, and the mechanical-power transmission system was eliminated along with most of its inefficiencies.[13] The switch from mechanical-power transmission to individual electric drive was a long process; many mills used mechanical-power transmission systems until after World War II.

The introduction of electric light and power permitted a reconsideration of basic mill design. The long, narrow, high textile mill was a response to four factors: the need to maximize the availability of natural light, to minimize the length of the mechanical-power transmission system, to minimize land costs, and to minimize construction costs. Electric light and electric power greatly reduced the importance of the first two constraints. Long-distance transmission of electric power also freed mills from their traditional sites, which by the twentieth century were cramped and expensive, and allowed mills to be built on inexpensive land in suburban areas. Multi-storey mills continued to be economical to build, but they involved inefficiencies in product flow, and by the 1920s it was recognized that single-storey mills might well be more efficient than multi-storey mills even if their initial costs were higher. Electric light and power made the single-storey mill practical.

Air conditioning was another factor that led to the redesign of the textile mill. Spinning and weaving were best done in a hot, humid environment. Nineteenth-century mills were generally steam heated and the humidity was often increased by releasing steam into the atmosphere. Towards the end of the century, improvements such as forced-air heating and primitive humidifying and air-cleansing systems were developed. However, the traditional multi-storey mill with its many windows proved a difficult structure in which to control temperature and humidity within the increasingly fine tolerances demanded by textile processing.

By the 1920s the suitability of the traditional mill form was being reconsidered. It was no longer necessary for efficient power distribution or lighting and was unsuited to modern air-conditioning requirements. Moreover the multi-storey building had inherent inefficiencies in machinery layout and product flow that could be overcome in a single-storey building. A single-storey, windowless, air-conditioned factory was built in Massachusetts in 1930.[14] Although it was a technical success, the new form was not generally adopted until after World War II.

The structure as well as the form of the textile mill changed. By the early twentieth century the increasing cost of good large-dimension timbers prompted a search for alternate building materials. Reinforced concrete became a popular building material in the United States in the late 1890s. Reinforced-concrete mills were fireproof, they were more rigid and durable than slow-burning mills, and they could be built with wider spans than was possible in slow-burning mills. They were more expensive to build than slow-burning mills (one source estimated the difference in 1922 at ten per cent),[15] but were better insurance risks. They were cheaper than mills built of structural steel in which the steel was properly protected against fire. The main objection to reinforced concrete was that it was difficult to attach machinery or shafting to it or to modify the structure.

With the exception of grain elevators, the first reinforced-concrete building in Canada was built in Halifax in 1904. In 1905 the Galt Knitting Company built a four-storey mill in Galt using reinforced concrete in the walls but heavy timber mill construction in the interior for floors, beams, and columns[16] (*see* Fig. 100). In 1907 the Eagle Spinning Company built a small brick and reinforced-concrete mill in Hamilton, Ontario[17] (*see* Fig. 110), and Wabasso built a considerably larger brick and reinforced-concrete mill in Trois-Rivières[18] (*see* Fig. 27). In 1910 Wabasso's subsidiary, Shawinigan Cotton, built a reinforced-concrete mill at Shawinigan and in 1916 Mercury Mills of Hamilton began what was probably Canada's largest reinforced-concrete textile mill[19] (*see* Fig. 50). Although reinforced concrete was a popular building material in the years 1905–30, it did not entirely supplant other forms of mill construction. Some large mills, for example the Mount Royal in Montréal (1907), were built using a modified slow-burning style using steel columns and beams with wooden floors and brick load-bearing walls.[20] As late as 1926 an addition to the Montmorency mill was built using traditional mill construction techniques (*see* Figs. 45 and 46). In the mid-1920s two large rayon mills, Courtaulds at Cornwall and Canadian Celanese at Drummondville, were built using reinforced-concrete floors in combination with steel frames encased in concrete. The Depression and World War II virtually stopped mill construction.

When construction resumed, both the old form and the old structural system were abandoned. In 1942 Canadian Industries Limited built a nylon-spinning plant at Kingston. The concrete and steel plant bore no resemblance to a traditional textile mill, but was readily recognizable as a modern industrial building. In the more traditional natural-fibres sector of the industry, Wabasso initiated the move to the modern mill at Grand-Mère, Quebec, in 1944. The one-storey Grand-Mère plant was 1000 feet long and 200 feet wide, with a partial basement and relatively few windows. In spite of its width it did not have skylights. The flat mill roof was supported by a steel frame.[21] Cotton was delivered at one end of the mill, processed through picking, carding, spinning, and weaving departments, and stored as cloth in a warehouse at the other end. Offices, fan rooms, lockers, storerooms, and other service facilities were located in a row along the north side. In 1945 Associated Textiles of Canada built a 400-foot-by-180-foot, windowless, air-conditioned weave shed at Louiseville, Quebec. The single-storey "fire resistive" structure had a concrete roof resting on steel columns.[22]

The Grand-Mère and Louiseville mills set the pattern for postwar construction. In large mills begun after 1945 the working areas were on one level, had few if any windows, and were at least partially air conditioned. The framework was usually steel with some form of fire-resistive roof and curtain walls. The older mills were not abandoned immediately. During the 1950s and early 1960s Dominion Textile made major investments in renovating and re-equipping its old mills, but when it began to build new mills in the mid-1950s, they were built in the new style.

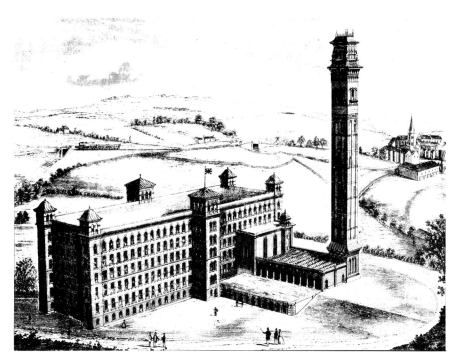

38 The India Mill, Over Darwen, England, about 1870. A first-class British fireproof mill with brick-arch floors and iron columns.
Evan Leigh, *The Science of Modern Cotton Spinning...*, Vol. 1 (Manchester: Palmer and Howe, 1873), Plate IX

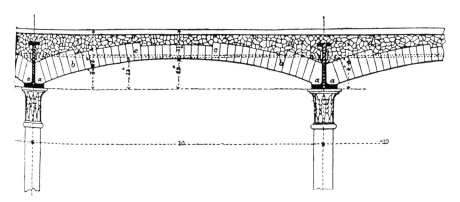

39 Detail of the construction of a brick-arch floor.
William Fairbairn, *On the Application of Cast and Wrought Iron for Building Purposes* (London: Longmans, Green and Company, 1870), p. 133

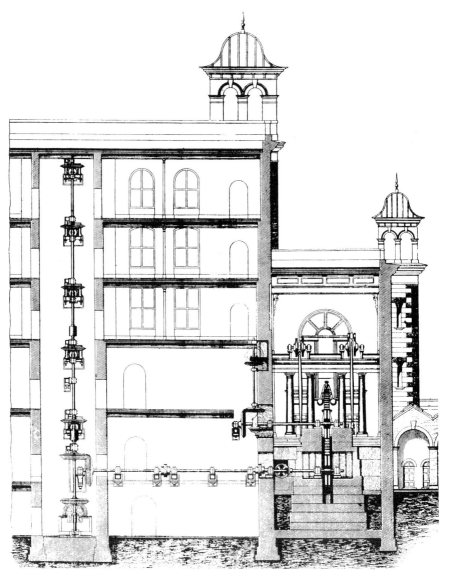

40 The India Mill's drive system, using a steam engine, gears, and shafts.
Evan Leigh, *The Science of Modern Cotton Spinning...*, Vol. 1 (Manchester: Palmer and Howe, 1873),
Plate XIII

41 The Harmony mill in Cohoes, New York, 1987.
Canadian Parks Service, 1987

42 Cross section of the Harmony mill about 1870. Although this was a modern mill, the use of joists and light flooring was not in the slow-burning style. Mansard roofs were popular at the time, but were soon found to be fire hazards. The Harmony mill was water powered; power was transmitted by a system of leather belts and iron shafts and pulleys.

Evan Leigh, *The Science of Modern Cotton Spinning...*, Vol. 1 (Manchester: Palmer and Howe, 1873), Plate XXI

43 The interior of the Canada Cotton Manufacturing Company mill at Cornwall, Ontario. Built in 1874, the mill is an example of the slow-burning, or mill-construction, style.
Heritage Recording Service, Canadian Parks Service, 1985

44 Transition between the mill-construction portion of the Canada mill in Cornwall and the reinforced-concrete portion of the mill. Note the difference in window area and the span between columns.
Canadian Parks Service, 1986

45 Construction work on a slow-burning-style mill or warehouse at Mont-morency, Quebec, 1927. The low windows probably indicate that this was a warehouse.
Notman Photographic Archives, McCord Museum of Canadian History, MP 2091 (5)

46   Roofing the mill/warehouse at Montmorency, Quebec, 1927.
Notman Photographic Archives, McCord Museum of Canadian History, MP 2091 (6)

23/8/27.

47 Construction work on a steel-frame mill with reinforced-concrete floors for Dominion Textile at Magog, Quebec, 1927.
Notman Photographic Archives, McCord Museum of Canadian History, MP 2089 (11)

48   The steel frame of the Dominion Textile mill at Magog, Quebec, 1927.
Notman Photographic Archives, McCord Museum of Canadian History, MP 2089 (16)

49 The interior of the Mercury mill in Hamilton, Ontario, a reinforced-concrete mill with characteristic high ceilings and large window area. This appears to be the sewing room, where various parts of knitted garments were assembled and finished.
National Film Board, B-58; National Archives of Canada, PA 180952

50 The exterior of the Mercury mill. The main building was built in 1916–17. A comparison of this photograph with one of a traditional mill-construction building, for example the Hudon mill (Fig. 56), shows the marked change in external appearance that the adoption of reinforced construction entailed. The Mercury mill was demolished in 1983.
Hamilton Public Library

51 A 1400-horsepower cross compound steam engine in a British mill about 1908. The main drive wheel is on the right, between the two cylinders of the engine and at the entrance to the rope race. This grooved wheel drove the ropes shown in the rope race (Fig. 52).

Charles J. Kavanagh, "Some Aspects of the Power Problem for the Textile Industry," *Cassier's Magazine*, August 1908, p. 372

52   The rope race. The ropes in turn drove the main shafts on each storey of the mill. Rope drives began to replace belt drives in the United States about 1870 and somewhat later in Britain.

Charles J. Kavanagh, "Some Aspects of the Power Problem for the Textile Industry," *Cassier's Magazine,* August 1908, p. 373

53 An early form of electric drive in the mule room of Wabasso at Trois-Rivières, Quebec, ca. 1915. A single large electric motor provided power for an entire floor of the mill. These appear to be concrete floors supported by cast-iron or steel columns.
Notman Photographic Archives, McCord Museum of Canadian History, 4981

54 A group drive arrangement at the St. Croix mill in Milltown, New Brunswick. One overhead electric motor drove four spinning machines.
National Film Board, B-5; National Archives of Canada, PA 800601

55 Individual motor drive in the spinning department of the Stormont mill, Cornwall, Ontario, 1930.
National Film Board, B-11; National Archives of Canada, PA 800607

Postwar Industry

Since World War II the textile industry, particularly the traditional sectors, has suffered major upheavals with serious losses in employment and market share. The story of this period is extremely complex and largely beyond the scope of this book. What follows is an attempt to describe a few major issues: the tendency to trade liberalization, the loss of market share to imports, the increasing use of synthetics at the expense of natural fibres, increasing mechanization, and declining employment in the traditional sectors.

The Second World War, like the First, was a prosperous period for the textile industry. Plants that had been under-utilized were run overtime; old plants, such as the St. Ann mill, that had been closed were reopened. Employment in the cotton sector increased by 9 per cent between 1940 and 1950; in the hosiery/knit-goods sector the figure was 8 per cent; in the woollen sector, 23 per cent; and in the silk/synthetic sector, 211 per cent. Between 1941 and 1948, prices were controlled at the 1940 level; during much of the period this was below the cost of production. Government subsidies made up the difference.[1] As a result during the late 1940s, return on net worth in the textile industry was 15.7 per cent compared to 14.1 per cent for manufacturing generally.[2] Dominion Textile's earnings per share in the 1940s were double what they had been in the 1930s and higher than they would be in the 1950s.[3]

Wartime prosperity continued with minor setbacks until 1951. Indeed, the years immediately after the war were exceptionally prosperous. However, this prosperity hid a number of trends that made the industry increasingly vulnerable. Many of these trends could be traced to the war or earlier.

During the war the nascent sales organizations that the larger firms had developed were allowed to atrophy and had to be rebuilt after the war. Similarly the long hours and unavailability of replacement machinery during the war left the industry with a worn-out, outdated plant in 1945; it took almost five years for the plant to be brought up to standard after the war. In the longer term the war accelerated the switch from natural fibres to synthetics, increased labour costs and militancy, and led to reductions in tariff levels and to the rise of foreign competition.

Rayon production began in Canada in the 1920s; nylon production began in Kingston in 1942. The synthetic sector continued to grow after the war and was less affected by recessions than were the natural-fibre sectors. Much of this growth was at the expense of the natural-fibre sectors. Between 1941 and 1951, while the per capita consumption of all textile fibres remained at about 29 pounds, the per capita consumption of synthetic fibres increased from about 3 to 6.8 pounds.[4] Because the growth of the synthetic sector was at the expense of the natural-fibre sectors it contributed little to the growth of employment in the industry as a whole; indeed, since synthetic production was more capital intensive than labour intensive, there was a tendency towards reduced employment.

Although both wages and prices were controlled during the war, wages were allowed to increase substantially; between 1938 and 1946 the labour cost per employee in the cotton sector increased by 70 per cent; in knitting the figure was 45 per cent.[5] These increases continued after the war. Once price controls were removed, wage increases were generally matched by price increases so that the general relationship of labour costs to gross value of production remained in a historical range of about one to four.

Compared to potential foreign competitors' labour costs, Canada's labour costs were high. An International Labour Office study found that of 30 major textile-producing countries in 1947–49, only the United States and Israel had higher hourly wage rates.[6] Wages were not the only problem Canadian manufacturers faced in meeting foreign competition. In order to supply the Canadian market they felt obliged to produce almost the same range of products as American and British manufacturers, who produced for much larger markets. As a result Canadian production runs were much shorter than comparable American or British runs and costs were proportionately higher.

Historically the threat from foreign producers had been countered by the tariff, but the war weakened support for the tariff. In 1940–41 the tariff on many British imports was reduced or eliminated as a measure of wartime co-operation, and the Atlantic Charter pledged the allies to support a postwar liberalization of trade. In 1947 Canada was a signatory of the General Agreement on Tariffs and Trade (GATT), which was intended to reduce tariff levels and non-tariff restraints on trade. As a result of the GATT Canada lowered its tariffs. The average level of duty collected on all dutiable imports fell from about 21 to 17.3 per cent. For cottons the decrease was from about 22.6 per cent in 1947 to 19 per cent in 1950. For woollens the decrease over the same period was from 23 to 18 per cent, and for synthetics from 37 to 26 per cent.[7]

Postwar trade liberalization resulted in significant increases in Canadian imports of textiles with no appreciable increase in exports. Import competition became particularly severe when the postwar boom ended and foreign firms sought markets for surplus production. In the 1930s and 1940s, imports had accounted for about 18 per cent of Canadian consumption; by 1951–54 they had 25 per cent of the Canadian market. The woollen and cotton sectors were more severely affected by import competition than was the synthetic sector, which retained about 85 per cent of the domestic market.[8] Competition in the woollen sector came primarily from Britain; in the cotton sector the Americans replaced the British as the principal competition for Canadian producers.

All of these factors — a weak sales organization, competition between natural fibres and synthetics, high costs, and falling tariff protection — exacerbated the effect of the general downturn that followed the postwar boom. For the textile industry the boom peaked in 1951 when employment in the primary industry, excluding knitting, reached 81 710 and gross value of production peaked at $846 million. By 1954, employment had fallen to 64 581 and production fell to $631 million. The value of production did not regain its 1951 level until 1961; employment has never regained the 1951 levels. The knit-goods/hosiery sector was also affected: employment peaked at 27 634 in 1948 and gross value of production peaked at $170 million in 1951. By 1954, employment was down to 21 622 and production had fallen to $147 million.[9] The woollen sector, already weak, was particularly hard hit; employment fell from 9200 in 1950 to 4500 in 1954.[10]

The textile industry's reaction to the recession of the early 1950s was varied. Many firms did not survive. The Rosamond Woollen Company, Dominion Woollens and Worsteds, Hamilton Cotton, and Canadian Cottons all went out of business in the 1950s or early 1960s. Although many of the mills owned by these firms were acquired by other firms, they were seldom long-term successes and most have now been closed and, in many cases, demolished.

Many of the weaker firms were absorbed by stronger firms. Dominion Textile acquired Montreal Cotton (which it had controlled for years) in 1948, acquired Caldwell Linen in 1956, and bought a 50-per-cent interest in Esmond Mills of Granby, Quebec. It also bought the remaining equipment of Canada Cottons and in 1965 bought Penmans and Tre-mont Worsteds.[11] In 1955 the Woods Manufacturing Company, which owned the Empire Mill at Welland, merged with Wabasso.[12] In 1985 the Wabasso name and some of its assets were acquired by Dominion Textile. Silknit Limited of Toronto acquired the Dominion Woollens and Worsteds plant at Hespeler, the Slingsby Manufacturing Company plant in Brantford, Ontario, and the fabric division of Riverside Silk Mills of Galt.[13] Canadian Celanese acquired Coaticook Textiles and Rayflex Corporation and in 1963 it merged with its principal competitor in producing acetate rayon, the Canadian Chemical Company, under the name Chemcell (1963) Limited.[14]

The industry leaders also made a major effort to increase efficiency through modernization. New equipment, such as high-speed and shuttleless looms, was installed and new products such as Dacron, spandex, and acrylic were developed. Dominion Textile accepted synthetics as a major part of its business, not simply a sideline as they had been in the 1930s.[15] The industry began to replace its oldest mills with completely new ones. The Hudon mill, built in 1873, was closed in 1953; between 1957 and 1967 Dominion Textile built new plants at Salaberry, Saint-Jean, Saint-Timothée, all in Quebec, and Long Sault, Ontario.[16] These plants were the first entirely new plants built by the company since its formation in 1905. It also modernized the best of its older plants: Montmorency, Valleyfield, and Magog.

The industry also appealed for a return to earlier levels of tariff protection. The Tariff Board investigated the woollen sector twice (1955 and 1958), the cotton sector (1958), and the knit-goods/hosiery sector (1961). Initially these appeals fell on deaf ears. In the case of the woollen sector, which was suffering from British imports, low tariffs on British woollens were intended as a means of ensuring access of Canadian raw materials to British markets. The United States, which was the principal foreign competitor of Canada's cotton sector, was also a major importer of Canadian raw materials. The election of a Progressive Conservative government in 1957 marked a slight shift away from the philosophy of exporting raw materials towards supporting traditional industries.[17] Under the GATT the government could not apply discriminatory tariffs, but it could negotiate voluntary export restraints (VER) with exporting nations. In 1958 Canada negotiated with Japan a VER that restricted clothing and textile imports. Similar agreements were negotiated and periodically renewed with other low-wage producers. VERs were not negotiated with the Canadian industry's traditional and still most important competitors, the United States and Britain, which were high-wage producers.

The combination of protection through import restraints, introduction of new product lines, corporate concentration, and increases in efficiency restored a measure of profitability and stability to the industry. However, the increased efficiency was achieved at a cost of major employment losses in the traditional textile sectors as more production was switched to synthetics. At the end of the war Dominion Textile employed 13 000; by 1968 it had only 8500 employees although sales had doubled. Losses in employment in the traditional textile sectors were just balanced by increases in employment in the synthetic sector. Overall, employment in primary textiles increased by about 8.5 per cent between 1958 and 1967; over the same period employment in manufacturing increased by about 13 per cent.[18]

The recovery was shortlived. During the 1960s the low-wage countries acquired the technology for the new synthetics, which were the basis of the Canadian recovery, and the quotas on imports became increasingly liberal. Between 1964 and 1976, imports were able to increase their share of the market, based on weight, from 36 to 60 per cent; based on value, their share was considerably lower.[19] Once again the industry appealed to the government for support. In 1970 the government established a Textile and Clothing Board that was to investigate alleged cases of harm caused by imports and recommend for or against protective action. In making its recommendations the board was to consider Canada's trade agreements, international trading conditions, the effect of action on employment and on consumers, and the viability of the industry requesting protection.[20] In the event that an industry was not considered viable, the government would either provide assistance to modernize it or to close it down. The intent was that the Canadian textile industry would concentrate its efforts in the areas where it was most competitive. In theory the new policy would hasten the rationalization and concentration that market forces had been causing since the early 1950s. It would also cushion the blow to those parts of the industry not judged viable.

The policy, with some changes, is still in effect. In some respects it has been successful. The industry is as efficient as modern equipment and scale of operation will make it. The major firms — Du Pont, Celanese, Courtaulds, and Dominion Textile — have expanded at the expense of smaller, weaker firms, and production is noticeably more concentrated.[21] In spite of these changes the industry has not achieved stability in the face of foreign competition. Between 1978 and 1984, Canadian industry's share of the Canadian market for yarn fell from 78 to 63 per cent; for fabrics the decline was from 47 to 43 per cent. In a report on the industry in 1985 the Textile and Clothing Board noted that in spite of earlier rationalizations, a further 22 200 jobs had been lost in the textile and clothing industry. It attributed two-thirds of these losses to imports and recommended more stringent quotas and controls of imports.[22]

Conclusion

The history of the textile industry in Canada is not one but several histories of distinct but related industries. This study has dealt with the four major sectors of the primary textile industry: the woollen, cotton, knit-goods/ hosiery, and silk/synthetic sectors. It has not dealt with the minor sectors of the textile industry such as rope making, carpets, or bags. It has said nothing about the secondary textile industry, the clothing industry, although until at least 1910, more than 50 per cent of all workers in the textile industry were employed in the secondary industry.

The textile industry has deep roots in Canada. It began in New France as home production of linens and woollens from locally grown flax and wool. Home production of woollens apparently peaked in the early nineteenth century and disappeared as an economically significant activity early in the twentieth century. The woollen sector, defined as the production of woollens in a factory setting, originated as a service industry to the home production of woollens. The more labour-intensive aspects of production, such as fulling and carding, began to be industrialized in the early nineteenth century. At about the same time professional weavers, working in a cottage-industry setting, became common. By the 1840s, integrated woollen mills, in which all the processes necessary for converting raw wool to cloth were performed by powered machinery, were in existence. During the 1850s, 1860s, and 1870s these small mills proliferated, especially in Ontario, which became the leading woollen-producing province. The small mills produced narrow ranges of products for local markets, were locally financed, and used locally grown wool.

During the 1860s and 1870s a number of larger companies developed, the most notable of which were the Rosamond Woollen Company at Almonte, the R. Forbes Company and A.W. Brodie Company at Hespeler, the Paton Manufacturing Company at Sherbrooke, and the Cornwall Manufacturing Company mill at Cornwall. These mills produced a variety of woollens and worsteds for the national market. The financial requirements of the large mills often were greater than local capital could supply, and most of them had links with Montréal capital markets. The large mill owners served as spokesmen for the entire sector and the large mills were the leaders in the introduction of new technology.

Under the National Policy the woollen sector enjoyed much the same protection as did the cotton sector, but it did not enjoy the same rapid growth during the 1880s. Tariff protection may, however, have offset the major problems that faced the industry: foreign competition and the declining market for woollens, particularly the coarse, heavy type in which the small mills specialized. When protection was reduced in 1897 the sector quickly succumbed to foreign competition. It recovered during World War I and again during the 1930s, but it has never regained the predominant place it had in the nineteenth century.

Cotton cloth has always been produced in a factory setting in Canada; there is no tradition of home production. Production began in 1844 but was insignificant until the 1860s. There was further growth during the 1870s and then a great burst of construction in the five years following the introduction of the National Policy in 1879. It took most of the 1880s to work out the resulting overcapacity in the sector. Balance was achieved through diversification and restriction of output. Initially output was restricted through voluntary agreements, but when these failed, two Montréalers, David Morrice and Andrew Gault, arranged a series of takeovers that by 1892 had brought most of the sector's capacity under their control. This control, based on the financial resources of Montréal, availability of labour and power, nearness to markets, and access to rail communication, ultimately led to the location of the larger part of the industry within a hundred-mile radius of Montréal. The consolidation produced a strong industry that remained relatively stable until after World War II.

Although the cotton and woollen sectors used similar technologies, they were distinguished by several characteristics. Cotton manufacturing was concentrated in Quebec, particularly in the Montréal area and the Eastern Townships, while woollen manufacturing was based in Ontario. Cotton mills were much larger, employed more hands, and required greater capital resources than did most woollen mills. When cotton mills were first established they often represented attempts by local capitalists to diversify their interests; when local resources proved inadequate the greater resources of Montréal led to the loss of the local mill's independence and, in some cases, to the loss of the mill. Consolidation never occurred in the woollen sector; restriction of output took place through the failure of individual companies. The different fates of the two sectors under the National Policy is one that deserves more investigation. Although both cotton and woollen mills relied heavily on cheap labour, particularly women and children, the use of women and children was more pronounced in the cotton sector in its first decades than in the woollen sector. The cotton sector appears to have had more labour troubles than the woollen sector.

The first knit-goods/hosiery mills were established in the 1840s and 1850s, often as sidelines for woollen or cotton mills. Although some important knitting firms (Penman Manufacturing, Joseph Simpson) were organized in the 1860s, the sector remained a minor one compared to woollens or cottons until the turn of the century. It experienced its most rapid growth during the years 1900–1920, when it replaced the woollen sector as the second most important employer in the primary textile industry.

The rapid growth was largely the result of an expanding market and new products; the early mills were generally hosiery mills, but by the end of the century, knitted undergarments and outerwear had become important products. The effect of tariff policy is difficult to gauge. During the nineteenth century, knit goods received the same tariff protection as cottons, but did not enjoy comparable growth. By the 1930s the knit-goods sector rivalled the cotton sector as an employer. Unlike the cotton sector, the knit-goods sector was primarily an Ontario-based industry until after World War II.

The early knitting mills were much smaller than cotton mills of the same period, but were larger than most woollen mills. Relatively small size and a moderate rate of expansion helped to keep ownership of the sector dispersed. Many firms were family owned; in several cases, ownership of important firms remained in the same family for three or four generations. The largest firms moved beyond family control; John Penman's firm was incorporated in 1882 and expanded through acquisition of smaller firms. In 1906 Penman sold his interest in the firm to a group associated with Dominion Textile and it remained within the orbit of Dominion Textile until it was finally absorbed in 1965. In the nineteenth century the knitting sector was Canadian owned, but during the expansive years of the early twentieth century a number of American hosiery firms established branches in Canada and took a share of the market.

Although the knit-goods/hosiery sector has been treated as a part of the primary textile industry, it had some characteristics of a secondary industry. Its products were clothing that required no further processing and were generally sold to retailers. The cotton and woollen sectors produced woven cloth, most of which was sold to converters for further processing. Knitting technology also differed from technology in the cotton and woollen sectors. In cotton and woollen mills yarn was converted to cloth using looms; in knitting mills yarn was converted to cloth and garments using a variety of knitting machines and sewing machines. Whether or not this difference in technology is related to the high proportion of women employed in the knit-goods sector in comparison to the cotton and woollen sectors is a matter that might be a rewarding subject of further research.

Although the silk and synthetic sectors are grouped together, this is largely a historical accident resulting from the fact that synthetic fibres were originally developed as a substitute for silk. The processes used and the historical development of the two sectors are distinct. The spinning and weaving of synthetic fibres uses machinery that is much the same as that used in the cotton or woollen sectors, but the actual production of synthetic fibre is a chemical process that has nothing in common with traditional textile technology. The spinning or throwing of natural silk uses different equipment from that used in spinning wool, cotton, or synthetics.

Natural-silk mills in Canada have been comparable in size to mid-size cotton mills and have employed an unusually high proportion of women; synthetic mills, by contrast, have been larger than all but the largest cotton mills and have employed proportionately fewer women than the textile industry as a whole.

Until recently the silk/synthetic sector has been substantially smaller than the other sectors considered here. Before World War I the industry consisted of three mills in Quebec. Although it expanded with mills in Quebec and Ontario after World War I, its real period of growth came after the establishment of synthetic (rayon) plants in Cornwall and Drummondville in the 1920s. The first silk mills in Canada were subsidiaries of American firms, but by the 1930s the bulk of silk production in Canada was controlled by Canadians. The two synthetic plants established in Canada before World War II were subsidiaries of American and British firms.

Four major themes — tariff policy, finance and ownership, labour history, and technology and architecture — give the history of the primary textile industry general interest and relevance. In the late nineteenth and early twentieth centuries the growth of the textile industry, particularly the cotton industry, was viewed as evidence of the beneficial effects of a protective tariff. Many Canadians still hold to this view, but the problems of the industry over the past 50 years provide an object lesson on the pitfalls of using tariff policy to aid domestic industries.

The financing and management of the textile industry provides a number of development models. The capital requirements of the woollen sector were small, and mills were usually locally owned and financed. Expansion could often be financed through internal capital accumulation. Perhaps as a result the typical woollen mill operated on a much smaller scale than the typical cotton mill. This pattern was apparently adequate during the nineteenth century, but in the twentieth century the woollen sector declined from being the leading sector in the primary textile industry to being a minor sector. How much of this decline was the result of economics of scale and inadequate financial resources and how much was the result of changing tastes and tariff policies is not clear.

Cotton mills required much larger capital investments than woollen mills and consequently were more likely to be organized by consortia of capitalists than by individuals. In the initial phase of the cotton sector's development, established mercantile and resource extraction capital in regional centres was pooled to establish regional mills. Within less than a decade these pools of regional capital proved inadequate to carry the mills through the hard times that resulted from initial excess capacity. Between 1890 and 1905, control of the sector was consolidated in the hands of a group of Montréal capitalists. The cotton sector has remained highly centralized and has extended its control into both the woollen and knit-goods/hosiery

154

sectors. The consolidation of the cotton sector preceded, and may have provided a model for, the great consolidation movement that swept Canadian industry in the years 1905-11.

The financial history of the knit-goods/hosiery sector falls between that of the woollen and cotton sectors. Initially much of the sector was organized on a small scale by individuals or partnerships. In the 1890s and early twentieth century there was a tendency to consolidation; this was balanced by the emergence of new firms and the growth of a number of independent older firms. In the early twentieth century a number of British and American hosiery firms established subsidiaries in Canada and gained about 45 per cent of the market; the knit-goods portion of the knit-goods/hosiery sector remained largely Canadian owned. The silk/synthetic sector has been characterized by extensive foreign ownership.

The textile industry was one of the earliest large employers of labour in a factory setting. It was a low-wage industry with a large proportion of semi-skilled and unskilled jobs; women and children filled the lowest paying job categories. Over most of its history 50 per cent or more of its employees were women or children. The proportion of children employed declined in the early decades of the twentieth century, but the proportion of women has fluctuated, rising during wartime labour shortages and falling in other periods. Working conditions in the industry were characterized by long hours, low wages, and unhealthy and occasionally dangerous working conditions. Given the conditions and the large numbers of employees grouped together, one might expect that textile mills would be fertile grounds for labour organization. However, in spite of periodic attempts to organize the industry and several rounds of serious strikes, the major firms were not effectively organized until after World War II.

Textile mills have evolved over the past century to meet the changing technological needs of the industry. Mills were long, narrow, and high; this form kept them compact and allowed the mechanical transmission of power from water wheels or steam engines. They also had numerous windows to provide the light necessary for textile processes. Structurally, early mills were modelled on traditional grist and flour mills. These mills were very susceptible to fire, and during the 1870s Canadian mill owners began to build in the "slow burning" or "mill construction" structural style that had been developed by the American textile industry. From 1880 until World War I, "mill construction" was the standard structural system used in textile mills and in most other buildings for light industry. In the early twentieth century, mill architects began to use reinforced concrete rather than brick and wood. In the 1920s some mills were built using structural steel and concrete. In spite of these changes in building materials, the external form remained the same; long, narrow, and high, with many windows. The introduction of electric lighting in the 1880s and of electric drive after 1900 rendered the old form obsolete, but it was not until after World War II that the industry began to build a new style of mill, the single-storey, windowless, air-conditioned mill that is now the standard light-industry plant.

Part II
The Physical Legacy
of the
Textile Industry

Introduction

Since the mid-nineteenth century the textile industry has played an important role in the labour, business, economic, and architectural history of central and eastern Canada. The woollen industry and the cotton industry were among the first Canadian businesses to employ large numbers of workers in a factory setting; this was particularly the case for women and youths. The industry provided a training ground for many Canadian businessmen who learned both the opportunities and the hazards of investment in manufacturing. It also provided, and continues to provide, many often-contradictory object lessons for businessmen, economists, politicians, and labour leaders who oppose or support government fostering of industrial development through tariff protection, subsidies, and legislation. Finally, in many communities the mills themselves, massive and enduring, helped to define the community in the same way that churches and public buildings did.

The contributions that the industry has made to Canadian life have not been entirely happy: working conditions were often deplorable by modern standards, the financial success of the industry was mixed at best, and the mills are often unpleasing agglomerations of ill-designed and badly maintained additions to originals that at best were strong and functional. Some Canadians would as soon forget the industry and move on. This would be a mistake. Good and bad, the story of textile manufacturing is a part of our story.

Recognition of the legacy of the textile industry can take many forms. Historical publications such as this are one form. The preservation of the records of the industry and of the experiences of textile workers is an acknowledgement of the importance of the industry and of the experiences of those involved in it as well as a service to future historians. Markers and plaques memorialize significant events, firms, and individuals. The preservation of artifacts, of machinery, of knowledge of processes, and of buildings associated with the industry is a fourth way of recognizing the importance of the textile industry in Canada.

A sound beginning has been made to save the heritage of the textile industry, but much remains to be done. There is a considerable body of literature on the history of textile manufacture in Canada, but there is no comprehensive survey of the entire industry. Many of the records of textile firms have been lost, some remain in private hands, a few have found their way into public archives. A beginning has been made in recording the experience of textile workers. Federal, provincial, and local agencies have taken steps to mark sites associated with the industry; for example, the

Marysville cotton mill in New Brunswick and the Rosamond woollen mill in Ontario have been declared to be of national architectural and historical significance. The centennial of the cotton industry was marked by a private plaque at Sherbrooke in 1944, and the site of the first cotton mill in Ontario has been marked in Thorold.

For many people the preservation of artifacts, skills, and structures associated with the industry is the most meaningful form of commemoration. Hand spinning and weaving is demonstrated at many pioneer village museums across the country. Small-scale factory production of woollen cloth using period machinery is undertaken at several sites where original mill buildings and equipment are preserved: the Asselstine mill at Upper Canada Village, the Ulverton mill in Quebec, and the Barrington mill in Nova Scotia are examples of the preservation and interpretation of relatively small-scale mills.

The physical legacy of the large-scale manufacture of textiles is threatened by rising land values, the cost of preserving threatened structures, and the opportunities of development. There are, however, a number of ways of limiting the loss of this important part of our industrial heritage. Many large mills have potential for conversion to alternative uses; most are solidly built and many occupy desirable waterfront locations. They can be converted to office use; the Marysville cotton mill complex in New Brunswick now houses government offices; the former Simpson knitting mill in Toronto has been converted to office and retail space under the name Berkeley Castle. Mills can also be converted to residential use; the Paton mill in Sherbrooke, the Belding-Corticelli mill in Montréal, and the Rosamond mill in Almonte are examples. While these conversions obscure the mills' industrial history, they preserve their architectural contributions to their communities.

Conversion to other uses does not rule out the possibility of interpreting the history of the industry. At Terrebonne, Quebec, a former grist, saw, and woollen mill complex has been converted to a cultural centre housing offices, an art gallery and library, and an interpretation centre. At Almonte, Ontario, where the main Rosamond mill has been converted to condominiums, a local association is developing an adjacent warehouse as a museum of the textile industry.

The mills can be saved, but time is running out. Since the 1950s many large mills built before World War I have been demolished or burned. The list includes the Hudon and Colonial mills in Montréal, Penmans' Saint-Hyacinthe mill, the Wabasso mill in Trois-Rivières, the St. Croix mill in Milltown, New Brunswick, Penmans' No. 9 mill in Paris, the Stormont mill in Cornwall, and the Mercury, Zimmerknit, Ontario, and Hamilton mills in Hamilton. Other mills have lost many of their early buildings; for example, most of the nineteenth-century buildings of the Montreal Cotton

Company were demolished in the 1970s. As recently as May of 1990 about half of the Forbes mill in Cambridge was razed.

The short histories that follow chronicle a number of sites where a substantial number of early buildings survive. The selection of mills reflects the geographical and historical development of the industry. Consequently most of the knitting and woollen mills described in it are in Ontario and most of the cotton mills are in Quebec. Obviously the histories do not represent a complete list of surviving textile mills in Canada, but I hope that they will provide information and, perhaps, inspiration to those interested in Canada's industrial and architectural heritage.

56 The Hudon cotton mill, built in 1874 at 3340 rue Notre Dame Est in Montréal, was the largest cotton mill in Canada during the 1870s and 1880s. It was closed in 1953 and demolished in 1978–79.
Notman Photographic Archives, McCord Museum of Canadian History, 4650

Montréal, Quebec

Montréal was, from the mid-1870s to after World War II, the leading cotton-manufacturing centre in Canada. Its mills were concentrated in two areas, the east end and along the Lachine Canal. The east-end mills were the Hudon, built in 1873–74, and the St. Ann, built in 1882–83. After 1885 the two mills were operated as a single unit, the Hochelaga Cotton Manufacturing Company. During the 1880s and 1890s the Hochelaga mills were the most important ones in Canada and they remained important, but not dominant, in the twentieth century. The Hudon mill was closed in 1953 and demolished in 1978–79 after being damaged by fire. The St. Ann mill was closed in 1983 and most of it was demolished in 1984.

The Lachine Canal emerged as one of Canada's first major industrial corridors in the 1850s and 1860s with flour mills, a shipyard, a sugar refinery, and other industries. One of the factories that contributed to the canal's growth as an industrial corridor was a cotton mill built by F.W. Harris at 572 rue William in 1854. Although the mill went out of business about 1875, the canal area developed as Montréal's seond textile district in the 1880s. The Merchants Manufacturing Company built a large cotton mill on the canal in 1881–82. In 1899 the Colonial Bleaching and Printing Company built a large plant on Saint-Ambroise a few blocks from the Merchants mill. In 1907 the Mount Royal Spinning Company built a third large mill on the other side of the canal about two kilometres above the Merchants mill. The Saint-Gabriel locks on the canal were also the site of a large woollen mill, the Montréal Woollen Mills Company, and after 1884, of the silk mill built by Belding Paul and Company. The Harris mill, the Montréal Woollen mill, and the Colonial plant have been demolished, but the main buildings of the Merchants Manufacturing Company, the Mount Royal Spinning Company, and the Belding Paul and Company plants still stand.

57 The St. Ann mill, at 2554–2618 rue Notre Dame Est, was built in three stages: the block on the left in 1882, the centre block in 1912, and the warehouse on the right in 1905. Only the warehouse survives.
Dominion Textile

Merchants Manufacturing Company
3970–4200 rue Saint Ambroise

The Merchants Manufacturing Company was organized in 1880 in response to the opportunity offered by the introduction of the National Policy. Although it shared some important backers with the Hudon and Montreal Cotton firms, its leading figures, Gilman Cheney, A.A. Ayer, the Hon. Robert Mackay, and Alexander Ewan, were not part of the group that formed around Andrew Gault and David Morrice.1 The Merchants mill remained independent until 1905, when it became part of Dominion Textile.

The company was capitalized at $400 000. It built a four-storey (plus basement) brick mill, 346 feet by 76 feet, in the Montréal suburb of Saint-Henri in 1881, and the mill went into production in 1882.[2] With 25 500 spindles and 635 looms in 1885, it was a medium-sized mill by Canadian standards. During the 1890s it was enlarged and by 1908 it had 2465 looms and 110 000 spindles.[3] It was the was the second-largest mill in Canada and held this position until World War II.

Although it was located along the Lachine Canal, the mill depended on steam power; by 1920 it had converted to electricity.[4] As an independent mill it produced bleached shirtings, grey and fancy cottons, sheets, pillowslips, cheese cloth, and other cottons using its own dyehouse and bleachery. As a unit in Dominion Textile it was sometimes described as a yarn mill although as late as 1941 it had 2388 looms.[5]

Its labour practices appear to have been representative of the industry. In 1888 the manager, R.W. Eaton, testified before the Royal Commission on the Relations of Labour and Capital that the mill employed about 420 men, women, and children; about 10 of the employees were under 14 years of age. The hours of work were from 6:30 A.M. to 6:30 P.M. with 45 minutes off at noon; on Saturday the plant closed at 3:00 P.M. The mill disciplined its employees through fines and dismissals; over the period 1882–87 it collected $1116.04 in fines and paid a total of $431 632.36 in wages. Eaton testified that in spite of the long hours worked and the low wages offered, he could not get anyone to leave the mill and work as a domestic for $13 per month and board.[6]

An account of a strike gives another view of labour-management relations and highlights what was to be a continuing problem in Quebec mills, the split between a largely French-speaking work force and English-speaking management. In October 1891 about 200 weavers struck in protest against the dismissal of the overseer, Mr. Duplessis. It was said that he had been dismissed because he was a French Canadian, the last French Canadian in a responsible position in the plant. A workers' delegation, acompanied by the mayor and the priest, met with the management and demanded his reinstatment. The workers also demanded a diminuition of fines for soiled goods, a maximum work week of 60 hours, better filling of the spools that were used in weaving, and the dismissal of a cloth inspector, Mr. Butterworth. All of their demands were rejected, and after a nearly a week the employees abandoned the strike.[7]

The mill was closed in 1967[8] and until recently was occupied by Coleco Canada. The nineteenth-century plant is almost intact although the addition of aluminium cladding and insulation in the late 1980s has greatly altered its appearance. Nevertheless it remains as an important part of an assemblage of major industrial structures (St. Lawrence Flour, Redpath Sugar, Northern Electric, Canada Malting) that contributed to the Lachine Canal's reputation as an early centre of Canadian industrialization.

58 The Merchants Manufacturing Company mill in 1885, shortly after it was completed.
Canadian Textile Directory, 1885, p. 261; National Archives of Canada, C 128001

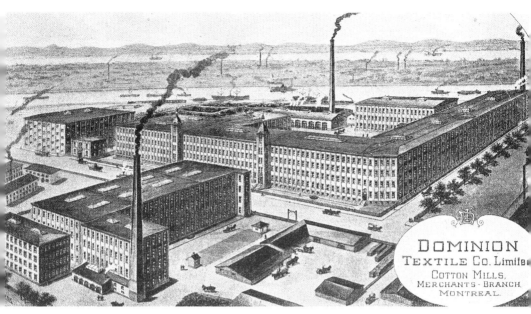

59 and **60**   The Merchants mill about 1920 (above) and about 1950 (below).
Canadian Textile Journal, 5 Dec. 1922, p. 495, National Library of Canada, NL 16977; Dominion Textile

61 and **62**   Although almost all of the Merchants mill survives, its appearance was altered by the addition of metal cladding and insulation between 1983 (above) and 1988 (left).
Quebec Regional Office, Canadian Parks Service, 1983, 1988

Belding-Corticelli Limited
184 rue Shearer

In 1876 the American silk-manufacturing firm Belding Brothers established a branch, Belding Smith and Company, in Montréal. In 1877 it was reorganized as Belding Paul and Company.[1] In 1884 the firm built a 155-foot-by-45-foot, four-storey brick mill, a two-storey dyehouse, and a 110-foot-by-45-foot building housing a workshop, wheelhouse, and boiler room at the Saint-Gabriel lock on the Lachine Canal.[2] The mill processed raw silk into thread and ribbons. In the 1880s and 1890s the mill also wove some silk cloth, but its main product remained thread and ribbons; this was true of all Canadian silk mills until the 1920s. Substantial additions, which probably tripled the mill's area, were made to the plant in 1893 and 1903. A large office and warehouse replaced the wheelhouse and boiler room in 1913; this completed major construction at the site.[3] The main buildings are extant although they are now undergoing renovations to convert them to condominiums.

In 1911 Belding Paul and Company merged with its only serious competitor, the Corticelli Silk Company, to form Belding Paul Corticelli. The Corticelli Silk Company had a mill at Saint-Jean, where it produced silk thread, laces, braid, and some piece goods.[4] Corticelli owned a subsidiary in Coaticook, Quebec, Cascade Narrow Fabrics, which became part of the new firm.[5]

Both the Belding Paul and Corticelli companies were subsidiaries of American firms, but when they merged in 1911, control passed to Canadians. Frank Paul, who had served as president of Belding Paul from 1877 to 1911, continued on as president of Belding Paul Corticelli until 1915, when he was replaced by A.O. Dawson, the president of Canadian Cottons and, from 1928, the president of Dominion Woollens and Worsteds. Dawson continued as president until his death in 1940.[6] The company was reorganized as Belding-Corticelli Limited in 1920.

By 1933 the firm employed 429 in its Montréal plant, 225 in Saint-Jean, and 181 in Coaticook. Although both the Bruck Silk Mills in Saint-Hyacinthe and the Associated Textiles mill in Louiseville employed more than any one of the Belding-Corticelli mills, Belding-Corticelli was the largest silk-producing firm in Canada.[7] It continued to produce thread and ribbons, but after the growth in the market for silk hosiery in the 1920s, it produced an increasing amount of hosiery. The Coaticook, Saint-Jean, and Montréal plants were all in operation in the early 1950s, but the last two have since been closed and a plant opened in Saint-Hyacinthe.

63   The Belding Paul silk mill about 1900.
E.J. Chambers, *The Book of Montreal* (Montréal: n.p., 1903), p. 183; National Library of Canada, NL 17008

64 The Belding Paul mill in the spring of 1988, when it was being converted to condominiums.
Canadian Parks Service, 1988

65 Detail of the exterior brickwork of the Belding-Corticelli mill, ca. 1980.
Quebec Regional Office, Canadian Parks Service

66   Interior construction of the Belding-Corticelli mill, ca. 1980.
Quebec Regional Office, Canadian Parks Service

172

The Eastern Townships, Quebec

The recorded history of the Canadian textile industry began in the Eastern Townships of Quebec at Magog, where Joseph Atwood established a woollen mill in 1824–25, and at L'Acadie, where Mahlon Willette built a woollen mill in 1826. In 1844 Sherbrooke also became the site of Canada's first cotton mill. Although woollen manufacture in the townships did not develop into a major regional industry as it did in Ontario, the Paton Manufacturing Company mill in Sherbrooke was the largest single mill in Canada in the 1880s and 1890s. During the 1880s the area also developed into a cotton-manufacturing area with a large print and cloth mill at Magog and a smaller mill at Coaticook. Still later it diversified into knit goods/hosiery and silk/synthetics with Penman and Consolidated Silk mills at Saint-Hyacinthe, Julius Kayser and Canadian Silk Products plants at Sherbrooke, and Canadian Celanese's huge rayon plant at Drummondville. It also had three large tire-cord plants: Canadian Connecticut Cotton Mills at Sherbrooke, Jenckes Canadian Company at Drummondville, and Canadian Manhasset Cotton Company in Saint-Hyacinthe.

67 Dominion Textile's Pacific Street mill in Sherbrooke. The two main buildings, which were built by Canadian Connecticut Cotton Mills in 1914 and 1920 to produce tire cord, are typical of mill-construction building in its most evolved form, with laminated plank floors on steel beams.
Canadian Textile Journal, 22 April 1955, p. 28; National Library of Canada, NL 16041

Paton Manufacturing Company
Belvedere and King, Sherbrooke

Andrew Paton emigrated from Scotland in 1855. For ten years he was involved in woollen mills in Galt and Waterloo. He sold some of his products to George Stephen, and in 1865 Stephen and a group of financiers from the Eastern Townships asked him to undertake the organization and management of a new mill in Sherbrooke. The new firm, operating under the title Andrew Paton and Company, built a brick woollen mill on the Magog River in 1866.[1] In 1868 the firm was expanded and reorganized as the Paton Manufacturing Company. In the new firm about two-thirds of the shares were held by Montréalers including George Stephen, who became vice-president. The rest of the shares were held by Eastern Townships investors such as A.T. Galt and R.W. Heneker, the commissioner of the British American Land Company.[2] Heneker served as president until about 1902.[3] Paton became a minor shareholder, but continued as managing director until his death in 1892, when he was succeeded by his son, W.E. Paton.

In 1871 the company, with 194 employees, was the second-largest woollen firm in Canada. In 1872 it doubled its capacity from 10 to 20 sets of cards and became Canada's largest mill. After the construction of a new worsted mill in 1892 the firm employed about 700 and produced a wide variety of products including tweeds, overcoatings, jersey cloth, shoe linings, rugs, shawls, flannels, and yarn.[4] The firm also had some knitting capacity and in 1909 it purchased an adjacent woollen mill, Adam Lomas and Son, and converted it to a knitting mill.[5] The Lomas firm was an old one, having been organized in the 1840s, and was the successor to an even older firm, the Goodhue mill, organized in 1826 as a saw, grist, and woollen mill.[6]

After 1905 Paton Manufacturing had close links with Dominion Textile. Senator Robert Mackay, one of the members of the syndicate that organized Dominion Textile and a director of Dominion Textile from 1905 to 1917, was a director of Patons in 1903 and vice-president in 1911; Sir Herbert Holt, vice-president of Dominion Textile from 1911 to 1941 and a son-in-law of Andrew Paton, was a member of Paton's board.[7] In 1923 the firm was reorganized as Paton Manufacturing Company Limited and came under the control of Dominion Textile. In 1965 the company was sold to Cleyn and Tinker; in 1978 the operations were moved to Huntingdon and the mill was closed.[8]

The original 1866 mill has been demolished, but the 1892 worsted mill and what is probably the 1871–72 expansion have been converted to residential units. A number of warehouses and outbuildings have also survived and await redevelopment. Most of the buildings on the Lomas mill site have been demolished.

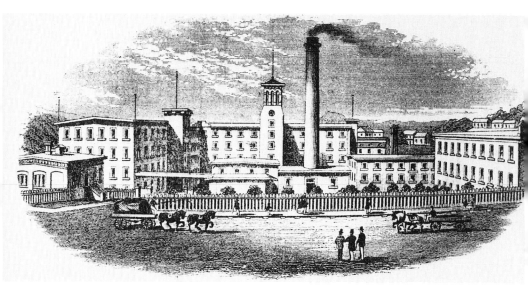

68 An 1885 view of the Paton Manufacturing Company mill in Sherbrooke. The original mill with the Italianate bell tower was built in 1866.
Canadian Textile Directory, 1885, p. 248; National Archives of Canada, C 127997

69 The Paton mill about 1950. The gradual accretion of structures often left mill sites cramped and unattractive. In the rehabilitation of this site, the original mill on the left was demolished and the 1871 expansion in the foreground and the 1891 worsted mill in the centre were converted to residential units.
Manual of the Textile Industry of Canada, 1951, p. 91; National Library of Canada, NL 17297

70 The refurbished worsted mill in 1987.
Canadian Parks Service, 1987

Magog Textile and Print Company
250 rue Principale, Magog

The Magog Textile and Print Company was organized by a group of investors from the Eastern Townships in 1883. It apparently had support from Montréal capital as the Honourable James K. Ward, a lumberman and investor in the Hudon, Montreal Cotton, and Coaticook mills, was its president.[1] The firm was organized to take advantage of the glut of grey cotton in Canada in the early 1880s. It bought (or perhaps accepted on consignment) grey cloth from Canadian mills, printed the cloth, and resold it. The mill was designed to produce about 15 million yards of cotton prints annually, an amount equal to the output of approximately 1500 looms.[2] Until 1899 it was the only print mill in Canada.

The original plan included spinning and weaving capacity, but it was not until 1888 that the plan was realized.[3] With 40 000 spindles and 600 looms in 1892,[4] it was the sixth-largest cloth mill in Canada, ranking behind the Montreal Cotton, Hudon, Merchants, Canada, and St. Croix mills. If its printing business is included in the calculation, it is probable that it was the third-largest mill in Canada.

The company was not a success and in 1889 it was sold to the Hochelaga Cotton Manufacturing Company. In 1890 the Hochelaga Company formed the core of the Dominion Cotton Mills Company, which included 11 previously independent mills. The Magog plant was expanded to provide printing and bleaching capacity for the other mills; its spinning and weaving capacity was also increased. By 1902 it employed 1000 hands; its 50 000 spindles and 1234 looms produced 13 million yards of cloth annually. In addition to its own production it printed 5 560 000 yards of cloth from other mills.[5] When Dominion Cotton merged with the Merchants, Montmorency, and Colonial Bleaching and Printing mills in 1905 to form Dominion Textile, printing equipment from the Colonial mill was transferred to Magog[6] and it continued to serve as the main printing facility for Dominion Textile.

Initially the plant was water powered,[7] but in 1896 a Taylor hydraulic air-compression system was installed. This was the first installation of this Canadian-designed system, which used water power to compress air; the compressed air was then used in much the same way as steam would have been to operate machinery. Initially compressed air was used to operate the printing presses, but its use was soon extended to the spinning and weaving mill.[8] How successful the system was is not clear; it was probably in use until 1908 and may have been replaced by a hydro-electric drive system in 1910.[9]

The Magog mills seem to have been strike free during the nineteenth century, but they were caught up in the round of strikes that convulsed the Quebec textile industry in the years 1900–1908.[10] In July of 1900, 400 workers in the cloth mill struck in protest against a change in the pay day and to support a demand for a 10-per-cent wage increase. Strikers stoned workers who attempted to enter the mill, and when the strikers attempted to enter the mill they were met by special police, the riot act was read, and shots were fired. Ultimately the militia was called out and the strike was broken.[11] In 1901 the mill was organized by the Union of Textile Workers; when the organizers were fired the plant was struck again. Labour unrest continued throughout the decade; between 1906 and 1911 the mills were struck five times. Three of these strikes involved 800 to 900 workers.[12] The Magog plant was also involved in the 1937 strike against Dominion Textile.

A 1917 recruiting pamphlet gives the company's view of labour practices and working conditions at the Magog mills. The company operated 65 000 spindles, 1800 looms, and 12 printing machines. It employed 550 men, 450 women, 100 boys, and 125 girls and had a monthly payroll of $60 000. The heating and air-cleansing systems in the mills were said to be the best on the continent and the work was steady. In addition to offering monetary benefits, the company operated a small farm that produced potatoes and beans that were sold at cost to employees; it also arranged for the supply of firewood, coal, and flour at cost. The company supported a clubhouse with recreation and reading rooms and a tennis court. The pamphlet also noted some of the amenities of the town: a healthy situation, good cheap water, a modern sewage system and street lighting, churches and schools, and a nun-operated daycare that provided accommodation for 200 children of working families. As a result of the installation of new machinery the company wished to recruit 100 families.[13]

Dominion Textile still operates a large textile plant at Magog. The modern plant encompasses a range of old and new buildings including the 1883 print mill.[14]

71 The Dominion Textile mill at Magog, ca. 1927.
Dominion Textile

72 The Magog mill, looking upriver towards the power plant.
Dominion Textile

180

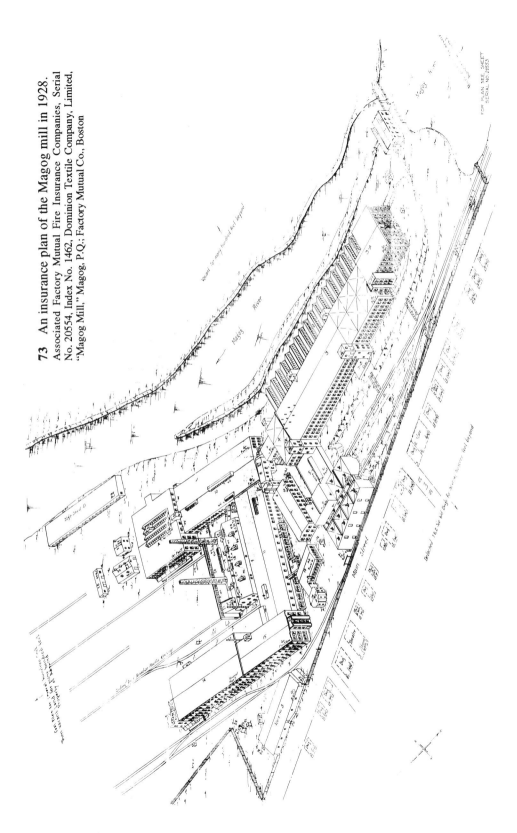

73 An insurance plan of the Magog mill in 1928.
Associated Factory Mutual Fire Insurance Companies, Serial
No. 20554, Index No. 1462, Dominion Textile Company, Limited,
"Magog Mill," Magog, P.Q.; Factory Mutual Co., Boston

Canadian Celanese Limited
Chemin Celanese, Drummondville

During the late nineteenth century several procedures were developed for breaking down cellulose fibres in plants and reconstituting them as artifical silk or rayon. Commercial production of rayon began in Europe in the late 1890s, but there were no major rayon plants in Canada until 1925–26.

In the 1920s Camille and Alfred Dreyfus developed a new process for producing rayon by dissolving cellulose in acetone. They organized firms for producing acetate rayon in Britain and the United States and in 1926 incorporated Canadian Celanese Limited with Camille Dreyfus as president. The firm built a new mill at Drummondville and in 1927 began the production of rayon fabric using imported cellulose yarn. In 1928 it began to produce yarn from cotton linters (short cotton fibres that were unsuitable for spinning) as the raw material.[1]

Drummondville was selected as a site because of its proximity to Montréal, its abundant and cheap hydro-electric power and wood, and a labour force that as a result of wartime work in chemical plants was relatively familiar with chemical processes.[2] Canadian Celanese may also have been influenced by the location of several substantial textile manufacturers — Butterfly Hosiery, Jenckes Canadian Company, and Dominion Silk Dyeing and Finishing Company — in Drummondville in the years after the First World War.[3]

In 1926 Canadian Celanese signed a $7 million contract for the construction of its first seven buildings. The mill was an immediate success and additions were made in 1928, 1930, 1935, 1943, 1946–47, 1964, and 1980.[4] Employment climbed from 1757 in 1933 to 2500 in 1939.[5] Unlike the Courtaulds mill, which sold most of its product as stock or yarn for further processing, the Celanese company processed most of its product and sold it as woven or knitted fabric. In 1935–37 Canadian Celanese produced about 15 million yards of rayon fabric; total Canadian production was about 32 million yards.[6]

During the late 1950s Canadian Celanese acquired a number of small textile firms. In 1963 it merged with the Canadian Chemical Company, a petrochemical and textile firm in Edmonton, to form Chemcell (1963) Incorporated. In 1971 Chemcell was reorganized as Celanese Canada; it is the largest Canadian producer of broad-woven man-made fabrics and the largest Canadian supplier of man-made fibres. It is also a major chemical producer.[7]

Photograph by Canadian Airways Limited

THIS IS THE CELANESE PLANT, 1939

$11,430,870 invested in site, improvements, machinery and equipment, December 31,1938 **2,500 JOBS**

The above photograph illustrates how investors, management, technicians have combined to build up a steadily expanding industry giving stability of employment to thousands of Canadian workers.

CANADIAN
CELANESE
LIMITED

74 An advertisement for Canadian Celanese.
Manual of the Textile Industry of Canada ... 1940, p. 117; National Library of Canada, NL 14664

Salaberry-de-Valleyfield, Quebec

Montreal Cotton Company
1 rue Saint Laurent

The Montreal Cotton Company was organized in 1874 and built a mill at Valleyfield in 1875–76. Production began in 1877; during the 1870s and 1880s the plant was the second-largest mill in Canada; only the Hudon (Hochelaga) mill was larger. Major building programs in 1882–83 (following the introduction of the National Policy), 1893, 1898, 1901, and 1905 made it the largest textile mill in Canada.[1] It remained the largest Canadian cotton mill until the 1960s, when Dominion Textile began to transfer operations to newer mills. The plant was shut down in stages; the last section to be closed down was the Gault mill, which was closed after 1983.

The company was organized by a group of Montréal and English financiers. The Montréalers, who subscribed about two-thirds of the original authorized capital of $500 000, included Hugh Allan, J.K. Ward, J.-Rosaire Thibodeau, and Andrew F. Gault. The principal English subscriber was probably Samuel Barlow, a Lancashire cotton machinery manufacturer.[2] Allan was president from 1874 to 1882; Gault was president from 1883 to 1903. From 1923 to 1928 and 1933 to 1939 Sir Charles Gordon, the chairman of Dominion Textile, was also president of Montreal Cotton. He was succeeded in both positions by his son, G. Blair Gordon, who incorporated Montreal Cotton into Dominion Textile in 1948.[3]

The original mill was a four-storey gray stone building about 190 feet by 90 feet.[4] It was was located at the upper end of the Beauharnois Canal and was powered by two 250-horsepower turbines that drove 27 000 spindles and 520 looms. By 1896 it had 17 water wheels yielding a total of 3600 horsepower.[5] Electric lights were installed in the mill in September of 1883 and in 1896–97 the mill began to use electric drive. This was almost certainly the earliest use of electric drive in a Canadian textile mill. By 1928 all of its operations were electrically driven.[6] The firm was technologically innovative in other ways; A.F. Gault, the company president, Louis Simpson, the mill manager, and others organized the Northrop Loom Company of Canada and began manufacturing automatic looms at Valleyfield in 1898. By 1908, 400 of the 5000 looms installed at Montreal Cottons were automatic.[7]

By 1908 the company employed 2500 men, women, and children when it was operating at full capacity. Part of the labour force was recruited locally and part was recruited in England. The company was active in what was described as welfare work; it provided recreational (bowling, billiards, skating, curling tennis, baseball) and educational facilities for its employees and operated a dairy to ensure a supply of pure milk.[8] In 1908 it owned 200 to 300 houses that it rented to employees.[9] In spite of its efforts to maintain a loyal and contented labour force, the company faced bitter, and occasionally violent, strikes in 1880, 1887, 1900, 1906, 1908, 1937, 1946, and 1952.[10]

Today only the Gault mill and the powerhouse, both built about the turn of the century, survive. Although the Gault mill is a large building, it and the powerhouse probably represent less than one-quarter of the original mill. The Gault mill is still owned by Dominion Textile and is used for storage. The rest of the site, including the headrace and tailrace, which have been filled in, is occupied by a shopping centre and parking lot.

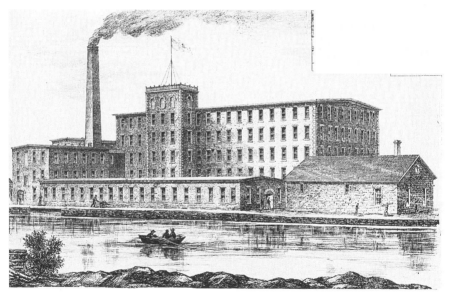

75 Montreal Cotton Company mill and bleachery in 1878.
Canadian Illustrated News, 12 Jan. 1878, p. 20; National Archives of Canada, C 67515

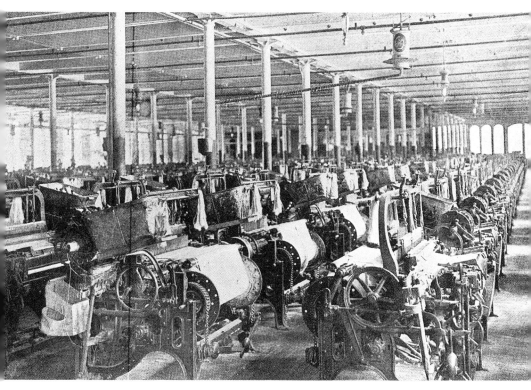

76 A weave room at Valleyfield about 1908.
Valleyfield Canada: The Cotton Factory Town of Canada (Valleyfield: Montreal Cotton Co., n.d.);
National Library of Canada, NL 16970

77 The Montreal Cotton Company mill in the 1950s. Only the Gault mills on the right and a powerhouse survive.
Dominion Textile

78 and **79**   The Montreal Cotton mill from the southwest about 1908 (above) and in 1986 (below).
Valleyfield Canada: The Cotton Factory Town of Canada (Valleyfield: Montreal Cotton Co., n.d.), National Library, NL 16971; Canadian Parks Service, 1986

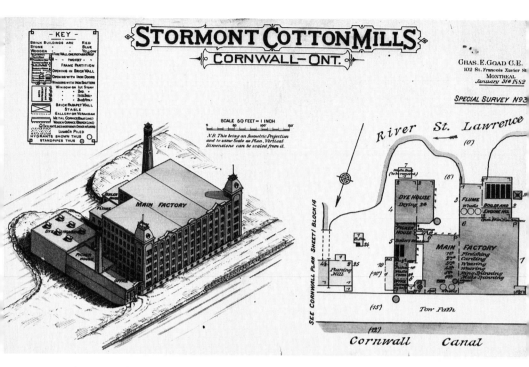

80 The Stormont mill, built in 1879 and expanded in 1881, was a six-storey building about 220 by 130 feet. The walls of the first storey were of stone, subsequent storeys were of brick; the walls tapered from 30 inches thick at the base to 16 inches thick at the top. The wall was strengthened with brick piers that projected six inches between each window. The internal structure was standard mill construction with floors 6.5 inches thick made up of four thicknesses of planking on 12-by-12-inch beams supported by posts 8 to 10 inches in diameter spaced 10 to 13 feet apart. The roof was an almost flat wooden truss; the stairs were enclosed in two brick towers at each end of the façade. The dye house, wheel house, boiler room, and engine room were at the back of the mill, and the head race passed beneath it. The mill burned on Hallowe'en, 1960.
National Archives of Canada, NMC 9380

Cornwall, Ontario

In the 1870s Montréal capitalists, seeking profitable fields of investment, took advantage of the proximity of Cornwall, Ontario, and its abundant waterpower and established three textile mills. In 1868 George Stephen and associates built a woollen mill, the Cornwall Manufacturing Company, on the Cornwall Canal; the mill operated for 34 years and then was converted to a cotton mill known as the Dundas mill. In 1870 the Gault Brothers built the Stormont cotton mill on the canal, about a mile west of the Dundas mill. In 1874 Donald Smith and others built a large cotton mill, the Canada mill, next to the Dundas mill. These three mills formed the basis of Cornwall's reputation as a mill town in the nineteenth century. In the twentieth century the reputation was bolstered when Courtaulds built a rayon mill in 1924–25. With the exception of the Stormont mill, parts of all of these mills survive.

81 The Stormont mill, undated photo.
National Archives of Canada, PA 179834, Merrilees Collection, C 20827

Canada Cotton Manufacturing Company
William and Edward streets

The Canada Cotton Manufacturing Company was organized in 1872 by a group of financiers and mill owners including Donald A. Smith and Edward Mackay of Montréal, Bennett Rosamond of Almonte, John Harvey of Cornwall, and Donald McInnes of Hamilton.[1] The original plant, completed in 1873, consisted of the main mill, a four-storey, 250-foot-by-90-foot, red brick mill-construction building with a mansard roof, warehouse, dyehouse, and gas plant.[2] The mill began operation in 1874 and by 1878 it had 20 000 spindles, 500 looms, and about 400 hands who produced about 100 000 yards of cloth per week.[3] In 1882 the company built a 550-foot-by-120-foot weave shed[4] and doubled the plant's capacity. With 40 000 spindles and 720 looms in 1885, the mill ranked with the St. Croix mill in Milltown, New Brunswick, as the third-largest textile mill in Canada.[5] In the twentieth century it was surpassed by a number of other mills (Merchants, Magog, Montmorency, etc.), but it continued to rank as a medium-size mill until it was closed.

In 1892 the mill became part of Canadian Coloured Cotton Mills Company, which had been organized by Andrew Gault and David Morrice to limit competition in the cotton industry. Gault was president of Canadian Coloured Cotton from 1892 to 1897; Morrice was president from 1898 to 1913. The Canada mill was considered the flagship mill of the company, which also owned the Stormont mill in Cornwall and, after 1904, the Dundas mill, which is across the street from the Canada mill. Considered together the three mills formed a major operating unit that rivalled the Hudon and Merchants mills.

The mill was on the Cornwall Canal and in 1878 it was powered by two 250-horsepower turbines with a Corliss steam engine in reserve. Direct-drive water power remained the primary motive force until at least 1918, when the mill utilized 1200 horsepower generated by water, 800 horsepower generated by steam, and 800 horsepower of purchased electricity.[6] The mill began using incandescent electric light in March 1883; it was the first large industrial plant in Canada to do so.[7]

The company employed about 500 to 700 in the 1880s; about half were women and 15 per cent were under 16 years of age. Originally most of the employees had been local people of Scottish descent, but by the late 1880s about half of the employees were French speaking; the overseers and handymen were all English speaking.[8] The mill suffered a brief strike in 1882 as a result of an attempt by the company to extend the work week beyond 60.5 hours. Four years later both the Canada and Stormont mills were organized by the Knights of Labour, and both mills were struck in 1887, 1888, and 1889 over hours, wages, and disagreements over implementing previous agreements.[9] The mill was not affected by the strikes of the early twentieth century, but its employees took part in the 1937 wave of strikes.

Canadian Cottons was liquidated in 1959, a victim of foreign competition, labour difficulties and, perhaps, a decision by management to salvage what capital it could from the company and shift it into another business.[10] When it closed in 1959 the Canada mill complex consisted of about ten large buildings. Most of these have been demolished, but the key buildings — the 1873 mill and the 1882 weave shed with a 1916 extension — survive. The original mansard roof on the main mill and the monitor roof on the weave shed have been replaced by flat roofs. Both buildings have some twentieth-century additions and interior renovations, but the basic structures are largely intact. The 1873 mill is the oldest surviving cotton mill in Canada. The 1882 weave shed is the finest surviving Canadian example of a large single-storey weave shed built in the nineteenth century.

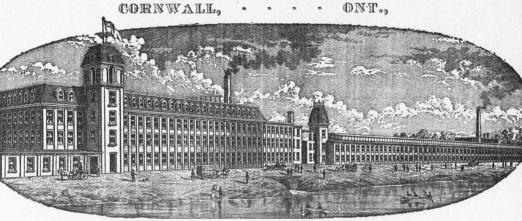

THE CANADA COTTON MANUFACTURING COMPANY,

CORNWALL, · · · · ONT.,

MANUFACTURERS OF

COTTONADES, WOVEN DUCKS, DYED DUCKS, WHITE DUCKS,

For Sails and Tents, in 7, 7½, 8, 9, 10 and 12 oz.

CANTON FLANNELS, BLEACHED, UNBLEACHED AND COLORED,

GRAIN BAGS, SUGAR BAGS, Etc.

he Wholesale Trade only Supplied.

JOHN FRASER, Agent,
42 St. John Street, MONTREAL.

82 An advertising cut showing the 1874 mill and the 1882 weave shed of the Canada Cotton Manufacturing Company at Cornwall.
Canadian Textile Directory, 1885, p. 278; National Library of Canada, C 12800

83 The Canada mill in 1985. The mansard roof was replaced about the turn of the century.
Canadian Parks Service, 1985

84 The interior of the weave shed (now used as a cabinet shop) at the Canada mill, 1986.
Heritage Recording Unit, Canadian Parks Service, 1986

Cornwall Manufacturing Company — Dundas Mill
William and Edward streets

The Dundas mill was built as a woollen mill. George Stephen, who was already a shareholder in the Rosamond mill at Almonte and the Paton mill at Sherbrooke, organized the Cornwall Manufacturing Company in 1868. Hugh Allan became president and Stephen was vice-president. The firm built a woollen mill on the Cornwall Canal.[1] The mill burned in 1870 and was rebuilt in 1872. At the time it burned it was probably the fourth-largest woollen mill in Canada; the Rosamond mill at Almonte, the Randall and Farr mill in Hespeler, and the Paton mill in Sherbrooke employed more people.[2] The Cornwall Manufacturing Company continued to be an important Ontario woollen producer until 1902, when it closed.

The original mill employed about 100 people with an annual wage bill of $18 000 and $200 000 in annual sales.[3] By 1888 it employed 60 men, 120 women, and 45 children and youths. It produced dress goods, tweeds, and overcoatings using Australian and South African wool. In 1892 the mill had ten sets of 60-inch cards and 28 broad and 45 narrow looms and was driven by both water and steam power.[4]

The mill closed in 1902 and was sold to Canadian Coloured Cotton, which converted it to a cotton mill in 1904.[5] Because much of its equipment had been transferred from the Dundas Cotton Company mill in Dundas, Ontario, it was known as the Dundas mill. As a cotton mill it was relatively small; in 1907 it ranked nineteenth out of 21 cotton mills in Canada and it never seems to have had more than 20 000 spindles or 200 looms.[6] After 1904 it operated in conjunction with the Canada mill across the street.

Although the Dundas mill was not a major cotton mill, its early history as a woollen mill and its membership in the group of mills that made Cornwall an important textile centre make it an interesting mill. Most of the mill was demolished in 1978, but parts of three large buildings, including the original mill, survive.

85 The Dundas mill in the foreground and the Canada mill in the distance. Ornate bell towers, such as the one on the Dundas mill, were often taken down during twentieth-century renovations. This photograph probably dates from the period 1900–20.
National Archives of Canada, PA 179833, Merillees Collection, C-20826

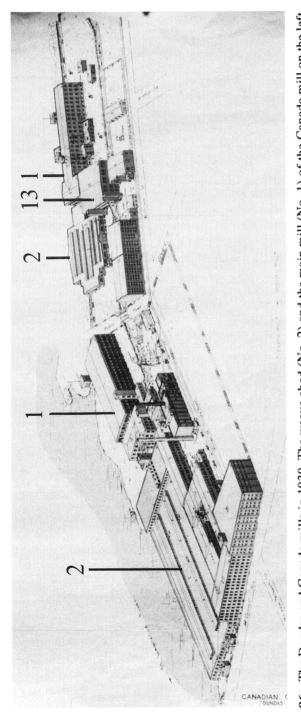

86 The Dundas and Canada mills in 1939. The weave shed (No. 2) and the main mill (No. 1) of the Canada mill on the left and parts of Nos. 1, 2, and 13 of the Dundas mill on the right survive.

Associated Factory Mutual Insurance Plan, Serial No. 29522, Index No. 2150, Canadian Cottons, Limited, "Dundas & Canada Mill," Cornwall, Ont.; copy on file, Cornwall Warehousing Ltd., Cornwall

197

Courtaulds (Canada) Limited
1150 Montreal Road

The processes by which the cellulose in wood and other vegetable matter can be broken down and reconstituted as synthetic fibres were developed in Europe in the late nineteenth century. In 1904 Samuel Courtauld and Company, a British silk-manufacturing firm, purchased the rights to manufacture rayon fibre by the viscose process. In the viscose process, bleached sulphite wood pulp is steeped in caustic soda, mixed and conditioned so that the wood fibres are broken down and reduced to a thick, amber, highly alkaline liquid. This liquid is then extruded into an acid solution that causes it to coagulate into filaments. Although these filaments can be used for weaving or knitting, they are usually cut into short lengths and then spun in much the same fashion as natural fibres. Courtaulds began production in England in 1905 and in 1909 organized a firm, American Viscose, to produce rayon in the United States.[1]

For 20 years Courtaulds exported relatively small amounts of rayon to Canada, but when the market began to expand in the 1920s the firm decided to produce rayon in Canada. Rayon had been admitted to Canada duty free, but in 1923 a 15-per-cent tariff was imposed as an incentive to Courtaulds to build. In 1924 Courtaulds began construction of a plant in Cornwall and production began in 1925.[2] The firm did not process its own yarn; it sold to other firms. Initially knit-goods firms were its major customers, but by 1936, 60 per cent of its sales were to weavers.[3]

The mill was an immediate success and additions were made in 1926–27, 1930, 1933–34, 1937–38, 1946, 1949, and 1951–53.[4] Expansion was the result of sustained growth in the market for synthetic products and continued and increasing tariff protection. Employment rose from 100 when the plant opened to 750 in 1926 and 1370 in 1933.[5] The mill was organized by the United Textile Workers of America in 1936 during a strike over wages and working conditions. Working conditions in synthetic mills tended to be particularly unpleasant and unhealthy because of the caustic substances used in producing rayon. Because of the continuous nature of rayon production, synthetic mills were vulnerable to work stoppages, and in 1937 Courtaulds recognized a local union affiliated with the Trades and Labour Council of Canada.[6]

The original mill and the 1926–27 extension, both of which are extant, have the external appearance of a traditional brick mill, but structurally they are a combination of reinforced concrete and structural steel. Subsequent additions tend to be steel frame, concrete, and cinder block.

87   Courtaulds rayon mill at Cornwall in the 1930s.
National Film Board, B-1; National Archives of Canada, C 46217

88 The Courtaulds mill in the late 1940s.
National Archives of Canada, PA 179679, Malak Collection, 967-11423

Almonte, Ontario

Rosamond Woollen Company
Mary and Ramsay streets

During the last half of the nineteenth century the Mississippi Valley of eastern Ontario was one of the most important wool-cloth-producing districts in Canada. The Rosamond Woollen Company was the area's most important firm.

James Rosamond, an Irish immigrant, established a mill on the Mississippi River at Carleton Place about 1830. Initially it was a saw and grist mill, but by the end of the 1830s it also did custom carding and fulling. In Carleton Place in 1846 Rosamond established an integrated mill that carded, spun, and wove. In 1849 he, in partnership with two other merchants, built the Ramsay Woollen Mill in Almonte, Ontario. This mill burned in 1852; Rosamond bought out his partners and built another mill, the Victoria Woollen Mill, in Almonte in 1857.

In 1862 he leased the Victoria mill to his sons, Bennett and William, who doubled its capacity. In 1866 they organized a new firm, B. and W. Rosamond and Company, with George Stephen of Montréal as a partner. In 1870 the firm was reorganized as the Rosamond Woollen Company.[1] About this time William Rosamond withdrew as an active partner in the firm. George Stephen continued to provide capital and marketing advice for the firm, but Bennett was the president and dominant partner.

In 1866 B. & W. Rosamond and Company built a stone mill on Coleman's Island in Almonte: this mill is now known as the Rosamond mill. The mill, six storeys high and 58 feet by 157 feet, was the largest woollen mill in Canada in 1871.[2] It employed 74 men, 105 women, and 30 youths and produced $350 000 worth of tweed annually.[3] Over the next 40 years several additions were made to it and it continued to rank as one of the largest woollen mills until World War I.

The Rosamond firm was progressive: it began production of worsted cloth in 1880 and concentrated on the production of high-quality cloth. Its products won several international prizes and enjoyed a small export market.[4] Bennett Rosamond was a recognized spokesman for the woollen industry. In 1890 he was president of the Canadian Manufacturers' Association and from 1892 to 1905 he was the member of Parliament for North Lanark.[5] In addition to the Rosamond Woollen Company the family had other textile interests. Bennett Rosamond and George Stephen organized the Almonte Knitting Company in 1882. Bennett was a shareholder in Stephen's Canada Cotton Manufacturing company at Cornwall and William was the co-owner of the Cobourg Woollen Company from 1875 until about 1900.[6]

The firm survived the recession of the late 1890s, but the death of Bennett Rosamond in 1910 and of his chosen successor, a nephew, Alexander, in France in 1916 deprived it of the forceful leadership that had been a major contribution to its success. Although the Rosamond family continued to operate the mill, it was not a major force in the woollen industry after World War I. In 1952 the family sold the mill to Artex Woollens.[7] It continued in use as a textile mill until 1987.

The main mill has been converted to residential condominiums; a warehouse, known as the Annex, has been acquired by the Mississippi Valley Textile Museum, which plans to develop it as a museum.

In 1990 the minister of the Environment recognized the company's importance in the history of the Canadian woollen industry by erecting a plaque at the mill site. The company has also been commemorated by the Ontario government, which erected a plaque at the Victoria mill.

89 The Rosamond Woollen Company mill about 1877 before wings were added to either end. The original mills often had a severe beauty that was lost as outbuildings were tacked onto them.
Ontario Archives, S15198, Accession 3023

90 The renovated Rosamond mill, 1991.
Canadian Parks Service, 1991

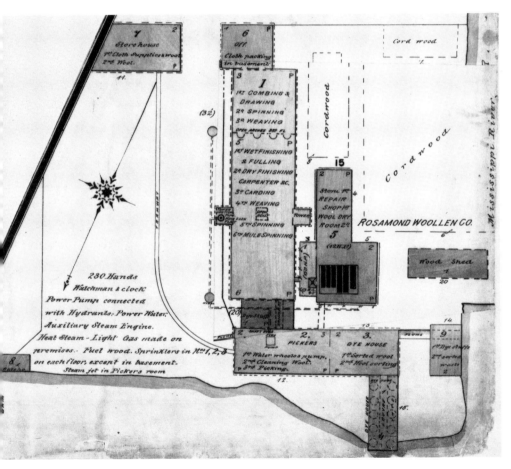

91 An 1884 insurance plan of the Rosamond mill showing the layout of its machinery and fire-fighting equipment. By 1884 the south wing of the mill had been built.
National Archives of Canada, NMC 93466, IP/PA/440/Almonte/1879 (1884), Sheet 13

203

West *(elevator)* Tower

East *(stair)* Tower

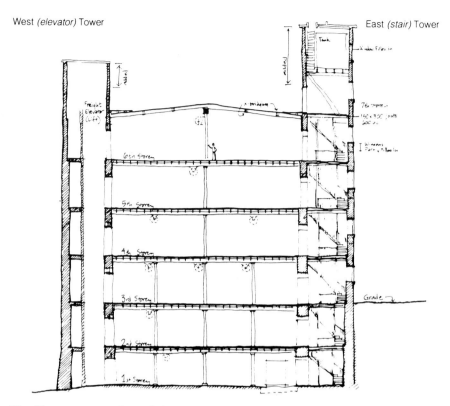

92   Transverse section of the main block of the Rosamond mill showing post and line shaft locations.
Drawing by D. Bouse

Cambridge, Ontario

During the later nineteenth century the upper Grand River Valley, with an abundance of water power, labour, locally produced wool, and easy access to markets, became the most important woollen- and knit-goods-producing area in Canada. The three towns, Hespeler, Preston, and Galt, that now make up the City of Cambridge were among the most important producers within this region. Hespeler had two large woollen mills, the Forbes mill and the Brodie mill, Preston had one large woollen mill, the Pattinson, and Galt had three mid-sized knitting mills, the C. Turnbull Company, Galt Knitting, and Newlands. The area's textile industry continued to expand in the early twentieth century with the establishment of two other important mills, Stauffer-Dobbie and Riverside Silk Mills.

93 The C. Turnbull Company knitting mill in Galt. The mill was demolished in the 1970s.
Canadian Textile Journal, 9 Sept. 1955, p. 7; National Library of Canada, NL 16018

R. Forbes Company
215 Queen Street, Hespeler

In 1863 George and Shubell Randall and Herbert Farr purchased the site of a sawmill on the Speed River in Hespeler, Ontario. They built a two-and-one-half-storey stone building, 54 feet by 146 feet, and established a knitting and weaving mill. By 1871 the water-powered mill employed 163 people (45 men, 44 women, and 74 children) and produced goods worth $200 000; it was the second-largest woollen mill in Ontario. In 1874 Jonathon Schofield and Robert Forbes bought the mill.[1]

Schofield and Forbes had been operating a woollen mill on Tannery Street in Hespeler since 1870. They closed their older mill and moved to the new property. In 1880 Forbes bought Schofield's interest in the firm and in 1888 the R. Forbes Company Limited was incorporated. The company, which in 1885 had six sets of cards and 27 looms, produced tweeds, flannels, hosiery, fancy knit goods, and yarn. It expanded gradually during the 1880s and more rapidly during the years 1890–1908. By 1908 it was a very large mill complex occupying about 500 000 square feet in more than 25 buildings.[2]

By the early twentieth century the Forbes company was slightly larger, based on the number of looms and spindles employed, than the Rosamond company, but smaller than the Brodie mill (also in Hespeler) and the Paton mill. However, when one considers that a large part of its capacity was devoted to knitting and that it occupied almost 500 000 square feet compared to about 250 000 for the Paton mill, it seems probable that by 1910 the mill was the largest textile mill in Canada excepting some cotton mills and, perhaps, Penmans' Paris, Ontario, and Saint-Hyacinthe, Quebec, knitting mills.

In the early twentieth century the company produced worsteds and serges, worsted and woollen yarns, and fancy knit goods. In 1938 it quit producing knitted goods and concentrated on weaving and on the production of yarn.[3] From as early as the 1880s it had its own marketing agency with sales representatives who travelled from the Maritimes to the Prairies;[4] most large mills sold their products through an agent such as David Morrice and Sons.

Under the Forbes family's management the company enjoyed labour peace. It encouraged a stable labour force through long-term employment contracts, the provision of company housing, and an employee benefit society. It also subsidized the immigration of skilled employees from Europe.[5] In 1933 the mill had its first organized strike.[6] The strike failed and when Dominion Woollens and Worsteds workers in Peterborough struck in 1937, the workers in the Hespeler plant refused to support them.

Perhaps because of their diversified interests the Forbes company survived and even prospered in the early years of the century when many woollen mills failed. The Forbes family retained control of the company until 1928, when they sold out to Dominion Woollens and Worsteds. At about the same time as they sold their interest in the firm, the Forbes family took over the management of the C. Turnbull Company, a major knitting firm in Galt.[7]

Dominion Woollens and Worsteds, with plants in Peterborough, Milton, and Hespeler, was the largest woollen firm in Canada. In 1933 it controlled 12.5 per cent of all sales in the woollen sector; the Forbes mill was its largest plant.[8] The company operated succcessfully through the 1930s and 1940s, but ran into difficulties in the 1950s. In 1958 Dominion Woollens and Worsteds went into receivership. Although the firm was reorganized and continued to operate until 1966, it was as a subsidiary and/or tenant of Silknit Limited, a major knitting firm that owned the buildings. After 1966 Silknit continued to operate the mill on a gradually decreasing scale until 1984, when it sold the mill to Waterloo Textiles, which in turn sold about 80 per cent of the mill to the City of Cambridge.[9] Part of the mill was demolished in 1990; part is still in use as a knitting mill and warehouse space. The original mill, built in 1864, survives.

94 The Randall-Farr and Company woollen mill in 1886. The main building survives but has been raised from two and a half storeys to three storeys. In front of the main building is a small sawtooth-roof weave shed. Sheds of this type were common in Britain but unusual in North America.
Canadian Textile Journal, 30 June 1933, p. 127; Hamilton Public Library

95 The Forbes mill in Hespeler, ca. 1947. The building nearest the dam is the original Randall-Farr mill. The five buildings beyond and to the right of the water tower were demolished in 1990.

Hespeler—1947: Old Boys' Reunion, June 30th–July 6th (Hespeler, Ont.: T&T Press, 1947), p. 12; National Library of Canada, NL 17006

96 Demolition of a portion of the Forbes mill, 1990.
Canadian Parks Service, 1990

George Pattinson and Company
498 Eagle Street, Preston

The Pattinson mill in Preston was built as a linen mill during the American Civil War by the firm of Elliott, Hunt, and Stephen. The Stephen in the firm was George Stephen, the Montréal dry-goods importer who had extensive interests in textile manufacturing. John Elliot had been associated with the Victoria Woollen Mills in Almonte. In spite of an investment of at least $120 000, the linen mill failed after the war.[1] In 1870 it was converted to a woollen mill by James Crombie. By 1871 it employed 31 men, 25 women, and 11 children, and produced $120 000 worth of woollens annually.[2] It was the sixth-largest mill in Ontario at the time.

In 1876 William Robinson, Daniel Howell, and others (all owners of the Galt Woollen Factory, subsequently the Galt Knitting Company) bought the mill and operated it until 1889. George Pattinson had an interest in the mill when Crombie owned it, and both he and the Hon. John Ferguson had an interest in it when William Robinson died.

On the death of Howell in 1889 they formed the firm of Ferguson and Pattinson to operate the mill. In 1898 Pattinson became the sole owner of the firm, George Pattinson and Company. In 1931 he was succeeded by his son, F.H. Pattinson, who operated the firm until 1958, when it moved to Jamaica. The move to Jamaica was prompted by high Canadian labour costs and foreign competition.[3]

In 1885 the mill had six sets of cards and 45 looms; it used both water and steam power. It expanded slghtly between 1885 and 1905; in 1910–12 its capacity was doubled. By 1933 it was the ninth-largest woollen mill in Canada on the basis of sales.[4] It produced tweeds, cheviots, overcoatings, and mackinaws, and sold directly to the public.

A substantial mill complex, estimated in 1958 at 200 000 square feet, survives. Much of the complex dates from 1910–12; what, if anything, survives from the nineteenth century is not clear. The complex is now occupied by a plastics firm.

The Pattinson mill was, throughout its history, a larger than average mill, but it was never among the largest. Similarly, although George Pattinson was respected in the industry, he does not seem to been a major industry spokesman. Although the mill was only a middle-sized one, it was an important factor in making the Cambridge area a leading textile producer.

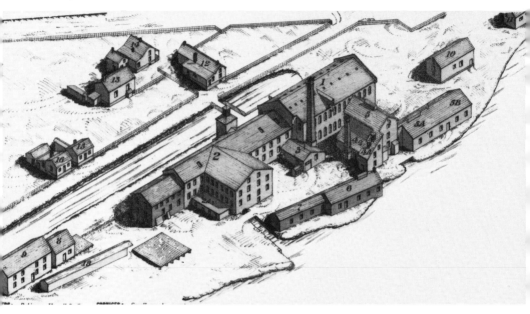

97   The Preston (Pattinson) Woollen Mill in 1884.
National Archives of Canada, NMC 9641

98   The mill in 1986. Most of the surviving mill apparently dates from the expansion of 1910–12.
Canadian Parks Service, 1986

Galt Knitting Company
35 Water Street South, Galt

In 1881 Adam Warnock organized the Galt Knitting Company with the assistance of some Montréal financiers. He purchased the Galt Woollen Factory at the confluence of Mill Creek and the Grand River in Galt and converted it to a knitting mill.[1] The Galt Woollen Factory had been built in stages in 1843, 1859, and 1867. From 1867 to 1881 it was operated by William Robinson and Daniel Howell.[2] The 1871 census reported that it employed 45 persons and produced $68 000 worth of woollen cloth annually.[3]

Warnock manufactured shirts and drawers on a moderately large scale by Canadian standards. By the turn of the century the company employed four cards, 1200 spindles, 14 knitting frames, 40 sewing machines, and about 110 people.[4] In 1933 it had annual sales of about $261 000 and employed 116; the median number of employees for Ontario knit-goods mills in 1933 was 43. Since the 1930s the firm has grown slowly; in 1984 it employed 270 and produced underwear, sportswear, and knitted fabrics.[5] Since about 1956 the firm has been known as Tiger Brand Knitting; Tiger Brand had been the Galt Knitting Company's brand name. It is still controlled by the Warnock family.

In 1905 the firm moved to a new factory directly across the street from the old Galt Woollen Factory. The new mill, four storeys high, plus basement, and about 124 feet by 130 feet, was built with reinforced-concrete walls and a mill-construction interior. Although the mill was built over Mill Creek, it was steam powered; as late as 1929, steam accounted for 120 horsepower and electricity for 87 horsepower in the mill.[6] The mill is still in use by Tiger Brand Knitting. The firm also owns the former Riverside Silk Mills plant in Galt and a mill in Pincher Creek, Alberta. Most of the buildings of the original Galt Woollen Factory have also survived; they are owned by the Grand River Conservation Authority and are being converted to offices and apartments.

99 Although most of the equipment in the Tiger Brand knitting mill is state of the art, a few Tompkins string needle knitting machines dating from the period 1910–30 are still used for special orders.
Canadian Parks Service, 1991

100 The Galt Knitting Company mill built in 1905.
Canadian Parks Service, 1985

Newlands and Company, Limited
31 Ainslie Street, Galt

In 1885 Andrew Newlands Sr. established a small (15 employees) knitting firm in Galt in partnership with Adam Warnock of Galt Knitting. In 1894 both men sold their interests in the firm to Andrew Newlands Jr. and Joseph Stauffer. The firm manufactured glove and shoe linings, jersey cloth, and sleigh robes using hand-powered machines. By the turn of the century Newlands and Company had adopted steam power and employed about 125 people.[1]

In 1916 Andrew Newlands Jr. sold his interest in the firm to George A. Dobbie. The firm was incorporated as Newlands and Company, Limited with Joseph Stauffer as president.[2] By the 1930s the company ranked eighth in terms of sales among Canadian knitting mills.[3] By the mid-1950s the company employed 450.[4]

Late in World War II Newlands replaced its old mill on South Ainslie Street with a new mill that is still in use. In 1946 the firm bought the C. Turnbull Company. George A. Dobbie, president of Newlands and of Stauffer-Dobbie, a subsidiary of Newlands, became president of the C. Turnbull Company. In 1951 George H. Dobbie, son of George A., bought out the Stauffer interests and took control of all three firms. Control remained in the hands of the Dobbie family until 1972, when Dobbie Industries, the holding company, went into receivership. The firm was re-organized as Newlands Textiles in 1980.[5]

Newlands produced a wide variety of knit goods including glove and shoe linings, robes, eiderdowns, jersey cloth, plush rayon, and hand-knitting yarns.

In 1903 Adam Newlands and Joseph Stauffer organized a subsidiary, the Galt Robe Company, for the manufacture of imitation buffalo robes. In 1920 the firm was incorporated as Stauffer-Dobbie Limited. The new firm specialized in weaving cotton and rayon towelling and cloth and by the 1950s employed about 400. It apparently operated as an independent firm, but in 1959 it came under the control of Dobbie Industries, which also controlled Newlands and the C. Turnbull Company. Its plant, which was on a different site than the Newlands plant, has been demolished since the present Newlands Textiles was organized to operate the mills owned by Dobbie Industries.[6]

101 Newlands' Ainslie Street mill in 1985.
Canadian Parks Service, 1985

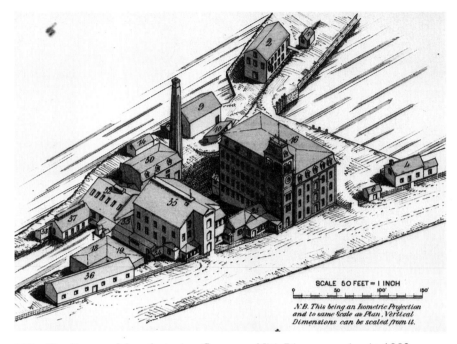

102 The Penman Manufacturing Company Nith River complex in 1882.
National Archives of Canada, NMC 9618

Paris, Ontario

Penman Manufacturing Company
Emily and West River streets

About 20 kilometres down the Grand River from Cambridge, the town of Paris also developed as a textile centre. Its main firm, the Penman Manufacturing Company, was the largest knit-goods firm in Canada.

John Penman was born in the United States. In the early 1860s the family moved to Woodstock, Ontario, where Penman's father established a small textile mill. John Penman may have worked with his father or have established his own small mill in Woodstock. In 1868 he moved to Paris, Ontario, where he purchased a mill on the Nith River and established a water-powered knitting mill in partnership with W.E. Adams. The partnership was dissolved in 1870.[1] The original mill burned and was replaced in 1874 by a four-storey brick mill, about 50 feet by 100 feet, with a mansard roof.[2] This mill, on the Nith River near the junction of Emily and West River streets, is still standing.

In 1882 the firm was incorporated as the Penman Manufacturing Company with an authorized capital of $250 000. In addition to John Penman the incorporators included W.D. Long, H.J. Long, and C.E. Newberry of Hamilton and David Morrice of Montréal.[3] In 1887 the firm bought a second mill in Paris, the Grand River Knitting, or Adams-Hackland, mill. The Adams-Hackland mill, or Grand River complex, was gradually expanded; by the the early twentieth century it was much larger than the original mill, the Nith River complex.[4]

In the 20 years after 1887, the Penman firm acquired the Peninsular Knitting Company of Thorold, Ontario; the Coaticook Knitting Company of Coaticook, Quebec; the Norfolk Knitting Company of Port Dover, Ontario; the Watson Manufacturing Company of St. Catharines, Ontario; the Canadian Woollen Mill Company of Saint-Hyacinthe, Quebec; and the Anchor Knitting Company of Almonte, Ontario.[5] Penman Manufacturing became much the largest knitting firm in Canada: in 1933 it had 17.6 per cent of all sales of knit goods in Canada. The next-largest firm, the Eaton Knitting Company of Hamilton, had 7.5 per cent of all sales.[6]

John Penman remained president of the firm until 1906, when he sold out to a Montréal syndicate that included Charles Gordon and David Morrice. He subsequently organized Hamilton's Mercury Mills Limited, which became by 1933 the fifth-largest knitting mill in Canada.[7] The Penman

Manufacturing Company was reorganized as Penmans Limited with David Morrice as president. He was succeeded by Charles Gordon, the president of Dominion Textile, in 1914.[8] Penmans remained closely linked to Dominion Textile until it was absorbed by the larger firm in 1965.

The mill employed 75 adults (55 women) in 1871 and 175 in 1882;[9] it was three to eight times larger than the average mill of the period. With the acquisition of the Adams-Hackland mill in 1887 and the expansion of both mill complexes, Penman Manufacturing became the major employer in Paris; by 1933 the two mill complexes employed over 700.[10] A significant number of the firm's employees were British immigrants; between 1906 and 1928 it recruited 700 workers in Britain for its Paris plants.[11] In general Penmans, and the knitting industry, seem to have enjoyed a more peaceful relationship with labour than did the large firms in the cotton industry. However, there is a record of three strikes at Penman's Paris mills. In 1907, 850 women and 150 men struck to support a demand that the Saturday half day, which until then had only been in effect during the summer, be extended to the whole year. After a week the company agreed to the demand. In 1922, 175 employees struck successfully to protest an 18-per-cent pay cut.[12]

During the 1907 and 1922 strikes the workers were not represented by a union. The United Textile Workers of America began to organize the company's Paris mills in 1946 and in 1948 was able to win a slim majority in a certification vote. The union demanded a 20-cent-an-hour increase and when the company refused, called a strike in 1949. The union was not able to take out the entire work force and the strike was long, bitter, and ultimately unsuccessful. The experience was so searing that the mills were never struck again.[13]

In 1970 Dominion Textile sold the original plant, the Nith River complex, to Pride of Paris, a textile firm that still owns the mill. The Adams-Hackland, or Grand River complex, has also been sold by Dominion Textile and has been demolished.[14]

103 The main mill at the Nith River complex in 1985.
Canadian Parks Service, 1985

104 John Penman, the founder of Penman Manufacturing Company and of Mercury Mills Limited.
Archives of Ontario, Penman Family Papers, AO 316

105 A part of Penmans Grand River complex in 1985. Built in 1900, it was demolished ca. 1988.
Canadian Parks Service, 1985

Toronto, Ontario

Joseph Simpson and Sons
2 Berkeley Street

Toronto was the single most important centre for the production of knit goods in Canada: in 1933 about 17 per cent of all knit-goods employees were in Toronto. This importance was due more to the presence of a number of medium-sized firms, such as Joseph Simpson and Sons, than to the presence of industry leaders; the largest firms in the knitting sector, Penmans and Julius Kayser, operated in smaller centres such as Paris, Saint-Hyacinthe, and Sherbrooke.

In 1865 Joseph Simpson, formerly of Richmond, Virginia, established a small knitting mill on Front Street in Toronto. In 1868 he built a larger, 95-foot-by-58-foot, three-storey brick mill near the corner of Berkley Street and the Esplanade. Another five major buildings were added to the mill between the 1880s and 1910, by which time the complex had reached its present form.[1] In 1919–20 Simpsons built a warehouse and a spinning mill at King and St. Lawrence, a few blocks east of the main mill.[2] The buildings in both complexes are of brick and timber, with some steel components in the later buildings.

The Simpson firm, which was also known as the Toronto Knitting and Yarn Factory, remained under the control of the Simpson family until 1945, when it was bought by Monarch Knitting of Dunnville.[3] The mill was closed in 1952 and used as low-cost warehousing, office, and work space. In the early 1980s A.J. Diamond and Partners renovated it as office and retail space under the name Berkeley Castle.[4] All of the major structures, including the 1868 mill, have been preserved.

In 1871 the Simpson company employed 77 persons (60 of them women), two more than Penman Manufacturing in Paris. It produced shirts, pants, jackets, and hosiery valued at $50 000 annually.[5] During the nineteenth century it was among the five largest knitting plants in Canada. Because of its downtown site it had reached its capacity by about 1910 and did not expand a great deal thereafter. Nevertheless, in terms of employment it was still the sixth-largest Canadian firm in 1933; in terms of sales it was ninth or tenth largest.[6]

The Simpson firm is credited with being the first Canadian knitting mill to use circular knitting machines. Initially the mill produced woollen underwear, but it gradually expanded its product line to include worsted, cotton, and woollen sweaters and yarn for sale to other knitting firms.[7] The mill was fully integrated, with carding and spinning capacity for wool and cottons as well as knitting capacity. Initially the mill was steam powered with a direct drive, but by 1906 the steam engine was connected to a Canadian General Electric generator that provided alternating current for the machinery.[8]

106   The Joseph Simpson and Sons knitting mill in 1906.
Canadian Journal of Fabrics, July 1906, p. 148; Hamilton Public Library

107 The Berkeley Castle development in 1991.
Canadian Parks Service, 1991

Hamilton, Ontario

Hamilton is known as a steel town, but from the 1880s to the 1950s it was also an important cotton and knitting centre. The first cotton mill in the area was the Dundas mill built at neighbouring Dundas in 1861. Two companies, the Hamilton Cotton Company and the Ontario Cotton Mills Company, built mills in Hamilton during the cotton boom, and a third, the Imperial Cotton Company, was built in 1900. Only the Imperial mill survives today. The city was also the site of several major knitting mills built during the late nineteenth and early twentieth century; in the 1930s four Hamilton firms, Chipman Holton Knitting, Eaton Knitting, Mercury Mills, and J.R. Moodie and Sons, were among the 12 largest knit-goods/hosiery firms in Canada. The Eaton and Mercury mills have been demolished, but portions of the Moodie and Chipman Holton mills survive.

108 Built in 1900, the Cosmos Imperial mill is the last survivor of Hamilton's three cotton mills.
Canadian Parks Service, 1986

J.R. Moodie and Sons Limited
Sanford Avenue between King and Wilson

Of the four large Hamilton knitting firms, J.R. Moodie and Sons, established in 1888, was much the oldest; the other firms all date from 1902 or later.

John and James Moodie organized the Eagle Knitting Company in 1888 and in 1890 they occupied quarters at the corner of Main and Macnab streets in Hamilton. The firm specialized in women's underwear and grew rapidly. By 1903 it employed about 325 and in 1907 it built a second mill, the Eagle Spinning Mill, on Sanford Avenue. At about this time John Moodie retired from the firm.[1] In 1909 J.R. Moodie and Sons was organized as a holding company to control Eagle Knitting, Eagle Spinning, and the Peerless Underwear Company, which operated as a distributor for the firm.[2] James R. Moodie was the president of the firm, but active management was in the hands of his three sons. The firm expanded at its Sanford Avenue site, and in 1928 the Main and Macnab street mill was closed. At the time the firm employed about 700 people and used 300 knitting machines and 400 sewing machines.[3] It was among the dozen largest knit-goods/hosiery firms in Canada. The firm continued under the direct control of the Moodie family until it closed in 1958.[4]

The Moodie family was innovative. John Moodie was a founder of the Cataract Power Company, which began generating hydro-electricity at De Cew Falls, about 35 miles from Hamilton, in 1898, and by 1899 the Eagle Knitting Company was using electric power.[5] The Sanford Avenue mill was of reinforced concrete with brick curtain walls.[6] When it was built in 1907, reinforced-concrete construction was just being introduced in Canada.

Little is known of the labour relations of the firm except that a 1922 article stated that it paid particular attention to welfare work and had a doctor who provided free medical care to employees at its mills.[7]

J.R. Moodie and Sons is a good example of a large family-owned urban knitting mill. Like the Simpson company, it remained independent throughout most of its existence and had no direct relationship with major figures in the textile industry. The Moodie family was somewhat more active in the industry than was the Simpson family. James Moodie Jr. was a director of the Canadian Woollen Manufacturers' Association and his brother, Robert, was chairman of the Ontario division of the Canadian Manufacturers' Association.[8]

The original mill at Main and Macnab has been demolished, but the Sanford Avenue complex has survived.

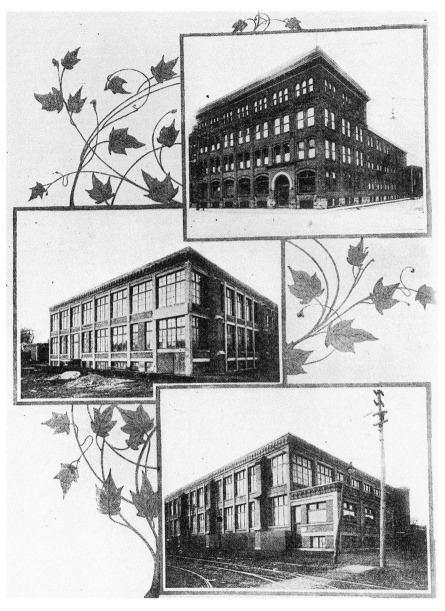

109 The three mills operated by J.R. Moodie and Sons, 1925. The mill at the top is the original plant at Main and Macnab. The two lower views are of the reinforced-concrete mills on Sanford Avenue. The one at the bottom was probably built in 1907.
Canadian Textile Journal, 16 Jan. 1925, p. 38; National Library of Canada, NL 16972

110 The former Eagle Spinning mill on Sanford Avenue in Hamilton. Although the original windows have been bricked in, the brick buttresses and blind arcade survive.
Canadian Parks Service, 1986

New Brunswick

Although the cotton industry was historically concentrated in Quebec, it had, particularly in the nineteenth century, a strong presence in New Brunswick. In 1891, Canadian cotton mills employed 8502 workers; of these, 20 per cent were in New Brunswick mills and 45 per cent were in Quebec mills. On a per capita basis 55 out of every 10 000 New Brunswickers worked in cotton mills. In Quebec the figure was 25, and in Canada as a whole, 18. There were two mills in Saint John, one in Moncton, one in Milltown, and one in Marysville near Fredericton. Two of the mills have been demolished, but three — one in Moncton, one in Saint John, and one in Marysville — survive.

111 The St. Croix mill in Milltown. The original mill in the centre was built in 1882; the weave shed on the left was added before 1922. The mill has been demolished.
Manual of the Textile Industry of Canada, 1953, p. 63; National Library of Canada, NL 16968

The Gibson Mill
8 River Street, Marysville

In 1862 Alexander Gibson bought two failing lumber mills on the Nashwaak River north of Fredericton. He expanded the mills and built a substantial town, Marysville, around them. He also invested in the New Brunswick Land and Railway Company. By the 1880s he was a wealthy man; his railway holdings alone were worth $800 000 in 1882.[1]

During the 1870s the New Brunswick shipbuilding and lumber industries suffered severe recession and Gibson began to look for alternative investments. One possible area was cotton manufacturing. The introduction of a protective tariff on manufactured cottons in 1879 helped to start a boom in the Canadian cotton industry. In 1878 there were 8 small cotton mills in Canada; between 1879 and 1884, 18 mills were built. Three of these new mills were built in New Brunswick: one in Saint John in 1880, another in Milltown in 1881, and one in Moncton in 1882. It is probable that Gibson was influenced by the boom and in 1882 he sold his interest in the New Brunswick Land and Railway Company and began to build a large cotton mill.

The main mill, designed by the Boston firm of Lockewood, Greene and Company, was a four-storey brick-pier building, 418 feet long by 100 feet wide, built on slow-burning principles. In addition Gibson built cottages for his employees as well as the village store and church. The mill began production in 1885 with 12 000 spindles and 272 looms; this put it in the middle range of Canadian mills. Initially it produced unbleached or grey cotton, but after a dyehouse was built in 1886 it produced sheetings, ginghams, tickings, and denims.[2]

The diversification in its product was essential; at the time the mill began production the industry was in a major slump as the result of overproduction. The leaders in the industry, David Morrice and Andrew Gault, attempted to reduce production through producers' cartels and by buying up mills and closing down excess capacity. Although Gibson was able to maintain ownership of his mill in 1892, he was forced to agree to market his cloth exclusively through David Morrice's firm. Finally, when he was 88 years old in 1907, Gibson sold the mill to Morrice, who incorporated it into Canadian Cottons Limited. Canadian Cottons operated the mill until 1954. Subsequently it was operated by a number of different companies until it came into the hands of the provincial government in 1980.[3]

When the mill was taken over by the government most of the original buildings were intact. They have since been converted to offices. In 1990 a Historic Sites and Monuments Board of Canada plaque declaring the mill to be of national historic and architectural significance was erected at the mill.

112 The Gibson mill at Marysville with company housing in the middle distance and a sawmill in the foreground.
Public Archives of New Brunswick, Jacob Mersereau Collection, P18/190

113 The Gibson mill, converted to office space.
New Brunswick Department of Tourism, Recreation and Heritage

Saint John Cotton Company
Dunlop Lane, Saint John

William Parks, a wholesale grocer, built the first cotton mill in the Maritimes at Saint John in 1861. In 1882–83 he built a second mill, a four-storey brick-pier building 205 feet long and 79 feet wide, at the end of what is now Dunlop Lane. The original mill was known as the New Brunswick mill; the second was known as the Saint John mill.[1]

The Saint John mill began producing in 1883, at the same time as many other new mills came into the market. The market collapsed and by 1885 the mill ceased production.[2] When it reopened in mid-1887 it employed about 200 people and was expected to produce about 70 000 yards of cloth per week. An 1892 report indicated that it had 300 looms and 12 600 spindles, and produced grey cottons, sheetings, drills, ducks, and tickings.[3]

By 1890 both mills were in trouble and were being operated by a court-appointed receiver; their principal creditor, the Bank of Montreal, was sueing for foreclosure and sale; and the newly formed Dominion Cotton Mills Company wished to buy the mills and close them.[4] The mills emerged from these challenges and by 1893 were back under the management of William Parks and Son. During 1893 the company made a profit of $55 000 on an output of $500 000 (from both mills) and built a new bleachery at the Saint John mill.[5]

In order to resume operations the firm had borrowed $200 000 from two local capitalists and when one of them died, it was unable to repay the loan and suspended operation in 1900 or early in 1901.[6] The mills were sold for $145 000 to the Saint John firm of Manchester, Robertson and Allison, which reorganized them as the Cornwall and York Cotton Mills Company with a capital of $500 000.[7] The company operated independently for a number of years, but by 1922 it had become a subsidiary of Canadian Cottons.[8]

The older New Brunswick mill was renamed the Cornwall mill and the Saint John mill became the York mill. Together the two mills operated 114 cards, 430 looms, and 27 700 spindles.[9] The Cornwall mill was closed in 1930. The York mill continued to operate as a spinning mill on a small scale; the 1939 *Canadian Textile Directory* indicates that it had only 66 cards, 6424 spindles, and 76 employees. The mill was closed in April of 1959 when Canadian Cottons wound up its operations.[10]

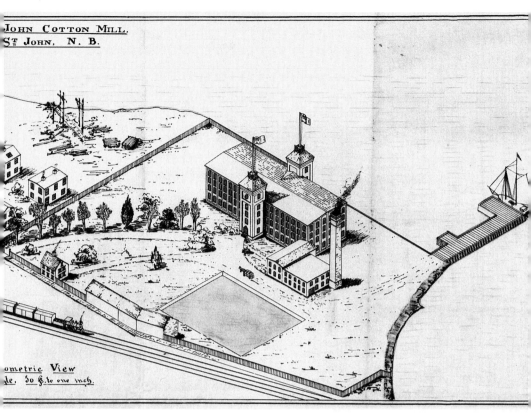

JOHN COTTON MILL,
S⪮ JOHN, N. B.

ometric View
le, 50 ft. to one inch.

114 The Saint John cotton mill built by William Parks and Son in 1882.
New Brunswick Museum, NBM 988.58.1

Nova Scotia

On a per capita basis the textile industry was not as important an employer in Nova Scotia as it was in the other provinces. Nevertheless, there were communities where textile manufacturing was important. In the 1880s three cotton mills were built in Halifax, Windsor, and Yarmouth. The Halifax mill was destroyed in the 1917 explosion and the Windsor mill was converted to a knitting mill in 1915 and is still in use. The Yarmouth mill is slated to be closed in 1991. In addition to these mills, Nova Scotia is home to one of Canada's most famous knitting mills, Stanfield's of Truro.

Stanfield's Limited
1 Logan Street, Truro

Charles E. Stanfield emigrated from Bradford, England, to Tyron, Prince Edward Island, in 1855. In Bradford he had apprenticed in his uncle's woollen mills and in Tyron he established the Tyron Woollen Mills. He sold the mill in 1866 and moved to Truro, Nova Scotia, where he established a felt-hat works. He was also involved in woollen mills at St. Croix and Farnham, Nova Scotia, before he established a knitting and weaving mill at Truro in 1882.[1]

By 1892 C.E. Stanfield was operating 24 knitting machines, four broad looms, and one set of cards. Although this probably made it an average-sized Canadian firm, it was much smaller than the industry leader, Penman Manufacturing, which operated 15 cards and 34 knitting machines in its two Paris plants.[2]

In 1896 C.E. Stanfield sold the firm to his two sons, John and Frank. The brothers stopped weaving and concentrated on knit goods, particularly underwear. They developed a pre-shrinking process for woollen underwear and were successful in marketing their brand of "unshrinkable" underwear during the Klondike gold rush. The company expanded rapidly: by 1907 it was operating ten sets of cards and 100 knitting machines. The plant was completely rebuilt between 1900 and 1906. In 1910 Stanfield's bought a large mill in Amherst, Nova Scotia, the Hewson Woollen Mills; Stanfield's continued to operate the plant under the name Amherst Woollen Mills.[3]

In 1906 the firm, which had operated under the name Truro Knitting Mills Company, was incorporated as Stanfield's Limited. Although John Stanfield remained president and Frank Stanfield was on the board of directors, the board also included the president and two directors of the Bank of Nova Scotia. The inclusion of three bank representatives suggests that Stanfield's, like many other growing firms, had brought in outside capital. Unlike many families in similar situations, the Stanfield family did not lose control of the firm and the presidency has remained in the family.

The firm has been innovative and the company history claims a number of firsts: the first cardigan jackets and stockinettes manufactured in Canada, the introduction to Canadians of heavy-rib underwear and the drop seat, the development of a shrink-proof process for woollen underwear, and the first packaging of underwear in cellophane.[4] In one respect at least it was remarkably conservative: it continued to use mules for spinning until about 1970.

In addition to its role in the knit-goods industry, the Stanfield family has been remarkable for its record of public activity. Frank Stanfield Sr., who was the active manager of the firm from 1906 to 1930, was the member of the Legislative Assembly for Colchester from 1911 to 1929 and lieutenant-governor of Nova Scotia, 1930–31. His brother, John, was member of Parliament for Colchester from 1907 to 1916 and was appointed to the Senate in 1921. Frank Jr., who became president of the company in 1930, was member of Parliament for Colchester-Hants from 1945 until 1953. Frank Jr.'s brother, Robert L. Stanfield, played no role in the company but served as premier of Nova Scotia from 1956 to 1967 and subsequently served as leader of the Opposition in the federal Parliament.

115 The Stanfield mill and John Stanfield about 1907.
Stanfield's Limited

116 The modern Stanfield's mill.
Stanfield's Limited

117 The modern mill.
Canadian Parks Service, 1985

238

Yarmouth Duck and Yarn Company Limited

233 Water Street, Yarmouth

In 1883 a group of Yarmouth shipbuilders and West Indies merchants organized the Yarmouth Duck and Yarn Company. W.D. Lovitt was the first president, S. Killam was vice-president, and Thomas Killam was secretary-treasurer.[1]

The firm built a small brick-pier mill, 90 feet by 76 feet and three storeys high. The mill was equipped with English machinery made by Howard, Bullough and Riley; its looms were built locally by the Yarmouth Cotton Machine Manufacturing Company.[2] The mill employed 80 and produced cotton duck at the rate of about 5000 pounds per week. The duck was used for products such as tents and sailcloth. The firm also developed a market for industrial canvas; the agricultural implement manufacturers Massey-Harris and International Harvester and papermaking companies became major customers.[3]

In 1902 the company name was changed from Yarmouth Duck and Yarn to the Cosmos Cotton Company. At about the same time, C.T. Grantham bought control of the company. Grantham had been involved in the firm in the 1890s, but had left to organize the Imperial Cotton Company in Hamilton, Ontario. Grantham's purchase was made in association with a New York commission agency, the J. Spencer Turner Company, and both Cosmos Cotton and Imperial Cotton soon became part of the Cotton Duck Company (which in 1913 became the International Cotton Mills and still later was reorganized as the New England Southern Mills), an American holding company with mills in New England and the American south.[4] In spite of the change of ownership, the management of Cosmos Cotton remained in local hands; in 1914 John Killam was president and Samuel Killam was manager.[5] In 1924 the Cosmos and Imperial companies were combined as Cosmos Imperial Mills, and in 1926 the firm was sold to a new firm, Cosmos Imperial Mills Limited. The sale is usually taken as marking the transfer of control of Cosmos Imperial to Canadian hands although it is probable that Americans maintained a large interest in the company until at least 1937.[6]

In 1892 the mill expanded by taking over a neighbouring woodworking firm and in 1907 and 1913 large additions were made to the original mill; by 1914 the main mill building was 515 feet long and 76 feet wide. Parts of it were of traditional slow-burning construction and parts were of brick and concrete. The older part of the mill was powered by the original steam engine; the newer part was electrically powered. The mill had 12 000 spindles and numerous looms; two of the looms, which were used for making paper-dryers' felts, wove cloth 17 and 13.8 feet wide.[7]

Over the period 1938–58 the company spent over $4 million remodelling and re-equipping the Yarmouth mill. In 1957 the Imperial mill in Hamilton was closed and much of its equipment was moved to Yarmouth, where it was installed in new buildings. In 1966 a subsidiary company, Yarmouth Industrial Fabrics, invested $2.5 million in a new single-storey weave shed across Water Street from the old mill. The new weave shed was designed to house 144 looms and employ 200.[8]

Dominion Textile purchased the Yarmouth mills in 1973 and operated them until January 1991, at which time it announced that the plant would be closed down between July and December of 1991.

118 The Yarmouth Duck and Yarn Company in the 1890s.
Canadian Textile Journal, March 1914, p. 79; National Library of Canada, NL 17463

119   The Cosmos Imperial mill at Yarmouth, probably in the 1930s.
National Archives of Canada, PA 42032

120 The mill in 1985.
Canadian Parks Service, 1985

Tables

Table 1
Employment in the Major Divisions of the Textile Industry, 1871–1950 (Number of Employees)

Year	Garment Trade	Cotton Textiles	Hosiery/ Knitting	Woollen Textiles	Silk/ Synthetics	Narrow Fabrics	Dyeing, Finishing	Misc.	Total
1871	16 878 68%	745 3%	245 1%	5 774 23%	–	–	–	1 040 4%	24 682
1881	28 584 66%	3 527 8%	1 556 4%	7 942 18%	211	–	ℐ	1 702 4%	43 522
1891	42 972 63%	8 734 12%	2 143 3%	9 223 13%	322	120	–	5 573 8%	70 087
1901*	37 509 58%	11 954 18%	3 687 6%	7 037 11%	–	–	548 1%	3 451 5%	64 186
1911*	40 729 63%	13 244 21%	8 050 11%	5 860 8%	594 1%	142	78	3 905 6%	72 602
1920	34 392** 39%	19 461 22%	14 572 16%	8 966 10%	1 165 1%	–	7 210 8%	2 976 3%	88 742
1930	42 544 39%	18 590 17%	18 570 17%	7 710 7%	5 393 5%	–	12 732 12%	4 037 4%	109 576
1940	57 071 41%	26 017 19%	23 438 17%	14 126 10%	8 512 6%	2 802 2%	1 210 1%	5 707 4%	138 883
1950	90 993 46%	28 430 14%	25 255 13%	17 357 9%	17 955 9%	2 058 1%	2 459 1%	12 069 6%	196 576

* In 1901 and 1911 only establishments employing 5 or more hands were included in the industrial census.
** From 1920, women's and men's custom-made-clothing establishments were not included in the industrial census.

Sources
Canada, *Census of Canada, 1870–71* (Ottawa: Printed by I.B. Taylor, 1875), Vol. 3, Tables 30 to 53; Canada. Dept. of Agriculture, *Census of Canada, 1880–81* (Ottawa: Printed by Maclean, Roger & Co., 1883), Vol. 3, Tables 31 to 54; Canada. Dept. of Agriculture and Statistics, *Census of Canada, 1890–91* (Ottawa: Queen's Printer, 1894), Vol. 3, Table 22; Canada. Dept. of Agriculture, *Fourth Census of Canada, 1901* (Ottawa: King's Printer, 1905), Vol. 3, p. xxv; Canada. Dept. of Trade and Commerce, *Fifth Census of Canada, 1911* (Ottawa: King's Printer, 1912), Vol. 3, Table 14; DBS, *The Textile Industries of Canada in the Decade 1917–26* (Ottawa: King's Printer, 1929), Tables 33, 54, 78, 87, 92, 98, 105, 110, 113, 118, 124, 131, 140, 144, 145; DBS, *The Textile Industries of Canada, 1929 and 1930* (Ottawa: King's Printer, 1932), Table 4; DBS, *The Textile Industries of Canada, 1940, 1941, and 1942* (Ottawa: King's Printer, 1945), Tables 3, 54, 78; DBS, *General Review of all Textiles, 1950* (Ottawa: King's Printer, 1952), pp. A-2 to A-5.

Table 2
Value Added in the Major Divisions of the Textile Industry, 1871–1940 (Thousands of Dollars)

Year	Garment Trade	Cotton Textiles	Hosiery/ Knitting	Woollen Textiles	Silk/ Synthetics	Narrow Fabrics	Dyeing, Finishing	Misc.	Total
1871	$6 302 64%	$320 3%	$106 1%	$2 782 28%	–	–	–	$395 4%	$9 905
1881	13 878 62%	1 983 9%	780 3%	4 790 21%	$158 1%	–	–	722 3%	22 311
1891	19 750 59%	4 629 14%	924 3%	5 152 15%	294 1%	$55	–	2 757 8%	33 561
1901*	17 615 50%	5 889 17%	1 980 6%	4 321 12%	–	–	$1 544 4%	3 566 10%	34 915
1911*	36 244 56%	11 241 17%	6 490 10%	4 970 8%	589 1%	89	163	5 036 8%	64 822
1920	63 651** 37%	44 152 25%	23 170 13%	21 840 13%	1 938 1%	–	12 333 7%	6 377 4%	173 462
1930	66 122 37%	25 499 14%	28 608 16%	13 416 8%	10 175 6%	–	22 665 13%	10 766 6%	177 251
1940	194 412 36%	115 559 21%	70 077 13%	77 136 14%	31 208 6%	11 987 2%	4 885 1%	42 187 8%	547 451

Value added = Value of production minus cost of materials.
* In 1901 and 1911 only establishments employing 5 or more hands were included in the industrial census.
** From 1920, women's and men's custom-made-clothing establishments were not included in the industrial census.
Sources
See sources for Table 1.

Table 3
Value of Production in the Major Divisions of the Textile Industry, 1871–1950 (Thousands of Dollars)

Year	Garment Trade	Cotton Textiles	Hosiery/ Knitting	Woollen Textiles	Silk/ Synthetics	Narrow Fabrics	Dyeing, Finishing	Misc.	Total
1871	$14 820 60%	$782 3%	$199 1%	$7 886 32%	–	–	–	$1 121 5%	$24 808
1881	23 621 60%	3 759 9%	1 386 3%	9 730 24%	275 1%	–	–	1 280 3%	40 051
1891	39 628 60%	9 127 14%	1 917 2%	10 076 15%	585 1%	131	–	4 688 7%	65 704
1901*	35 346 52%	12 144 18%	3 858 6%	8 251 12%	–	–	$2 052 3%	6 045 9%	67 696
1911*	72 892 54%	25 681 19%	13 394 10%	9 157 7%	1 009 1%	169	316	13 285 10%	135 903
1920	151 511** 36%	107 290 26%	58 099 14%	48 510 12%	5 377 1%	–	14 168 3%	31 220 8%	416 175
1930	147 577 41%	58 587 16%	54 118 15%	27 498 8%	17 809 5%	–	25 473 7%	30 754 8%	361 815
1940	194 412 36%	115 559 21%	70 077 13%	77 136 14%	31 208 6%	11 987 2%	4 885 1%	42 187 8%	547 451
1950	587 988 40%	267 078 18%	146 226 10%	157 359 11%	147 048 10%	13 704 1%	12 354 1%	134 203 9%	1 465 960

* In 1901 and 1911 only establishments employing 5 or more hands were included in the industrial census.
** From 1920, women's and men's custom-made-clothing establishments were not included in the industrial census.

Sources
See sources for Table 1.

Table 4
Cotton Yarn and Cloth Sector: Employment and Value of Production by Regions, 1871–1980

	1871	1881	1891	1901	1911	1920	1930	1940	1950	1960	1970	1980
No. of Employees												
Canada	745	3 527	8 502	12 029	13 041	17 624	16 999	23 616	26 967	16 841	13 298	9 247
Ontario	495	1 683	2 495	2 362	2 353	3 969	4 236	6 199	–	–	–	–
Quebec	123	1 500	3 792	6 695	8 173	11 327	11 195	15 876	17 847	12 155	8 933	–
New Brunswick	127	344	1 752	2 172	1 828	–	–	–	–	–	–	–
Nova Scotia	–	–	463	800	687	–	–	–	–	–	–	–
Other	–	–	–	–	–	2 328	1 568	1 541	9 120	4 686	4 365	–
Value of Production (Thousands of Dollars)												
Canada	$782	$3 760	$8 452	$12 033	$24 585	$92 490	$48 693	$103 390	$257 384	$209 503	$282 533	$661 755
Ontario	492	1 875	2 619	2 907	4 134	19 020	11 187	25 012	–	–	–	–
Quebec	129	1 609	3 656	6 150	16 741	63 401	34 322	72 240	171 168	153 164	217 170	–
New Brunswick	161	276	1 750	2 228	2 673	–	–	–	–	–	–	–
Nova Scotia	–	–	427	747	1 036	–	–	–	–	–	–	–
Other	–	–	–	–	–	10 069	3 185	6 138	86 216	56 339	65 353	–

Sources
See Sources for Table 1 and DBS, *Cotton Textile Industries, 1950* (Ottawa: 1952), Table 11; DBS, *Cotton Yarn and Cloth Mills, 1960* (Ottawa: 1962), Table 1; Statistics Canada, *Cotton Yarn and Cloth Mills, 1970* (Ottawa: Information Canada, 1972), Table 1; Statistics Canada, *Cotton Yarn and Cloth Mills, 1980* (Ottawa: Dept. of Supply and Services, 1982), Table 1.

Table 5
Woollen Cloth Sector: Employment and Value of Production by Regions, 1871–1980

	1871	1881	1891	1901	1911	1920	1930	1940	1950	1960	1970	1980
No. of Employees												
Canada	4 453	6 877	7 156	6 795	4 512	5 534	3 875	7 798	9 159	6 060	5 542	4 767
Ontario	3 696	5 221	5 191	4 324	3 108	4 524	3 075	5 079	5 116	2 543	1 611	1 484
Quebec	556	1 226	1 410	2 103	903	602	–	–	3 070	3 189	3 690	3 009
New Brunswick	97	139	105	118	–	–	–	–	–	–	–	–
Nova Scotia	104	221	319	196	396	–	–	–	–	–	–	–
Other	–	70	131	54	78	408	800	2 719	973	328	241	274
Value of Production (Thousands of Dollars)												
Canada	$5 508	$8 112	$8 088	$7 360	$5 739	$28 019	$12 348	$41 851	$68 680	$66 791	$96 443	$235 712
Ontario	4 589	6 077	5 874	4 657	4 017	23 583	9 882	28 730	33 786	26 662	27 300	64 404
Quebec	692	1 532	1 583	2 327	1 105	2 491	–	–	30 029	37 308	66 320	157 120
New Brunswick	127	91	87	115	–	–	–	–	–	–	–	–
Nova Scotia	100	304	369	214	504	–	–	–	–	–	–	–
Other	–	108	175	–	–	1 945	2 466	13 121	4 865	2 821	2 823	14 188

Sources
See Sources for Table 1 and DBS, *The Woollen Textile Industry, 1950* (Ottawa: 1952), Table 15; DBS, *Woollen Mills, 1960* (Ottawa: 1962), Table 27; Statistics Canada, *Wool Yarn and Cloth Mills, 1970* (Ottawa: Information Canada, 1972), Table 16; Statistics Canada, *Wool Yarn and Cloth Mills, 1980* (Ottawa: Dept. of Supply and Services, 1982), Table 1.

Table 6
Hosiery and Knit-Goods Sector: Employment and Value of Production by Regions, 1871–1970

	1871	1881	1891	1901	1911	1920	1930	1940	1950	1960	1970
No. of Employees											
Canada	245	1 554	2 143	3 896	8 364	14 004	18 615	23 225	25 255	20 765	23 735
Ontario	244	1 301	1 522	3 342	6 320	–	12 650	13 153	13 303	8 186	7 355
Quebec	1	218	408	434	1 554	–	4 481	8 521	–	10 889	14 372
New Brunswick	–	1	25	–	–	–	–	–	–	–	–
Nova Scotia	–	33	183	–	–	–	–	–	–	–	–
Other	–	1	5	–	–	–	1 034	1 551	11 952	1 690	2 008
Value of Production (Thousands of Dollars)											
Canada	$199	$1 385	$1 917	$3 858	$13 394	$56 737	$53 043	$69 427	$146 226	$198 160	$414 690
Ontario	198	1 253	1 426	3 277	10 063	–	36 911	40 761	78 427	77 830	105 259
Quebec	–	122	426	397	2 273	–	13 005	24 006	–	106 784	280 401
New Brunswick	–	–	8	–	–	–	–	–	–	–	–
Nova Scotia	–	10	56	–	–	–	–	–	–	–	–
Other	–	–	1	–	–	–	2 659	4 660	67 798	13 546	29 030

Sources
See Sources for Table 1 and DBS, *Hosiery, Knitted Goods and Fabric Glove and Mitten Industry, 1950* (Ottawa: 1952), Tables 7 and 19; DBS, *Hosiery and Knitting Mills, 1960* (Ottawa: 1962), Tables 10 and 23; Statistics Canada, *Knitting Mills, 1970,* (Ottawa: Information Canada, 1972), Table 1.

Table 7
Home Production of Woollen and Linen Cloth, Raw Wool, and Flax and Hemp, 1827–1891

Year	Thousands of Yards of Cloth			Yards of Cloth Produced per Capita	Thousands of Pounds	
	Woollen	Linen	Total		Raw Wool	Flax & Hemp
Quebec						
1827	2 130	1 150	3 280	6.95	–	–
1844	1 401	858	2 259	3.24	1 121	–
1851	1 591	928	2 519	2.82	1 429	1 189
1861	2 134	1 021	3 156	2.84	1 967	976
1871	3 340	1 559	4 899	4.11	2 763	1 270
1881	2 958	1 130	4 088	3.01	2 731	865
1891	2 205	568	2 773	1.86	2 547	576
Ontario						
1842	1 161	167	1 328	2.73	1 302	–
1848	1 923	72	1 995	2.75	2 340	42
1851	1 728	15	1 742	1.83	2 710	60
1861	2 093	37	2 130	1.53	3 660	1 226
1871	1 775	26	1 801	1.11	6 411	1 165
1881	1 427	14	1 440	.75	6 013	1 073
1891	525	5	530	.25	4 605	17 887
New Brunswick						
1851	622	–	622	3.21	–	–
1861	–	–	–	–	634	14
1871	1 051	74	1 125	3.94	796	39
1881	808	51	860	2.68	760	27
1891	452	25	476	1.48	693	11
Nova Scotia						
1851	1 129	–	1 129	4.08	–	–
1861	1 321	–	1 321	3.99	–	–
1871	1 476	112	1 588	4.09	1 132	112
1881	1 330	68	1 398	3.17	1 142	64
1891	734	26	760	1.69	1 072	16

Table 7. Continued

| Year | Thousands of Yards of Cloth | | | Yards of Cloth Produced per Capita | Thousands of Pounds | |
	Woollen	Linen	Total		Raw Wool	Flax & Hemp
Prince Edward Island						
1861	427	–	427	5.28	–	–
1871	579	–	579	6.16	–	27
1881	515	30	545	5.00	552	25
1891	402	9	412	3.77	538	4

Sources

Statistics on cloth production are adapted from Table I-A-1, Table I-A-2, and Table I-A-5 of Gilbert Rousseau, "Évolution de la production textile au Canada depuis ses origines jusqu'à aujourd'hui," Baccalauréat spécial, Sciences économiques, Université du Québec à Montréal, Montréal, 1980.

Figures for production of wool and flax are from *Census of Canada, 1870–71*, Vol. 3, Tables XXII and XXIV, and Vol. 4; *Census of Canada, 1880–81*, Vol. 3, Tables XXII and XXV; Census of Canada, 1890–91, Vol. 4, Tables 3 and 4.

Table 8
Employees in the Cotton, Woollen, and Knit-Goods/Hosiery Sectors per 10 000 Population

	1871	1881	1891	1901	1911	1921	1931	1941
Cotton								
Canada	2	8	18	22	18	20	16	21
Ontario	3	9	12	11	9	14	12	16
Quebec	1	11	25	41	41	48	39	48
New Brunswick	4	11	55	66	52	–	–	–
Nova Scotia	0	0	10	17	14	–	–	–
Woollens								
Canada	12	16	15	13	6	6	4	7
Ontario	23	27	25	20	12	15	9	13
Quebec	5	9	9	13	4	3	–	–
New Brunswick	3	4	3	4	–	–	–	–
Nova Scotia	3	5	7	4	8	–	–	–
Knit Goods/Hosiery								
Canada	1	4	4	7	12	16	18	20
Ontario	2	7	7	15	25	–	37	35
Quebec	–	2	3	3	8	–	16	26
New Brunswick	0	–	1	–	–	–	–	–
Nova Scotia	0	1	4	–	–	–	–	–

Sources
Calculated from Table 1.

Table 9
Value of Woollen and Cotton Imports, Exports, and Manufactures, and Apparent Consumption in Current Dollars and Constant Dollars (Values in Thousands of Dollars)

	1870	1880	1890	1900	1910	1920	1930	1940
Imports								
Cotton manufactures	$9 208*	$7 820	$4 236	$6 977	$18 696	$64 036	$22 753	$25 474
1900 dollars	4 675	5 896	4 480	6 977	13 657	–	–	–
1935–39 dollars	8 770	8 223	5 611	10 275	23 877	25 863	19 820	21 570
Wool manufactures	8 448	6 409	11 104	9 827	23 038	55 108	30 572	34 018
1900 dollars	9 103	6 797	10 898	9 827	19 538	–	–	–
1935–39 dollars	8 046	6 739	14 707	14 517	19 423	22 257	26 631	28 804
Raw Cotton	341*	1 496	3 762	4 229	9 385	28 542	12 080	25 058
1900 dollars	173	1 018	2 736	4 229	5 241	–	–	–
Raw Wool	800	1 685	1 729	1 575	1 587	10 658	3 068	12 945
1900 dollars	852	1 539	1 741	1 575	2 515	–	–	–
All textiles	19 683	22 233	29 476	36 377	78 427	243 606	130 717	147 328
1900 dollars	18 417	19 506	27 034	36 377	64 661	–	–	–
1935–39 dollars	18 746	23 379	39 041	53 574	100 162	98 387	113 865	124 749
Exports								
Cotton manufactures	4*	14	121	424	410	3 432	853	9 411
1900 dollars	2	11	128	424	299	–	–	–
1935–39 dollars	4	15	160	626	524	1 386	743	7 968

Table 9. Continued

	1870	1880	1890	1900	1910	1920	1930	1940
Woollen manufactures	35	48	51	62	93	6 255	627	1 022
1900 dollars	38	51	50	62	79	–	–	–
1935–39 dollars	33	50	68	91	118	2 527	546	865
Raw Wool	770	950	249	421	553	2 452	442	961
1900 dollars	464	715	210	421	1 087	–	–	–
All textiles	926	1 214	898	1 703	3 552	21 411	7 901	4 602
1900 dollars	997	912	755	1 703	3 315	–	–	–
1935–39 dollars	882	1 277	1 189	2 508	4 536	8 647	6 882	3 897
Domestic Manufactures								
Cottons	782	3 759	9 127	12 144	25 681	107 290	58 587	115 559
1900 dollars	397	2 834	9 653	12 144	18 759	–	–	–
1935–39 dollars	745	3 953	12 089	17 885	32 798	43 332	51 034	97 848
Woollens	7 886	9 730	10 076	8 251	9 157	48 510	27 498	77 136
1900 dollars	8 497	10 319	9 889	8 251	7 766	–	–	–
1935–39 dollars	7 510	10 231	13 346	12 152	11 695	19 592	23 952	65 314
All textiles	24 808	40 051	65 704	67 696	135 903	416 175	361 815	547 451
1900 dollars	23 212	35 139	60 261	67 696	112 048	–	–	–
1935–39 dollars	23 627	42 115	87 917	99 700	173 567	168 084	315 170	463 549

Table 9. Continued

	1870	1880	1890	1900	1910	1920	1930	1940
Apparent Consumption								
Cottons	9 986	11 565	13 242	18 697	43 967	167 894	80 487	131 622
1900 dollars	5 010	8 720	14 005	18 697	32 117	–	–	–
1935–39 dollars	9 510	12 161	17 539	27 536	56 152	67 809	70 111	111 450
Woollens	16 299	16 091	21 129	18 016	32 102	97 363	57 443	110 132
1900 dollars	17 563	17 065	20 737	18 016	27 225	–	–	–
1935–39 dollars	15 523	16 920	27 985	26 533	40 999	39 322	50 037	93 253
All textiles	43 565	61 070	94 282	102 370	210 778	638 370	484 631	690 177
1900 dollars	40 848	53 579	86 471	102 380	173 781	–	–	–
1935–39 dollars	41 490	64 217	124 877	150 766	269 193	257 823	422 152	584 401
Wholesale Price Index for Textiles								
1935 = 100	105.0	95.1	75.5	67.9	78.3	247.6	114.8	118.1
Canadian Population in Thousands								
	3 689	4 325	4 833	5 371	7 207	8 788	10 377	11 507
Apparent Consumption per Capita (Dollars)								
Cottons	2.71	2.67	2.74	3.48	6.10	19.10	7.76	11.44
1900 dollars	1.36	2.02	2.88	3.48	4.46	–	–	–
1935–39 dollars	2.58	2.81	3.63	5.13	7.79	7.72	6.76	9.69

Table 9. Continued

	1870	1880	1890	1900	1910	1920	1930	1940
Woollens	4.42	3.72	3.63	3.35	4.45	11.08	5.54	9.57
1900 dollars	4.76	3.95	4.29	3.35	3.78	–	–	–
1935–39 dollars	4.21	3.91	5.79	4.94	5.69	4.47	4.82	8.10
All textiles	11.81	14.12	19.51	19.06	29.25	72.64	46.70	59.98
1900 dollars	11.07	12.39	17.89	19.06	24.11	–	–	–
1935–39 dollars	11.25	14.85	25.84	28.07	37.35	29.34	40.68	59.79
Imports as a Percentage of Apparent Consumption of Textile Products in Canada								
Cottons	92%	68%	69%	36%	43%	38%	28%	19%
Woollens	52	40	52	55	72	57	53	30
All textiles	45	66	31	36	37	38	27	21

* Statistics for 1871.

Sources

Imports and Exports, 1870 to 1910: K.W. Taylor and H. Michell, *Statistical Contributions to Canadian Economic History*, Vol. 2 (Toronto: Macmillan, 1931), Tables V and VI.

Exports of Cotton and Woollen Manufactures: Canada, *Sessional Papers*, "Tables of Trade and Navigation," published annually.

Imports and Exports, 1920, 1930, and 1940: Canada, *Sessional Papers, 1922*, No. 11, "Rapport annuel du ministère des Douanes et de l'Accise, 31 mars 1921"; DBS, *Trade of Canada (Imports for Consumption and Exports) Calendar Year 1930* (Ottawa: King's Printer, 1931); DBS, *Trade of Canada, Year Ended December 31, 1940*, Vol. 3, Imports (Ottawa: King's Printer, 1941). The import and export figures include knitted cottons and woollens as well as knitting yarn.

Domestic Manufactures, 1870–1940: *see* Table 3.

Explanatory Notes
The 1900 dollar series was calculated for imports and exports in Taylor and Michell, *Statistical Contributions to Canadian Economic*

History, Tables V and VI. The ratios arrived at by them have been used to calculate 1900 dollars for domestic manufactures, consumption, and per capita consumption.

The 1935 dollar series is based on the wholesale price index for textiles found in M.C. Urquhart and K.A.H. Buckley, *Historical Statistics of Canada* (Toronto: Macmillan, 1971), J-38. Because the 1900 dollar series was calculated separately for different types of textiles and textile fibres, it is more reliable than the 1935–39 index, which is more broadly based.

Population statistics are from Urquhart and Buckley, *Historical Statistics of Canada*, A-2.

Trade statistics were reported on the basis of the fiscal year, which until 1906 ended 30 June. From 1906 to 1939 it ended 31 March. From 1939, trade statistics were reported on the basis of the calendar year. The manufacturing statistics taken from the census were reported on the basis of the census year, which until 1901 ended about 1 April and since 1911 has ended about 1 June.

Because of the difference in the reporting periods, the figures for apparent consumption can only be taken as approximations.

Table 10
Imports of Raw Cotton and Wool in Constant (1900) Thousands of Dollars

Year	Cotton	Wool	Year	Cotton	Wool
1869		$403	1890	$2736	$1741
1870		852	1891	2938	1535
1871	$173	938	1892	3452	2000
1872	131	1211	1893	3046	2055
1873	153	1237	1894	2658	1401
1874	271	736	1895	4072	1515
1875	291	1554	1896	2876	1758
1876	426	708	1897	3153	1116
1877	430	901	1898	4707	2304
1878	558	1218	1899	4204	1840
1879	728	974	1900	4229	1575
1880	1018	1539	1901	3777	1675
1881	1233	1572	1902	4948	2026
1882	1456	1886	1903	5233	1536
1883	2181	1917	1904	3746	1435
1884	1558	1210	1905	4365	1489
1885	1773	1517	1906	5237	1234
1886	2378	2339	1907	5574	1234
1887	2496	2353	1908	4024	1197
1888	2532	1641	1909	5028	1111
1889	2926	2086	1910	5241	1515

Source
Taylor and Michell, *Statistical Contributions to Canadian Economic History*, pp. 22–33.

Table 11
Tariff Rates on Cottons, Woollens, Silks, and Synthetics, 1851–1939

Year	Cottons	Woollens	Silks	Synthetics	All Dutiable Textiles
1851	12.5%	12.5%			
1856	15.0	15.0			
1859	20.0	20.0			
1866	15.0	15.0			
1874	17.5	17.5			
1880–81	22.1	26.8			
1889–90	29.6	28.7			
1895–96	28.5	31.8	30.3%		
1900–01	23.6	25.7	29.5		
1905–06	24.5	29.3	26.5		
1910–11	23.9	28.0	23.7		
1920–21	24.9	26.1	26.7		24.8%
1925–26	23.8	23.4	28.1	18.8%	23.2
1927–28	22.2	21.6	28.7	24.1	24.5
1931–32	30.9	41.4	37.2	53.9	36.0
1933–34	26.7	35.2	34.7	47.9	32.4
1936–37	22.7	27.2	28.0	35.6	26.1
1938–39	23.5	27.4	27.9	40.1	26.9

Sources
Canada. Dept. of Finance, *Tables of Trade and Navigation for the Province of Canada, 1851* (Quebec: Hunter, Rose and Co., 1852), Table 17; Canada, *Statutes*, 19 Victoria c. 10, An Act to Amend the Acts imposing duties of customs, 1856; Canada, *Statutes*, 22 Victoria c. 76, An Act to amend the law relative to Customs and Excise..., 1859; Canada, *Statutes*, 29–30 Victoria c. 6, An Act to amend the Acts respecting duties of customs..., 1866; Canada, *Statutes*, 37 Victoria c. 6, ... Customs and Excise ..., 1874; Canada, *Sessional Papers, 1882*, No. 1, "Trade and Navigation," Table 2; Canada, *Sessional Papers, 1891*, No. 4, Table 2; Canada, *Sessional Papers, 1897*, No. 5, Table 2; Canada, *Sessional Papers, 1902*, No. 11, Part 1, Table 13; Canada, *Sessional Papers, 1907*, No. 11, Table 14; Canada, *Sessional Papers, 1912*, No. 11, Table 14; Canada, *Sessional Papers, 1922*, No. 11, Table 15; DBS, *The Textile Industries of Canada ... 1917–26*, Table 31; DBS, *The Textile Industries of Canada, 1928* (Ottawa: King's Printer, 1930), Table 21; DBS, *The Textile Industries of Canada, 1931 and 1932* (Ottawa: King's Printer, 1935), Table 25; DBS, *The Textile Industries of Canada, 1933, 1934, and 1935* (Ottawa: King's Printer, 1938), Table 22; DBS, *The Textile Industries of Canada, 1936 and 1937* (Ottawa: King's Printer, 1941), Table 19; DBS, *The Textile Industries of Canada, 1938 and 1939* (Ottawa: King's Printer, 1942), Table 18.

Table 12
Average Annual Costs Per Mill in the Woollen Cloth, Cotton Yarn and Cloth, Hosiery and Knit-Goods, and Silk/Synthetic Industries, 1871–1940

	No. of Mills	Hands per Mill	Wages per Mill	Value of Product per Mill	Capital per Mill
1871					
Woollens	270	16	$3 399	$20 398	$10 284
Cottons	8	93	16 175	97 725	79 000
Knit goods	11	22	3 567	4 775	18 102
1881					
Woollens	1281	5	1 080	6 333	4 116
Cottons	18	196	39 680	208 888	193 139
Knit goods	83	19	3 817	16 687	7 600
1891					
Woollens	377	19	4 999	21 453	24 821
Cottons	22	386	95 673	384 169	600 369
Knit goods	281	8	1 652	6 822	4 771
1901					
Woollens	157	43	13 161	46 876	66 791
Cottons	20	601	195 340	601 653	914 935
Knit goods	52	75	20 383	74 183	71 600
1911					
Woollens	87	52	18 652	65 962	88 020
Cottons	26	502	185 713	945 574	1 727 744
Knit goods	68	123	41 392	196 968	175 559
1920					
Woollens	66	84	81 617	424 524	345 199
Cottons	31	569	447 120	2 983 548	2 464 958
Knit goods	128	109	86 499	217 318	329 012
Silk/Synthetics	5	233	163 488	1 075 350	980 336
1930					
Woollens	46	84	74 049	268 428	439 191
Cottons	33	515	394 085	2 380 085	1 475 541
Knit goods	158	115	93 325	335 714	403 400
Silk/Synthetics	25	216	188 744	712 344	1 220 242

Table 12. Continued

	No. of Mills	Hands per Mill	Wages per Mill	Value of Product per Mill	Capital per Mill
1940					
Woollens	66	118	123 982	634 111	417 985
Cottons	37	638	624 617	2 794 321	2 366 995
Knit goods	172	135	120 323	403 647	330 050
Silk/Synthetics	27	315	324 351	1 155 845	1 430 187

Sources

Woollens: DBS, *The Textile Industries of Canada, 1943, 1944 and 1945* (Ottawa: King's Printer, 1946), Table 62. The 1881 figures apparently include cottage weavers. From 1901, "hands" includes owners, salaried employees, and wage earners, and wages include both salary and wage figures; it is not known if this was true before 1901.

Cottons: DBS, *The Textile Industries of Canada, 1943, 1944 and 1945*, Table 25. From 1901 the figures for hands and wages have been adjusted to include salaried employees. For 1871 and 1881 "Capital per Mill" has been taken from the census reports.

Knit Goods: 1871–1911: *See* Table 1. **1920:** DBS, *Textile Industries of Canada ... 1917–26*, Table 78; **1930:** DBS, *Textile Industries of Canada, 1938–39*, Table 107; DBS, *Textile Mills, Knitting Mills, Clothing, 1953* (Ottawa: Queen's Printer, 1956), "The Hosiery and Knit Goods Industries," Table 1.

Silk/Synthetics: 1920: DBS, *Textile Industries of Canada ... 1917–26*, Table 92. **1930:** DBS, *Textile Industries of Canada, 1929–30*, Table 4. **1940:** DBS, *Textile Industries of Canada, 1940, 1941, and 1942*, Table 3.

Table 13
Average Annual Wages in Four Major Sectors of the Textile Industry

Year	Woollens	Cottons	Knit Goods/ Hosiery	Silk/ Synthetics
1871	$ 212	$174	$162	
1881	216	202	201	
1891	263	248	206	
1901	306	325	271	
1911	359	370	336	
1920	972	786	794	$702
1930	882	765	812	874
1940	1051	979	819	1030

Source
Derived from Table 12.

Table 14
Proportions of Men, Women, and Children Employed in the Wool Cloth, Cotton Cloth and Yarn, Hosiery and Knit-Goods, and Silk/Synthetic Sectors, 1871–1941

Year	Sector	16 Years of Age and Over		Under 16 Years of Age
		Male	Female	
1871	Woollens	46%	35%	19%
	Cottons	22	41	37
	Hosiery/Knit Goods	21	67	7
	Totals	41	38	21
1881	Woollens	44	43	13
	Cottons	28	41	31
	Hosiery/Knit Goods	24	66	10
	Totals	37	45	18
1891	Woollens	44	42	14
	Cottons	37	45	18
	Hosiery/Knit Goods	24	60	16
	Totals	38	46	16
1901	Woollens	49	43	8
	Cottons	45	40	15
	Hosiery/Knit Goods	22	62	6
	Totals	44	45	11
1911	Woollens	53	41	7
	Cottons	46	39	15
	Hosiery/Knit Goods	46	51	3
	Totals	47	43	10
1920	Woollens	53	47	
	Cottons	54	46	
	Hosiery/Knit Goods	30	70	
	Silk/Synthetics	23	77	
	Totals	44	56	
1931	Woollens	56	43	2
	Cottons	59	38	3
	Hosiery/Knit Goods	40	59	1
	Silk/Synthetics	53	44	2
	Totals	53	46	2

Tables

Table 14. Continued

Year	Sector	16 Years of Age and Over		Under 16 Years of Age
		Male	**Female**	
1941	Woollens	58	40	2
	Cottons	63	36	>1
	Hosiery/Knit Goods	39	60	>1
	Silk/Synthetics	62	37	>1
	Totals	57	42	>1

Sources
1871–1911: *See* Table 1. **1920**: DBS, *The Textile Industries of Canada ...
1917–26*, Tables 37, 71, 78, and 92. **1931**: DBS, *Seventh Census of Canada,
1931* (Ottawa: King's Printer, 1936), Vol. 7, Table 56, pp. 670–72. **1941**:
DBS, *Eighth Census of Canada, 1941* (Ottawa: King's Printer, 1946), Vol. 7,
Table 18, pp. 518–26.

Table 15
Weekly Wage Rates and Distribution by Sex in Different Departments of Two Mills, 1887 and 1927

			Weekly Wages in the Paton Woollen Mill, Sherbrooke, 1887			
	Average	No. of	Percentage of Employees			
Department	Wage	Employees	Males	Females	Boys	Girls
Miscellaneous	$19.44	65	71%	2%	21%	6%
Dyeing	15.54	18	89	–	11	–
Wool sorting	14.67	11	69	–	31	–
Warping	12.77	9	22	–	–	78
Finishing	10.01	104	21	7	34	38
Carding	9.94	41	30	5	23	58
Picking	9.72	14	54	–	46	–
Weaving	9.11	168	10	6	15	69
Waste	8.25	22	40	–	32	28
Spinning	7.85	43	29	–	16	53
Spooling	7.77	14	8	8	–	84
Winding	6.86	18	3	10	–	87
Twisting	6.44	18	4	–	9	87
	10.75	540	27	4	18	51

	Weekly Wages (50-Hour Week) in the Empire Cotton Mill, Welland, 1927			
	Average	No. of	Percentage of Employees	
Department	Wage	Employees	Males	Females
Mechanical	$31.00	15	100%	–
Cloth room	24.30	7	86	14%
Warehouse	23.35	3	100	–
Yard	20.65	3	100	–
Beaming	20.15	10	50	50
Weaving, beam	19.93	45	33	67
Weaving, creel	19.00	10	70	30
Carding	18.12	37	54	46
Spinning	17.50	39	23	77
Twisting	17.48	21	10	90
Winding	17.36	8	12	88
Spooling	17.20	20	15	85
General	14.70	5	40	60
	21.20	223	41	59

Sources
Paton Mill: Canada. Parliament, *Report of the Royal Commission on the Relations of Labour and Capital in Canada, Evidence Quebec* (Ottawa: Queen's Printer, 1889), pp. 1245–46.
Empire Mill: NA, RG 36, Vol. 34, File 64-19.

Table 16
Geographic Distribution of Mills, 1871–91*

	No. of Census Districts	No. with Carding Mills	No. with Woollen Mills	No. with Cotton Mills	No. with Knitting Mills	No. with Weavers
1851						
Ontario	48	37	28			
Quebec	38	34	13			
Nova Scotia	–	–	–			
New Brunswick	–	–	–			
Total	86	71	41			
1871						
Ontario	90	56	68	4	8	
Quebec	83	66	15	1	1	
Nova Scotia	19	18	5	–	–	
New Brunswick	14	13	5	1	–	
Total	206	153	93	6	9	
1891						
Ontario	88	31	66	6	42	68
Quebec	62	49	22	4	12	34
Nova Scotia	19	18	7	2	5	15
New Brunswick	13	13	4	5	1	7
Total	182	111	99	17	60	124

* Based on the number of census districts that reported at least one mill.
Sources
Canada, *Census of the Canadas, 1851–52* (Quebec: John Lovell, 1853), Appendices 13 and 14; Canada, *Census of Canada, 1870–71*, Vol. 3, Tables 30 to 53; Canada, *Census of Canada, 1890–91*, Vol. 3, Table 1.

Table 17
Relative Size of Canadian Textile Mills, 1933, by Employees

No. of Employees	Ontario		Quebec		New Brunswick		Nova Scotia	
	Knit Goods	Hosiery	Knit Goods	Hosiery	Knit Goods	Hosiery	Knit Goods	Hosiery
Knit-Goods/Hosiery Mills								
751 to 800	1		1	1				
701 to 750	2							
651 to 700								
601 to 650								
551 to 600	1		1					
501 to 550								
451 to 500	1							
401 to 450	1			1				
351 to 400								
301 to 350	2	1						
251 to 300	1	1	1	1			1	
201 to 250	1	5	2					1
151 to 200	2	3			1			
101 to 150	7	3		2			1	
51 to 100	7	3	1	3				
0 to 50	24	3	10	4				
Total mills	50	19	16	12	1	0	2	1
Total employees	7 153	2 838	2 267	2 187	200		391	217
Average employees	143	149	142	182	200		195	217
Median	54	168	42	96	200		195	217

Table 17. Continued

No. of Employees	Ontario	Quebec	New Brunswick	Nova Scotia
Woollen Mills				
651 to 700				
601 to 650	1			
551 to 600				
501 to 550				
451 to 500				
401 to 450	1			
351 to 400	1	1		
301 to 350	3	1		
251 to 300	3			
201 to 250	3			
151 to 200	4	1		
101 to 150	5	1		
51 to 100	5	1	1	
0 to 50	5	4		1
Total mills	31	9	1	1
Total employees	5 531	1 187	95	40
Average employees	178	132	95	40
Median	153	77	95	40

Table 17. Continued

No. of Employees	Ontario	Quebec	New Brunswick	Nova Scotia
Cotton Mills				
1901 to 2000		1		
1801 to 1900				
1701 to 1800				
1601 to 1700				
1501 to 1600		1		
1401 to 1500		1		
1301 to 1400				
1201 to 1300				
1101 to 1200		1		
1001 to 1100				
901 to 1000				
801 to 900	1	1		
701 to 800	1	1		
601 to 700	1	1		
501 to 600	1	1		
451 to 500	1			
401 to 450			1	
351 to 400		1	1	
301 to 350	1	2		
251 to 300	1	1		
201 to 250	1	2		
151 to 200	1			1

Table 17. Continued

No. of Employees	Ontario	Quebec	New Brunswick	Nova Scotia
101 to 150	1			1
51 to 100	1		1	
0 to 50		1		
Total mills	10	15	3	1
Total employees	3 745	10 618	1 119	248
Average employees	374	708	290	248
Median	316	361	378	248

Sources

Knit-Goods/Hosiery Mills: Canada. *Report of the Royal Commission on Price Spreads* (Ottawa: King's Printer, 1935), pp. 2847, 2864–65, 2911–12, 2930–31.

Woollen Mills: Canada. *Report of the Royal Commission on Price Spreads*, pp. 2799, 2822–23.

Cotton Mills: Canada. *Report of the Royal Commission on Price Spreads*, pp. 2693–94.

Table 18
Sources of Power in Cotton, Woollen, and Knitting Mills, 1901–1940 (Horsepower)

	Steam Engines	Other*	Water Wheels/ Turbines	Electric Motors	Total	Purchased Power	% Electric
1901							
Cottons	12 061	0	12 352	7 076	31 489	2 709	22%
Knitting	1 444	5	1 200	144	2 793	5	5
Woollen goods	6 089	104	7 682	475	14 350	212	3
Woollen yarns	115	0	107	0	222	0	0
Totals	19 709	109	21 341	7 695	48 854	2 926	16
1911							
Cottons	14 179	80	13 436	15 651	43 346	4 457	36
Knitting	3 152	484	2 005	1 986	7 627	138	26
Carding	125	26	594	0	745	0	0
Woollen goods	4 096	92	3 535	1 389	9 112	275	15
Woollen yarns	370	33	280	100	783	0	13
Totals	21 992	715	19 850	19 126	61 613	4 870	31

Table 18. Continued

1920 / 1924

	Steam Engines	Other*	Water Wheels/Turbines	Electric Power			% Electric
				Purchased	Generated on Site	Total	
1920							
Cotton yarn & cloth	10 520	105	13 420	25 217	10 250	59 512	60%
Cotton thread						1 337	
Other cottons						1 445	
Woollen yarn						4 486	
Woollen cloth						11 256	
1924							
Knitting	3 409	1 013	1 947	7 860	983	15 212	58

1930

	Steam Engines	Other*	Water Wheels/Turbines	Purchased Electric Power	Total	Electric Power Generated on Site	Total Electric Power	% Electric
1930								
Cotton yarn & cloth	9 162	0	23 900	43 684	76 746	22 331	66 015	86%
Cotton thread	0	0	0	1 987	1 987	0	1 987	100
Knitting	3 745	935	1 804	10 011	16 495	2 513	12 524	76
Woollen cloth	1 852	45	1 661	8 000	11 558	670	8 670	75
Woollen yarn	381	30	552	22 420	23 383	800	23 220	99
Totals	15 140	1 010	27 917	86 102	130 169	26 314	112 416	86

Table 18. Continued

1940	Steam Engines	Other*	Water Wheels/ Turbines	Purchased Electric Power	Total	Electric Power Generated on Site	Total Electric Power	% Electric
Cotton yarn & cloth	10 367	800	12 460	84 247	107 873	28 211	112 457	104**
Cotton thread	0	0	0	2 127	2 127	0	2 127	100
Knitting	3 046	764	2 559	11 916	18 285	3 999	15 915	87
Woollen cloth	365	42	1 410	13 949	15 766	724	14 673	93
Woollen yarn	589	103	667	7 101	8 460	1 131	8 232	93
Totals	14 367	1 709	17 096	119 339	152 511	34 065	153 404	101**

* Primarily internal combustion engines.
** This anomaly is inherent in the statistics in the published report.

Sources
Canada, Census of Canada, 1901, Vol. 3, Table 12; Canada, Census of Canada, 1911, Vol. 3, Table 6; DBS, The Textile Industries of Canada ... 1917–26, Tables 33, 41, 49, 60, 66, 82; DBS, Report on the Cotton Textile Industry in Canada 1930 (Ottawa: 1932), pp. 21, 25; DBS, Report on the Cotton Textile Industry in Canada 1940 (Ottawa: 1942) pp. 26–27, 33; DBS, Report on the Hosiery, Knit Goods and Fabric Glove Industry in Canada, 1930 (Ottawa: 1932) p. 13; DBS, Report on the Hosiery, Knitted Goods and Fabric Glove and Mitten Industries in Canada, 1940 (Ottawa: 1942), p. 15; DBS, Report on the Woollen Textile Industry in Canada, 1930 (Ottawa: 1931) pp. 19, 24; DBS, Report on the Woollen Textile Industries in Canada, 1940 (Ottawa: 1942), pp. 21, 29.

Table 19
Productivity per Employee in Constant Dollars
(Base 1935–39)

	Textile Price Index	Cottons	Knit Goods	Woollens
1871	112.5	$382	$385	$428
1881	85.6	657	586	705
1891	69.0	768	625	810
1901	65.1	757	825	943
1911	76.2	1114	1058	1113
1920	247.6	916	642	984
1930	114.8	1195	1342	1516
1940	118.1	3761	2532	4624

Sources
Calculated from Tables 1 and 2. Textile price index from
Urquhart and Buckley, *Historical Statistics of Canada*, J38.

Notes

Abbreviations

CJD	*Canadian Journal of Fabrics*
CTD	*Canadian Textile Directory*
CTJ	*Canadian Textile Journal*
DBS	Canada. Dominion Bureau of Statistics.
DCB	*Dictionary of Canadian Biography*
DDGR	*Dominion Dry Goods Report*
MTIC	*Manual of the Textile Industry of Canada*
MVTM	Merrimack Valley Textile Museum
NA	Canada. National Archives.
RCLC	Canada. Parliament. Royal Commission on the Relations of Labour and Capital.

Part I
The History of the Primary Textile Industry

Introduction

1 DBS, Industrial Statistics Branch, *The Textile Industries of Canada in the Decade 1917–26* (Ottawa: F.A. Acland, King's Printer, 1929), p. 6.

Technological Developments in the Textile Industry, 1750–1850 and 1850–1950

1 The descriptions of technological processes and developments are based primarily on the following volumes: MVTM, *Homespun to Factory Made: Woollen Textiles in America, 1776–1876* (North Andover, Mass.: 1977); MVTM, *All Sorts of Good Sufficient Cloth: Linen-Making in New England, 1640–1860* (North Andover, Mass.: 1980); W. English, *The Textile Industry: An Account of the Early Inventions of Spinning, Weaving, and Knitting Machines* (London: Longmans, Green and Co., 1969); J. Genaint Jenkins, ed., *The Wool Textile Industry in Great Britain* (London: Routledge and Kegan Paul, 1972); Chris Aspin, *The Cotton Industry* (Aylesbury, Eng: Shire Publications, 1981); Anna P. Benson, *Textile Machines* (Aylesbury, Eng.: Shire Publications, 1983).
2 MVTM, *Homespun to Factory Made*, p. 60.
3 Ibid., p. 70.
4 English, *Textile Industry*, p. 143.
5 Benson, *Textile Machines*, pp. 3–4.
6 Jenkins, *Wool Textile Industry*, pp. 103–10.
7 William Lazonick, "Industrial Organization and Technological Change: The Decline of the British Cotton Industry," *Business History Review*, Vol. 57, No. 2 (Summer 1983), p. 198.
8 Charles Singer, E.J. Holmyard, A.R. Hall, and Trevor I. Williams, *A History of Technology*, Vol. 5, The Late Nineteenth Century c. 1850–c. 1900 (Oxford: Clarendon Press, 1958), p. 577.
9 MVTM, *All Sorts of Good Sufficient Cloth*, pp. 24–26.
10 MVTM, *Homespun to Factory Made*, p. 82; Jenkins, *Wool Textile Industry*, pp. 130–31.
11 *DDGR*, April 1884, p. 139; *DDGR*, Feb. 1893, p. 34; Jean-Pierre Kesteman, "Histoire de Sherbrooke," Tome 1, L'âge de l'eau, manuscript on file, Quebec Regional Office, Canadian Parks Service, Quebec, 1979, pp. 169–71.
12 Melvin T. Copeland, *The Cotton Manufacturing Industry of the United States* (Cambridge, Mass.: Harvard Univ. Press, 1912), pp. 24, 101; English, *Textile Industry*, pp. 16–20.
13 Jenkins, *Wool Textile Industry*, p. 163.
14 MVTM, *Homespun to Factory Made*, p. 94.
15 Ibid., p. 96.
16 Edward Baines, *History of the Cotton Manufacture in Great Britain* (New York: Augustus M. Kelley, 1971), pp. 246–49, 253.
17 Ibid., p. 265.
18 W.S. Pepperell, "Cotton Mill Costs in 1850 and Today," *Textile World*, 4 April 1925, p. 2294.
19 *CJF*, Dec. 1896, pp. 365–36.

20 Lars G. Sandberg, "American Rings and English Mules: The Role of Economic Rationality," *Quarterly Journal of Economics*, Vol. 83, No. 1 (Feb. 1969), p. 25.

21 Canada. Parliament, *Report of the Royal Commission on the Textile Industry* (Ottawa: J.O. Patenaude, King's Printer, 1938), p. 41.

22 DBS, *The Textile Industries of Canada, 1943, 1944, and 1945* (Ottawa: Edmond Clouthier, King's Printer, 1945), p. 83; DBS, *Report on the Hosiery and Knitted Goods Industry in Canada, 1940* (Ottawa: 1942), Table 15.

23 George Otis Draper, "The Present Development of the Northrop Loom," New England Cotton Manufacturers Association *Transactions*, No. 59 (24–25 Oct. 1895), pp. 92–93; "New Automtic Shuttle Changing Loom," *CJF*, Aug. 1901, pp. 241–43.

24 Thayer Lincoln, "The Cotton Textile Machine Industry: American Loom Builders," *Harvard Business Review*, Vol. 12 (1933), p. 100.

25 Copeland, *The Cotton Manufacturing Industry of the United States*, p. 86; Irwin Feller, "The Diffusion and Location of Technological Change in the American Cotton Textile Industry, 1890," *Technology and Culture*, Vol. 15, No. 4 (Oct. 1974), pp. 573–74; Irwin Feller, "The Draper Loom in New England Textiles, 1899–1914: A Study of Diffusion of an Innovation," *Journal of Economic History*, Vol. 26, No. 3 (Sept. 1966), p. 320; International Correspondence Schools, *The Cotton Textile Worker's Handbook: A Reference Book Dealing With the Spinning of Cotton Yarns, the Weavinq of Cotton Fabrics, and the Yarn and Cloth Calculations Incidental thereto* (Philadelphia: The John C. Winston Co., 1921), p. 273; *CJF*, Sept. 1911, p. 247.

26 Brief by J.C. Mcruer, K.C., counsel to the Royal Commission on the Textile Industry. In the Commission's papers, Labour Canada Library, Ottawa, pp. 157–59.

27 Canada, *Report of the Royal Commission on the Textile Industry*, pp. 177–78.

28 Lincoln, "The Cotton Textile Machine Industry: American Loom Builders," p. 101.

29 Feller, "The Draper Loom," p. 344.

30 *CJF*, Oct. 1898, pp. 308–9.

31 Canada, *Report of the Royal Commission on the Textile Industry*, p. 41; Feller, "The Draper Loom," p. 320.

32 Arthur H. Cole, *The American Wool Manufacture* (Cambridge, Mass.: Harvard Univ. Press, 1926), Vol. 2, pp. 96–97.

33 DBS, *The Textile Industries of Canada, 1943, 1944, and 1945*, pp. 83–84.

34 William King, *Principles of Cotton Manufacture* (Gardenvale, Que.: Garden City Press, 1938), p. 67.

35 Thomas R. Navin, *The Whitin Machine Works Since 1831: A Textile Machinery Company in an Industrial Village* (Cambridge, Mass.: Harvard Univ. Press, 1950), pp. 513–19; George S. Gibb, *The Saco-Lowell Shops — Textile Machinery Building in New England, 1813–1949* (Cambridge, Mass.: Harvard Univ. Press, 1950), pp. 560–65.

36 Singer et al., *A History of Technology*, Vol. 5, pp. 597–99.

Homespun Cloth Production

1 Personal communication, Eugene Arima, Canadian Parks Service, Ottawa.

2 Harold B. and Dorothy K. Burnham, *'Keep Me Warm One Night': Early Handweaving in Eastern Canada* (Toronto: Univ. of Toronto Press, 1972), pp. 7–8; Gilbert Rousseau, "Évolution de la production textile au Canada depuis ses origines jusqu'à aujourd'hui," Baccalauréat spécial, Sciences économiques, Université du Québec à Montréal, 1980, p. 12.

3 Burnham, *'Keep Me Warm,'* pp. 7–8.

4 David-T. Ruddell, "The Domestic Textile Industry in the Region and City of Québec, 1792–1835," *Material History Bulletin*, No. 17 (Spring 1983), p. 100; Rousseau, "Évolution de la production textile," pp. 186–87, 192.
5 Robert-L. Séguin, *La civilisation traditionelle de l'habitant aux 17ᵉ et 18ᵉ siècles* (Montréal: Fides, 1973), p. 493; Burnham, *'Keep Me Warm,'* pp. 7–9.
6 Ruddell, "Domestic Textile Industry," pp. 96, 106–7.
7 Rousseau, "Évolution de la production textile," p. 190.
8 Ibid., p. 193.
9 Jean-Pierre Kesteman, "Une bourgeoisie et son espace: Industrialisation et développement du capitalisme dans le district de Saint-Francois (Québec), 1823–1879," thèse présentée à l'Université du Québec à Montréal comme exigence partielle du doctorat en Histoire, Oct. 1985, p. 202; Patrick C.T. White, *Lord Selkirk's Diary, 1803–1804. A Journal of his Travels in British North America and the Northeastern United States* (Toronto: Champlain Society, 1958), pp. 178–79, 182–83.
10 Canada (Province), *Census of the Canadas, 1851–2*, Vol. 2 (Quebec: Lovell and Lamoureux, 1855), pp. 262–63, 392–93. Statistics on employment and value of production in census years prior to 1920 have generally been taken from census reports.
11 Richard Reid, "The Rosamond Woolen Company of Almonte: Industrial Development in a Rural Setting," *Ontario History*, Vol. 75, No. 3 (Sept. 1983), pp. 298–99.
12 Judy Boss, *The Restoration of the Wile Carding Mill* (Halifax: Nova Scotia Museum, 1975), pp. 8–21.
13 Janine Grant and Kris Inwood, "Gender and Organization in the Canadian Cloth Industry, 1870," in P.A. Baskerville, ed., *Canadian Papers in Business History* (Victoria: Public History Group, Univ. of Victoria, 1989), Table 3. The percentage figures given in Table 3 of the Grant and Inwood paper have been compared with the dollar figures for factory production of wool and cotton cloth given in Tables 4 and 5 of this book to arrive at a figure for all of Canada.

Early Growth

1 The Canadian Encyclopedia, Vol. 3 (Edmonton: Hurtig Publishers, 1985), s.v. "Textile Industry"; *DDGR*, April 1885, p. 163.
2 Kesteman, "Une bourgeoisie et son espace," pp. 203–4.
3 *DDGR*, April 1884, p. 139; "Earnestown Cloth Factory," Kingston *Chronicle*, 19 July 1828; Brockville *Recorder*, 10 May 1832.
4 *CJF*, Feb. 1903, p. 48; *CJF*, June 1906, p. 16; John N. Jackson, *St. Catharines, Ontario: Its Early Years* (Belleville: Mika Publishing, 1976), p. 232; W.P.J. Millar, "George P.M. Ball: A Rural Businessman in Upper Canada," *Ontario History*, Vol. 66, No. 2 (June 1974), pp. 66–67.
5 *CJF*, Oct. 1887, pp. 278–79.
6 NA, MG ll, CO 221, Vol. 41, "Return of Manufactures...," reel B–1525.
7 *DDGR*, April 1885, p. 163.
8 *DDGR*, April 1884, p. 139; *DDGR*, Feb. 1893, p. 34; Kesteman, "Histoire de Sherbrooke," pp. 169–71.
9 There is some confusion as to whether this mill was at Chambly or at Saint-Athanase. Harold A. Innis and Arthur R.M. Lower, *Select Documents in Canadian Economic History, 1783–1885* (Toronto: Univ. of Toronto Press, 1933), pp. 299–304.
10 Kesteman, "Histoire de Sherbrooke", pp. 172–76.
11 *CJF*, April 1900, p. 98.

12 Larry McNally, "Water Power on the Lachine Canal, 1846–1900," Microfiche Report Series, No. 54, Parks Canada, Ottawa, 1982, pp. 40–43; *Lovell's Montreal Directory, 1874–75*, p. 45.
13 Joseph N. Fauteux, *Essai sur l'industrie au Canada sous le régime français* (Québec: Proulx, 1927), pp. 469–70.
14 Kesteman, "Histoire de Sherbrooke," p. 170.
15 *DDGR*, March 1885, p. 129.
16 Felicity L. Leung, "Catalogue of Significant Extant Textile Mills Built in Canada Before 1940," Microfiche Report Series, No. 350, Parks Service, Environment Canada, Ottawa, 1986, p. 116.
17 *CTJ*, 30 June 1933; George R. Stevens, *The Belding-Corticelli Story, 1876–1951* (Montréal: Belding-Corticelli, 1951), pp. 9–10, 14–15, 22; Canada, *Report of the Royal Commission on the Textile Industry*, p. 47.
18 "Flax Manufacturing in Canada," Article 3, *CJF*, Aug. 1904, pp. 164–65.
19 "The Flax Industry in Canada," Article 2, *CJF*, June 1904, pp. 127–28.
20 J.B. Bartram, "Canada's Opportunity in the Flax and Linen Industry," *CTJ*, 5 Dec. 1922, pp. 555–56.
21 Canada, *Census of Canada, 1890–91*, Vol. 3 (Ottawa: Queen's Printer, 1894), Table 1, Flax Mills; Canada, *Fourth Census of Canada, 1901*, Vol. 3, Manufacturers (Ottawa: King's Printer, 1905), pp. lxvi–lxvii; Canada, *Fifth Census of Canada, 1911* (Ottawa: Printed by C.H. Parmalee, 1913), Vol. 3, Table 14.

Crisis and Consolidation

1 Canada, *Report of the Royal Commission on the Textile Industry*, pp. 34–35.
2 *DDGR*, Nov. 1883, p. 2; *DDGR*, Jan. 1884, p. 50.
3 *DDGR*, Jan. 1884, p. 50.
4 Canada, *Report of the Royal Commission on the Textile Industry*, p. 35.
5 Thomas W. Acheson, "The Social Origins of Canadian Industrialism: A Study in the Structure of Entrepreneurship," PhD thesis, Univ. of Toronto, Toronto, 1971, p. 148; *DDGR*, Nov. 1883, p. 3.
6 Peter Delottinville, "The St. Croix Cotton Manufacturing Company and its Influence on the St. Croix Community, 1890–1892," MA thesis, Dalhousie Univ., Halifax, 1980, p. 13.
7 *DDGR*, May 1884, p. 169; *DDGR*, March 1885, p. 131; *DDGR*, Aug. 1886, p. 277; *DDGR*, July 1889, p. 20; Delottinville, "The St. Croix Cotton Manufacturing Company," p. 23.
8 *DDGR*, Nov. 1883, p. 3; *DDGR*, Jan. 1884, p. 51.
9 *CJF*, Oct. 1888, p. 294.
10 Barbara J. Austin, "Life Cycles and Strategy of a Canadian Company — Dominion Textile: 1873–1983," PhD thesis, Concordia Univ., Montréal, 1985, pp. 103, 213–14; *CTD, 1899*, p. 418.
11 Canada, *Report of the Royal Commission on the Textile Industry*, p. 35.
12 *CJF*, June 1887, p. 177.
13 Delottinville, "The St. Croix Cotton Manufacturing Company," pp. 15–18.
14 *CJF*, Feb. 1889, p. 62; *CJF*, April 1889, p. 126; *CJF*, May 1890, p. 29.
15 *CJF*, April 1889, p. 126.
16 *CJF*, Dec. 1890, p. 22; Acheson, "Social Origins of Canadian Industrialism," pp. 150–51.
17 Acheson, "Social Origins of Canadian Industrialism," pp. 150–51.
18 Based on total number of cotton spindles, 543 200, in Canada. *CTD, 1892*.

19 *CJF*, May 1892, p. 132.
20 Austin, "Life Cycles," pp. 168, 170.
21 Acheson, "Social Origins of Canadian Industrialism," p. 174.
22 Ibid., p. 284.
23 Canada, *Report of the Royal Commission on the Textile Industry*, p. 51.
24 RCLC, *Report of the Royal Commission on the Relations of Labour, and Capital in Canada. Evidence Quebec* (Ottawa: Queen's Printer, 1889), pp. 374–81.
25 Saint John (N.B.) *Globe*, 28 May 1897; W.R. Houston, *Annual Financial Review: Canadian, 1901* (Toronto: Houston's Standard Publications, 1901), pp. 82–83.
26 Jacques Rouillard, *Les travailleurs du coton au Québec, 1900–1915* (Montréal: Les presses de l'université du Québec, 1974), p. 35.
27 Austin, "Life Cycles," p. 331.
28 Based on Table 9.
29 *DDGR*, Nov. 1883, p. 5; *DDGR*, Dec. 1883, p. 26; *DDGR*, Jan. 1884, p. 49.
30 *CJF*, Nov. 1888, p. 352; *CJF*, Aug. 1889, p. 246.
31 *MTIC, 1899*, pp. 437, 442, 444, 453; Henry J. Morgan, ed., *The Canadian Men and Women of the Time*, 2nd ed. (Toronto: William Briggs, 1912), p. 144; Jacques Ferland, "Le rôle des déterminismes sociaux dans le développement des forces productives de l'industrie textile du Canada, 1870 à 1910," MA thesis, McGill Univ., Montréal, 1982, pp. 59–61; "The Woollen Mill Combination," *CJF*, Feb. 1900, p. 42.
32 *CTJ*, May 1904, pp. 101–2; *CTJ*, June 1904, pp. 121–22; *CTJ*, July 1904, pp. 149–50.
33 Douglas Rudyard Annett, *British Preference in Canadian Commercial Policy* (Toronto: Ryerson Press, 1948), pp. 32–34.
34 Canada, *Report of the Royal Commission on the Textile Industry*, p. 43; Canada. Tariff Board, *Canadian Wool Cloth Industry (Woollens and Worsteds) Reference No. 116* (Ottawa: Queen's Printer, 1955), pp. 49–50.
35 DBS, *The Textile Industries of Canada in the Decade 1917–26*, p. 95.
36 Emory Donald Nesbitt, "Fluctuations in the Economic Growth of Carleton Place," Dept. of Geography, Carleton Univ., Ottawa, 1970, p. 34; *MTIC, 1928*, pp. 254, 259.
37 John M. Merriman, "History, Development of Penmans Limited," *CTJ*, 16 July 1954, p. 22.
38 *DDGR*, Dec. 1883, p. 26; *DDGR*, March 1884, p. 107.
39 Merriman, "History and Development of Penmans Limited," pp. 21–22; Leung, "Catalogue," p. 131.
40 Austin, "Life Cycles," pp. 390, 894, 896; *CJF*, Sept. 1906, p. 1877; *CTJ*, March 1914, p. 94; *Who's Who in Canada, 1938–39*, p. 354, s.v. "Morrice, Robert Bruce"; Abram Ernest Epp, "Cooperation Among the Capitalists: The Canadian Merger Movement, 1909–1913," PhD thesis, Johns Hopkins Univ., Baltimore, 1973, pp. 414–15.
41 "York Knitting Mills, Limited and Woods Underwear, Limited with their afilliated companies, The Toronto Hosiery Company and The Dupont Textiles, Limited," *CTJ*, 3 Sept. 1926, pp. 899–900; Houston, *Annual Financial Review: Canadian, 1932*, pp. 1167–68; Houston, *Annual Financial Review: Canadian, 1941*, pp. 1170–71.
42 Canada, *Report of the Royal Commission on the Textile Industry*, 1938, pp. 53–54.
43 Cole, *The American Wool Manufacture*, Vol. 2, pp. 151–52.
44 Copeland, *The Cotton Manufacturing Industry of the United States*, pp. 23–25.
45 *CTJ*, 30 June 1933, p. 43.
46 Estimated from reports of imports of woollen and cotton knitted goods in Canada, *Sessional Paper*, 1894, No. 5, Trade and Commerce, Table 2, pp. 20–25, 119–23; Canada, *Sessional Paper*, 1903, No. 10, Trade and Commerce, Table 11, pp. 44–49, 150–55; and Canada, *Sessional Paper*, 1914, No. 10, Trade and Commerce, Table 18, pp. 72–73, 190–95, and from Table 3, Value of Production in the Major Divisions of the Textile Industry, 1870–1950.

47 Calculated from Table 13.

Causes of Growth: Tariffs and Finances

1 Estimated from reports of imports of woollen and cotton knitted goods in Canada, *Sessional Paper*, 1894, No. 5, Trade and Commerce, Table 2, pp. 20–25, 119–23; Canada, *Sessional Paper*, 1914, No. 10, Trade and Commerce, Table 18, pp. 72–73, 190–95, and from reports of domestic production in Table 3 of this book.
2 NA, MG 24, D16, Buchanan Papers, Vol. 2, pp. 1262–72, Barber and Brother to I. Buchanan, 11 May 1860.
3 Rousseau, "Évolution de la production textile," p. 61.
4 Orville J. McDairmid, *Commercial Policy in the Canadian Economy* (Cambridge, Mass.: Harvard Univ. Press, 1948), pp. 151–52.
5 Canada, *Sessional Paper*, 1891, No. 4, Trade and Navigation Reports, Table 2.
6 Michael Hinton, "The National Policy and the Growth of the Canadian Cotton Textile Industry," paper presented at the 13th Conference on Quantitative Methods in Canadian Economic History, Wilfrid Laurier Univ., Waterloo, Ont., March 1984, p. 14.
7 Ibid., p. 13.
8 Reid, "The Rosamond Woolen Company of Almonte," p. 269.
9 Ronald Rudin, "The Development of Four Quebec Towns, 1840–1914; A Study in Urban Economic Growth in Quebec," PhD thesis, York Univ., Toronto, 1977, pp. 41–42.
10 Thomas W. Acheson, "The National Policy and the Industrialization of the Maritimes, 1880–1910," *Acadiensis*, Vol. 1, No. 2 (Spring 1972), pp. 9 and 11; Acheson, "Social Origins of Canadian Industrialism," pp. 199–201; Austin, "Life Cycles," p. 120; Brian J. Young and G. Tulchinsky, "Allan, Sir Hugh," in *DCB* (Toronto: Univ. of Toronto Press, 1964–), Vol. 11, 1881 to 1890, p. 10; Elinor K. Senior, *From Royal Township to Industrial City: Cornwall, 1784–1984* (Belleville: Mika Publishing, 1983), pp. 226–28; Reid, "Rosamond Woolen Company," p. 269.
11 David G. Burley, "Gordon, John," in *DCB*, Vol. 11, 1881 to 1890, pp. 361–63; *DDGR*, March 1884, p. 113; B. Forster, "McInnes, Donald," *DCB*, Vol. 12, 1891 to 1900, pp. 631–34.
12 J.D. St-Aubin, *Salaberry de Valleyfield, 1842 à 1972: Histoire religieuse, municipale, scolaire, commerciale et industrielle* (Valleyfield, Que.: G. Brault, printer, 1973), pp. 45–49; Austin, "Life Cycles," p. 238. St-Aubin identifies "Mr. Bullough," an English manufacturer of textile machinery, as the English shareholder. Mr. Bullough could have been a member of the textile machinery manufacturing firm of Howard and Bullough; however, Austin, "Life Cycles," p. 238, identifies Samuel Barlow as the English investor. As Ms. Austin has had access to the Montreal Cotton Company minute books, Barlow seems the most probable.
13 Austin, "Life Cycles," pp. 129, 179–84.
14 Acheson, "Social Origins of Canadian Industrialism," p. 148; Morgan, ed., *The Canadian Men and Women of the Time*, 1912, p. 824.
15 Morgan, ed., *The Canadian Men and Women of the Time* (1898), pp. 370–71; *CTD*, *1899*, p. 436.
16 Austin, "Life Cycles," p. 238.
17 Delottinville, "St. Croix Cotton Manufacturing Company," pp. 31–32; *CJF*, May 1892, p. 132; *CJF*, June 1894, p. 172.
18 Saint John, N.B., *Globe*, 28 May 1897; *CJF*, June 1905, p. 28.

19 *Hamilton Spectator*, 4 July 1967; *CTJ*, "The Story of Cosmos at Yarmouth," 5 Sept. 1958, pp. 21–26; *CJF*, Dec. 1901, p. 335; Samuel B. Lincoln, *Lockwood Greene: The History of an Engineering Business, 1832–1958* (Brattleboro, Vermont: The Stephen Greene Press, 1960), pp. 559–60; Cotton Institute of Canada, "The Primary Cotton Textile Industry in Canada," brief submitted to the Royal Commission on Price Spreads, 1935, p. 18.
20 *DDGR*, Oct. 1884, p. 334; Austin, "Life Cycles," p. 167; R.T. Naylor, *The History of Canadian Business, 1867–1914* (Toronto: J. Lorimer, 1975), Vol. 2, p. 137.

Maturity, 1906–1945

1 Canada, *Report of the Royal Commission on Price Spreads* (Ottawa: King's Printer, 1935), p. 2789.
2 Canada, *Sessional Paper*, 1914, No. 10, Trade and Commerce, Table 18, pp. 72–73, 190–95, and Table 9 of this book.
3 *MTIC, 1928*, pp. 252–53; ibid., *1939*, pp. 130–32; *CTJ*, 29 March 1921, p. 176; "Chronology of the Textile Manufacturing Industries of Canada, 1883–1983," *CTJ*, June 1983, pp. 125, 126.
4 "Among the Mills," *CJF*, July 1900, p. 208; Cotton Institute of Canada, "The Primary Cotton Textile Industry in Canada," p. 20.
5 Austin, "Life Cycles," pp. 207–8.
6 *CTJ*, 28 Sept. 1920, p. 513.
7 Austin, "Life Cycles," pp. 207–8.
8 *CTJ*, Oct. 1897, p. 309.
9 *MTIC, 1928*, p. 253; NA, RG 36, No. 11, Advisory Board on Tariffs and Taxation, 1926–36, Vol. 33, file 64–10; DBS, *The Textile Industries of Canada in the Decade 1917–26*, p. 57; *MTIC, 1939*, pp. 66–67, 90; John M. Merriman, "The Wabasso Cotton Company Limited ... Its History, Growth and Progress," *CTJ*, 12 July 1957, pp. 21–29.
10 Merriman, "The Wabasso Cotton Company," p. 25.
11 DBS, *The Textile Industries of Canada in the Decade 1917–26*, pp. 78, 83–84.
12 Ibid., pp. 72–74.
13 Ibid., p. 96.
14 Canada, *Report of the Royal Commission on the Textile Industry*, pp. 53–54; *MTIC, 1928*, p. 262.
15 *CTJ*, "Jubilee Edition," 30 June 1933, p. 44; *CTJ*, 5 Dec. 1922, p. 549; *MTIC, 1928*, p. 264; Canada, *Report of the Royal Commission on Price Spreads*, p. 2737.
16 "New Canadian Raw Silk Factory," *CJF*, May 1904, pp. 107–8.
17 Canada, *Report of the Royal Commission on Price Spreads*, pp. 2736, 2791; Canada, *Report of the Royal Commission on the Textile Industry*, p. 49.
18 Austin, "Life Cycles," pp. 885–86; *Canadian Who's Who, 1939*, p. 330; "Who Owns Canada," *Grain Grower's Guide*, 25 June 1913.
19 Austin, "Life Cycles," p. 898; "Chronology," *CTJ*, June 1983, p. 129.
20 *Canadian Who's Who, 1936–37*, p. 277, s.v. "Dawson, A.O."; Stevens, *The Belding-Corticelli Story*, p. 48; Houston, *Annual Financial Review: Canadian, 1927*, pp. 328–29.
21 Austin, "Life Cycles," p. 886.
22 Canada, *Report of the Royal Commission on the Textile Industry*, p. 140.
23 Ibid., p. 97.
24 Ibid., pp. 26, 253; Roland Renner, "The Development of Unions in the Canadian Primary Textile Industry," MA thesis, McGill Univ., Montréal, 1977, p. 54; Réjean

Boucher, *Les 55 ans de la Celanese à Drummondville, 1926–1981* (Drummondville: Les Publications de la Societé historique du centre du Québec, 1981) p. 14.

25 Austin, "Life Cycles," pp. 379–80; Canada, *Report of the Royal Commission on the Textile Industry*, p. 53.

26 DBS, *The Textile Industries of Canada, 1938 and 1939* (Ottawa: King's Printer, 1942), pp. 50 and 110.

27 Canada, *Report of the Royal Commission on the Textile Industry*, pp. 138–39.

28 "The Story of Penmans Limited Spans a Century of Progress," *CTJ*, 21 June 1968, pp. 26–27.

29 "The Home of Monarch Knit," *CTJ*, Feb. 1913, pp. 41–43; *CTJ*, 14 Dec. 1945, p. 25.

30 Houston, *Annual Financial Review: Canadian, 1930*, p. 1140; ibid., *1932*, pp. 1167–68; ibid., *1941*, pp. 1170–71; Harvey Woods, *The Harvey Woods Story* (n.p.: n.p., n.d.); *CTJ*, 3 Sept. 1926.

31 Woods, *The Harvey Woods Story*; Canada, *Report of the Royal Commission on the Textile Industry*, pp. 53–54.

32 "The Textile Industry Who's Who," *MTIC, 1929*, pp. 48, 51; "Woollen Merger's Stock Issue," *CTJ*, 5 Aug. 1919, p. 328; "Changes in Canadian Woollen's Directorate," *CTJ*, 25 Nov. 1919, p. 555.

33 Houston, *Annual Financial Review: Canadian, 1927*, pp. 328–29; ibid., *1941*, pp. 522; Canada, *Report of the Royal Commission on the Textile Industry*, p. 52; "Chronology," *CTJ*, June 1983, p. 140.

34 *CTJ*, March 1915, p. 81; *CTJ*, 10 Feb. 1956, p. 25.

35 *MTIC*, 1939, p. 135; "Patons and Baldwins New Spinning Plant in Operation," *CTJ*, 8 April 1932.

36 Canada, *Report of the Royal Commission on the Textile Industry*, p. 47; Canada, *Report of the Royal Commission on Price Spreads*, pp. 2756–57.

37 Canada, *Report of the Royal Commission on the Textile Industry*, pp. 54–55.

38 *CJF*, May 1891.

39 Austin, "Life Cycles," p. 891.

40 Epp, "Cooperation Among the Capitalists," pp. 411–13; Houston, *Annual Financial Review: Canadian, 1911*, pp. 162–63.

41 *CJF*, April 1896, p. 101.

42 Canada, *Report of the Royal Commission on Price Spreads*, pp. 2722–23, 2804, 2851, 2914.

43 Austin, "Life Cycles," pp. 110, 165.

44 "The Textile Industry Who's Who," *MTIC, 1929*, p. 48.

45 Austin, "Life Cycles," p. 198; *CTD, 1907–08*, p. 263.

46 Canada, *Statutes*, 3 Edward VII, c. 15, s. 5.

47 Ibid., 4 Edward VII, c. 2, s. 16.

48 Ibid., 6–7 Edward VII, c. 2.

49 "Tariff History and Textiles — A Review of the Canadian Tariffs from 1878 to Date," *MTIC, 1931*, p. 113.

50 Ibid., pp. 113–14; Tom Traves, *The State and Enterprise: Canadian Manufactures and the Federal Government, 1917–1931* (Toronto: Univ. of Toronto Press, 1979), pp. 94–99.

51 "Tariff History and Textiles," *MTIC, 1931*, pp. 114–15; Table 11.

52 D.C. Coleman, *Courtaulds. An Economic and Social History* (Oxford: Clarendon Press, 1969), Vol. 2, pp. 310–12.

53 M.C. Urquhart and K.A.H. Buckley, *Historical Statistics of Canada* (Toronto: Macmillan, 1965), J-38.

54 *CTJ*, 26 Feb. 1924, pp. 181–82.

55 Canada, *Report of the Royal Commission on the Textile Industry*, p. 49.

56 Ibid., pp. 65–92; *DBS, The Canada Year Book, 1936* (Ottawa: King's Printer, 1936) pp. 484–87; *MTIC, 1939*, pp. 39–42; DBS, *The Textile Industries of Canada, 1938 and 1939*, Table 18.
57 Urquhart and Buckley, *Historical Statistics of Canada*, Q-2, Q-55, Q-61.
58 Yves Foisey, "Considerations économiques sur l'industrie lainière au Canada," *Études économiques*, Vol. 7 (1937), p. 88.
59 Canada, *Report of the Royal Commission on the Textile Industry*, pp. 13–14.
60 Ibid., pp. 5, 18–19.
61 Ibid., p. 30.
62 Ibid., p. 28.
63 Ibid., pp. 119, 127.
64 Ibid., p. 126.
65 *Hansard*, 22 June 1938, p. 4135; Austin, "Life Cycles," p. 403; Canada, *Exchequer Court Reports*, 1940, Dominion Textile Company Limited and the Minister of National Revenue.
66 *Hansard*, 23 Feb. and 30 May 1939, pp. 1228, 4758–61.

Labour and Working Conditions

1 Canada, *Census of Canada, 1870–71*, Vol. 3 (Ottawa: King's Printer, 1875), Tables 28 to 53; Canada, *Fifth Census of Canada, 1911*, Vol. 3, Table 1.
2 RCLC, *Evidence Ontario*, pp. 979–83, 1245, 1068–70.
3 Canada, *Report of the Royal Commission on Price Spreads*, pp. 2737, 2789.
4 Urquhart and Buckley, *Historical Statistics of Canada*, C-16, C-17.
5 Ibid., D-116, D-130.
6 RCLC, *Evidence Ontario*, pp. 877–80; Ontario. Bureau of Industries, *Annual Report of the Bureau of Industries, 1884* (Toronto: Queen's Printer, [1884]), Table XXIV.
7 Canada, *Report of the Royal Commission on the Textile Industry*, p. 161. *See* ⹂ 14, p. 291, and Table 29, p. 302, of the commission's report for further evidence ⹂ the disparity in male-female wages.
8 Ibid., p. 892.
9 William Lazonick, "Industrial Relations and Technical Change: The Case of the Self-Acting Mule," *Cambridge Journal of Economics*, Vol. 3, No. 3 (Sept. 1979), pp. 249–50.
10 Joy Parr, "Disaggregating the Sexual Division of Labour: A Transatlantic Study," *Queen's Papers in Industrial Relations, 1987–5* (Kingston, Ont.: Queen's Univ., 1987), pp. 33–34.
11 Rouillard, *Les travailleurs du coton*, pp. 56–57.
12 Ontario, *Statutes*, 47 Victoria, c. 39, 1884; ibid., 58 Victoria, c. 50, 1895; Rouillard, *Les travailleurs du coton*, pp. 56–57, 59.
13 Canada, *Report of the Royal Commission on the Textile Industry*, p. 149.
14 Gail Cuthbert Brandt, "The Transformation of Women's Work in the Quebec Cotton Industry, 1920–1950," in Bryan D. Palmer, *The Character of Class Struggle; Essays in Canadian Working Class History, 1850–1985* (Toronto: McClelland and Stewart, 1986), p. 127.
15 *CJF*, Oct. 1899, p. 307; Rouillard, *Les travailleurs du coton*, p. 54; Edith Abbott, "History of the Employment of Women in the American Cotton Mills," *Journal of Political Economy*, Vol. 16 (Nov. 1908), pp. 610–11; Brandt, "The Transformation of Women's Work," p. 124.
16 Brandt, "The Transformation of Women's Work," pp. 121, 126–27.
17 *CJF*, April 1886, p. 185.

18 Canada. Parliament, *Report of the Royal Commission to Inquire into Industrial Disputes in the Cotton Factories of the Province of Quebec* (Ottawa: King's Printer, 1909), p. 25.
19 Canada, *Report of the Royal Commission on the Textile Industry*, pp. 185–86, 276.
20 Rouillard, *Les travailleurs du coton*, pp. 43–44; Ferland, Le rôle des déterminismes sociaux," pp. 116–17.
21 Rouillard, *Les travailleurs du coton*, pp. 41–43.
22 Ferland, "Le rôle des déterminismes sociaux," pp. 99–100.
23 Joy Parr, "The Skilled Emigrant and Her Kin: Gender, Culture and Labour Recruitment," *Canadian Historical Review*, Vol. 68, No. 4 (Dec. 1987), pp. 531.
24 Austin, "Life Cycles," pp. 815–16; Peter Delottinville, "Trouble in the Hives of Industry: The Cotton Industry Comes to Milltown, New Brunswick, 1879–1892," *Canadian Historical Association, Historical Papers, Montréal, 1980*, p. 112.
25 *CJF*, Aug. 1907, p. 113.
26 Rouillard, *Les travailleurs du coton*, p. 49.
27 Austin, "Life Cycles," pp. 129, 144–47.
28 Morgan, ed., *The Canadian Men and Women of the Time*, 1898, p. 410–11; Houston, *Annual Financial Review: Canadian, 1901*, pp. 90–91.
29 Austin, "Life Cycles," pp. 269–70; Houston, *Annual Financial Review: Canadian, 1901*, pp. 90–91.
30 Canada, *Report of the Royal Commission on the Textile Industry*, p. 274.
31 RCLC, *Evidence Ontario*, pp. 1058–62.
32 Canada, *Report of the Board of Inquiry into the Cost of Living* (Ottawa: King's Printer, 1915), Vol. l, pp. 628–33.
33 Canada, *Report of the Royal Commission on the Textile Industry*, p. 153.
34 Ibid., p. 152.
35 Parr, "Disaggregating the Sexual Division of Labour," p. 23.
36 Urquhart and Buckley, *Historical Statistics of Canada*, p. 93.
37 RCLC, *Evidence Nova Scotia*, pp. 21–24.
38 Ibid., *Evidence Ontario*, pp. 1058–62, 877–80; ibid., *Evidence Nova Scotia*, pp. 124–26.
39 Canada, *Fifth Census of Canada, 1911*, Vol. 3, Tables 1 and 3.
40 Urquhart and Buckley, *Historical Statistics of Canada*, D-287.
41 Canada, *Report of the Royal Commission on the Textile Industry*, p. 156.
42 Réjean Charbonneau et al., *De fil en aiguille: Chronique ouvrière d'une filature de coton à Hochelaga en 1880* ([Montréal]: Société Saint-Jean-Baptiste (Section Maisonneuve), [1985]); "Among the Mills," *CTJ*, June 1901, p. 176; Delottinville, "The St. Croix Cotton Manufacturing Company," pp. 167–68; Rouillard, *Les travailleurs du coton*, p. 75; Ontario. Bureau of Industries, *Report, 1884–85*, Table XLl.
43 *CTJ*, 14 Oct. 1919, pp. 472, 480.
44 Austin, "Life Cycles," pp. 516, 553; Canada, *Report of the Royal Commission on the Textile Industry*, p. 191.
45 *CTJ*, Dec. 1897, pp. 369–70; Leung, "Catalogue," p. 111.
46 *CTJ*, 22 Jan. 1924, pp. 73–75.
47 Rouillard, *Les travailleurs du coton*, p. 62.
48 Ralph Ellis, "Textile Workers and Textile Strikes in Cornwall, Sherbrooke, and St. Grégoire de Montmorency, 1936–1939," paper read at the Canadian Historical Association conference, Montréal, May 1985, p. 8.
49 Daniel Nelson, *Managers and Workers: Origins of the New Factory System in the United States, 1880–1920* (Madison: Univ. of Wisconsin Press, 1975), p. 26.
50 *CJF*, Aug. 1891, p. 15.

51   Charles Lipton, *The Trade Union Movement of Canada, 1827–1959* (Toronto: NC Press, 1973), p. 75; R.C.B. Risk, "This Nuisance of Litigation: The Origin of Worker's Compensation in Ontario," in David Flaherty, ed., *Essays in the History of Canadian Law* (Toronto: Published for the Osgoode Society by the Univ. of Toronto Press, 1983), p. 424.
52   "Constitution of the 'Relief Society of the Star Woollen Mills,'" *CJF*, July 1888, p. 219.
53   Canada, *Sessional Papers*, 1882, No. 42, p. 7.
54   RCLC, *Evidence Quebec*, pp. 374–81.
55   Ibid., *Evidence Ontario*, pp. 1010–11.
56   Ibid., pp. 1075–77; *CJF*, Aug. 1895, p. 249.
57   RCLC, *Evidence New Brunswick*, pp. 30–32; ibid., *Evidence Quebec*, p. 1246.
58   Ibid., *Evidence Quebec*, p. 640; ibid., *Evidence Ontario*, p. 1074.
59   Ibid., *Evidence Nova Scotia*, pp. 129–30, 203–4.
60   Ibid., *Evidence Quebec*, pp. 1198–99, 1163–69.
61   Ibid., *Evidence Nova Scotia*, pp. 70, 76, 200–201.
62   NA, RG 36, No. 11, Vol. 34, file 64–19; *CTJ*, 28 Sept. 1920, p. 505.
63   *CTJ*, Aug. 1913, pp. 230–31; *MTIC, 1946*, p. 71.
64   Reid, "The Rosamond Woolen Company of Almonte," p. 282.
65   Bryan D. Palmer, *A Culture in Conflict; Skilled Workers and Industrial Capitalism in Hamilton* (Montréal: McGill-Queen's Univ. Press, 1979), pp. 155–60; Delottinville, "Trouble in the Hives of Industry," pp. 110–11; RCLC, *Evidence Ontario*, pp. 1002–11.
66   Delottinville, "The St. Croix Cotton Manufacturing Company," p. 225; *CJF*, July 1887, p. 212; *CJF*, April 1888, p. 123; Senior, *From Royal Township to Industrial City: Cornwall*, pp. 235–45.
67   *CJF*, June 1890, p. 23; Palmer, *Culture in Conflict*, pp. 55–56.
68   See *CJF*, 1883–99; Rouillard, *Les travailleurs du coton*, p. 62.
69   Canada, *Report of the Royal Commission to Inquire into Industrial Disputes in the Cotton Factories of ... Quebec*, pp. 25–27.
70   Rouillard, *Les travailleurs du coton*, p. 83.
71   Canada, *Royal Commission to Inquire into Industrial Disputes in the Cotton Factories of ... Quebec*, pp. 4–6, 37; Rouillard, *Les travailleurs du coton*, pp. 89–103.
72   Renner, "The Development of Unions," p. 81.
73   Lipton, *Trade Union Movement*, p. 75.
74   Rouillard, *Les travailleurs du coton*, pp. 80–82; Lipton, *Trade Union Movement*, pp. 221–23.
75   Ferland, "Le rôle des déterminismes sociaux," pp. 112–15, 148.
76   Canada, *Report of the Royal Commission on the Textile Industry*, p. 183; Canada. Dept. of Labour, *Rapport annuel sur les organisations du travail au Canada, 1929* (Ottawa: [1930]); Renner, "The Development of Unions," p. 80.
77   *The Labour Gazette*, March 1937, Table X, "Detailed List of Strikes and Lockouts in Canada, 1936"; *The Labour Gazette*, March 1938, Table X, "Detailed List of Strikes and Lockouts in Canada, 1937."
78   Canada, *Report of the Royal Commission on the Textile Industry*, pp. 185–86; *Labour Gazette*, March 1936, "Strikes and Lockouts"; *Labour Gazette*, March 1937, "Strikes and Lockouts"; Renner, "The Development of Unions," p. 103.
79   Canada, *Report of the Royal Commission on the Textile Industry*, pp. 186–87; Ellis, "Textile Workers and Textile Strikes," pp. 7–11.
80   Canada, *Report of the Royal Commission on the Textile Industry*, pp. 187–88; Ellis, "Textile Workers and Textile Strikes," pp. 11–13; Elwood Jones and Bruce Dyer,

Peterborough, the Electric City: An Illustrated History (Windsor, Ont.: Windsor Publications [Canada], 1987), pp. 77–78; NA, RG 27, Vol. 388, Strike 176.

81 NA, RG 27, Vol. 388, Strikes 5 and 196; *Labour Gazette*, March 1938, "Strikes and Lockouts."

82 NA, RG 27, Vol. 388, Strike 176.

83 *Labour Gazette*, March 1938, "Strikes and Lockouts"; NA, RG 27, Vol. 380, Strike 196.

84 Canada, *Report of the Royal Commission on the Textile Industry*, pp. 188–90; Ellis, "Textile Workers and Textile Strikes," pp. 16–22; *Labour Gazette*, March 1938, "Strikes and Lockouts."

85 Canada, *Report of the Royal Commission on the Textile Industry*, pp. 273–77.

86 Renner, "The Development of Unions," p. 112; Ellis, "Textile Workers and Textile Strikes," pp. 26–27.

87 Denyse Baillargeon, "Histoire des ouvriers unis des textiles d'Amérique (1942–1952)," thèse de M.A., Université de Montréal, 1981, pp. 57–58; Michele Ouimet, "L'industrie textile et les grèves de 1946 et 1952 à la Montréal Cottons Limited, Valleyfield, Québec," thèse de M.A., Université du Québec à Montréal, 1979, p. 65.

88 *Labour Gazette*, March 1947, "Strikes and Lockouts"; Jocelyn St. Pierre, *Les travailleurs Québecois, 1940 à 1971. Chronologie* (Québec: Institut supérieur des science humaines, Université de Laval, 1974), pp. 45–47.

89 DBS, *The Canada Year Book, 1952–53* (Ottawa: Queen's Printer, 1953), pp. 731–32.

90 Ellis, "Textile Workers and Textile Strikes," pp. 27–28.

91 Canada, *Report of the Royal Commission on Price Spreads*, p. 127.

Geographical Distribution

1 This chapter is based primarily on the published census returns and on data in the report of the royal commission on price spreads.

2 Canada, *Report of the Royal Commission on Price Spreads*, pp. 2822, 2828.

3 Ibid., pp. 2847–70, 2911-40.

4 Ibid., pp. 2695–96.

5 Acheson, "The National Policy and the Industrialization of the Maritimes," pp. 11–12.

6 Rouillard, *Les travailleurs du coton*, pp. 43–44; Renner, "The Development of Unions," pp. 24–25.

Structures

1 S. Stevenson and R. Wilcox, "Barrington Woollen Mill Restoration, Interim Report," manuscript prepared for the Nova Scotia Museum, Halifax, Aug. 1980; Leung, "Catalogue," p. 3.

2 Charles T. Main, "Approximate Cost of Mill Buildings," *Engineerinq News*, Vol. 63, No. 4 (7 Jan. 1910), pp. 96–97.

3 *See* Neil Cossons, *The BP Book of Industrial Archaeoloqy* (Newton Abbott, Eng.: David and Charles, ca. 1975), pp. 260–72, for an outline of British mill development.

4 John Winter, *Industrial Architecture: A Survey of Factory Building* (London: Studio Vista, 1970), pp. 45–68; Bryant F. Tolles, "Textile Mill Architecture in East Central New England: An Analysis of Pre–Civil War Design," *Essex Institute Historical Collections*, Vol. 107, No. 3 (July 1971), pp. 223–53.

5 Marsha Hay Snyder and Mary Cullen, "The Marysville Cotton Mill," agenda paper, 1984-21 Historic Sites and Monuments Board of Canada, Ottawa, 1984, p. 333.

6 Detailed fire insurance plans are excellent sources of information the layout of processes in a mill.

7 NA, National Map Collection, NMC 9381, IP/PA/440/Cornwall/1895, 9 of 12; Associated Mutual Insurance Company plan, Serial No. 13144, Index No. 2152, Canadian Cottons Ltd., "Canada Mill," Cornwall, Ontario, 13 Aug. 1918.

8 Initial capital costs for water power might be higher than for steam power, but operating costs would be lower. The relative costs of steam power, particularly for larger engines, decreased through the nineteenth century. Jennifer Tann, *The Development of The Factory* (London: Cornmarket Press, 1970), p. 67; Peter Temin, "Steam and Water Power in the Early 19th Century," *Journal of Economic History*, Vol. 26, No. 2 (June 1966), pp. 187–205.

9 *CTD, 1907*, p. 263.

10 Dennis Carter-Edwards, "The Canada Cotton Mill," in *Heritage Cornwall, Examples of the City's Historic Architecture* (Cornwall: Cornwall LACAC Publication, n.d.), p. 43; A.J. Lawson, "Generation, Distribution and Measurement of Electricity For Light and Power," Canadian Society of Civil Engineers *Transactions*, Vol. 4 (1890), pp. 183, 186.

11 *CJF*, March 1897, p. 66; *CJF*, Dec. 1897, pp. 368–69.

12 *CTJ*, 1 Feb. 1921; R.H. Wilmot, "Electrical Drive of Weaving Sheds Equipped with Plain Cotton Looms," *Textile Institute Journal*, Vol. 20 (Oct. 1929), p. T-296.

13 George Wrigley, "Electric Drive in Cotton Mills," *CTJ*, 14 March 1922, p. 112; "Modern Knitting Mill Construction," *CTJ*, 26 Oct. 1920, p. 568.

14 H.M. Rogers and J. Robert Potter, "New Mill Design—Old Mill Modernization (Part I)," *Sixth Canadian Textile Seminar, Queen's University, Kingston, Ontario, 11-12 September 1958* (Montréal: Textile Technical Federation of Canada, n.d.), n.p.

15 Wrigley, "Electric Drive in Cotton Mills," p. 112.

16 T. Ritchie, *Canada Builds, 1867–1967* (Toronto: Univ. of Toronto Press, 1967), p. 245; "The Galt Knitting Co. Limited," *CJF*, Sept. 1906, p. 195; personal communication, J.E. Warnock Jr., general manager, Tiger Brand Knitting Co.

17 "J.R. Moodie and Sons Ltd.," *CTJ*, 5 Dec. 1922, p. 518, states that the Eagle Spinning mill was built in 1904, but a search of Hamilton assessment records indicates that the company did not own the land until 1906 and that it was not until 1907 that there were buildings on it.

18 Merriman, "The Wabasso Cotton Company Limited," pp. 21–22; NA, National Map Collection, IP/PA 340/Trois Rivières/1955, Sheet 47.

19 *CTJ*, Nov. 1910, p. 225; W.A. Craick, "Features of a New Hamilton Plant," *Industrial Canada*, Vol. 18, No. 11 (March 1917), pp. 1277–79.

20 "Mount Royal Spinning Co.," *CJF*, May 1907, p. 82; Insurance plan, Factory Mutual Engineering Association, Serial No. 58782A, Index No. 1818, 23 April 1984, Dominion Textile Inc., "Mount Royal."

21 Merriman, "The Wabasso Cotton Company Limited," p. 27; NA, National Map Collection, IP/PA 340/Grand'mére/1966.

22 *CTJ*, 10 Aug. 1945, p. 25.

Postwar Industry

1 Austin, "Life Cycles," p. 469.

2   Canada. Royal Commission on Canada's Economic Prospects, *The Canadian Primary Textile Industry*, prepared by the National Industrial Conference Board ([Ottawa]: 1956), Table A.
3   Financial Post Information Service, "Dominion Textile Inc.," (card file).
4   Canada, *The Canadian Primary Textile Industry*, p. 21.
5   DBS, *Textile Mills, Knitting Mills, Clothing, 1953* (Ottawa: Queen's Printer, 1956), pp. C-5, L-4.
6   Canada, *The Canadian Primary Textile Industry*, p. 78.
7   DBS, *Trade of Canada, 1947*, Vol. 3, Imports. Merchandise. Trade (Ottawa: Statistics Canada, External Trade Division, 1947); ibid., *1955*.
8   Canada, *The Canadian Primary Textile Industry*, pp. 35–41.
9   M.C. Urquhart and K.A.H. Buckley, *Historical Statistics of Canada*, rev. ed. (Ottawa: Published by Statistics Canada in joint sponsorship with the Social Science Federation of Canada, ca. 1983), R-261, 242, 244, 231, 235.
10 Rianne Mahon, *The Politics of Industrial Restructuring: Canadian Textiles* (Toronto: Univ. of Toronto Press, 1984), p. 50.
11 Ibid., p. 52; Financial Post Information Service, "Dominion Textile Inc.," (card file).
12 *CTJ*, 12 July 1957, p. 25.
13 Financial Post Information Service, "Silknit Limited," (card file).
14 Mahon, *The Politics of Industrial Restructuring*, p. 54; Financial Post Information Service, "Celanese Canada Inc.," (card file).
15 Austin, "Life Cycles," pp. 532–33.
16 [Dominion Textile], "A Profile of Dominion Textile Inc.," manuscript history provided by Dominion Textile, Montréal, n.d., pp. 16–17.
17 Mahon, *The Politics of Industrial Restructuring*, pp. 58, 66.
18 Austin, "Life Cycles," p. 493; Urquhart and Buckley, *Historical Statistics of Canada*, 1983 ed., R-2, R-231, R-248.
19 GATT-Fly, *The Textile and Clothing Industries in Canada: A Profile* (Toronto: 1980), p. 27.
20 Caroline Pestieau, *The Canadian Textile Policy: A Sectorial Trade Adjustment Strategy* (Montréal: C.D. Howe Research Institute, 1976), p. 20.
21 Mahon, *The Politics of Industrial Restructuring*, Table A2.
22 Ibid., Table A2; Canada. Textile and Clothing Board, *Textile and Clothing Inquiry: Report to the Minister of Regional Industrial Expansion, October 1985*, Vol. 1 (Ottawa: 1985), pp. 1–4 (Oct. 1985).

Part II
The Physical Legacy of the Textile Industry

Merchants Manufacturing Company

1   Austin, "Life Cycles," pp. 179–84.
2   Ibid., pp. 179–84; Associated Mutual Insurance Company, plan, Serial No. 14041, Index No. 1795, Dominion Textile Co., Limited, "Merchants Branch," 28 July 1920.
3   *CTD*, 1885, p. 260; *CTD, 1907–08*, pp. 256–63.
4   *CTD, 1907–08*, p. 262; Associated Mutual Insurance Company, plan, Serial No. 14041, Index No. 1795, Dominion Textile Co., Limited, "Merchants Branch," 28 July 1920.
5   *CTD, 1899*, p. 410; *MTIC, 1941*, p. 142.
6   RCLC, *Evidence Quebec*, pp. 392–98, 734.

6 RCLC, *Evidence Quebec*, pp. 392–98, 734.
7 "Cotton Mill Strike," *CJF*, Oct. 1891, p. 18.
8 "Chronology," *CTJ*, June 1983, p. 152.

Belding-Corticelli Limited

1 G.R. Stevens, *The Belding-Corticelli Story* (n.p.: n.p., ca. 1951), pp. 6–7.
2 "Belding Paul and Co's Silk Factory," *DDGR*, May 1884, p. 269.
3 "Belding Corticelli 75th Anniversary," *CTJ*, 9 Nov. 1951, p. 52; Stevens, *The Belding-Corticelli Story*, pp. 17, 24.
4 "Belding Corticelli 75th Anniversary," *CTJ*, 9 Nov. 1951, p. 52; "The Silk Industry," *CTJ*, 30 June 1933, p. 44.
5 "Belding Corticelli 75th Anniversary," *CTJ*, 9 Nov. 1951, p. 52.
6 Stevens, *The Belding-Corticelli Story*, pp. 22, 48.
7 Canada, *Report of the Royal Commission on Price Spreads*, p. 2737.

Paton Manufacturing Company

1 "Andrew Paton," *CJF*, Nov. 1892, p. 331; Kesteman, "Une bourgeoisie et son espace," p. 334; R.E. Rudin, "Paton, Andrew," in *DCB*, Vol. 12, 1891 to 1900, pp. 827–28.
2 "The Paton Manufacturing Company," *CJF*, Dec. 1893, p. 356; Rudin, "The Development of Four Quebec Towns," pp. 41–42.
3 R. Rudin, "The Transformation of the Eastern Townships of Richard William Heneker," *Journal of Canadian Studies*, Vol. 19, No. 3 (Autumn 1984), p. 34.
4 NA, RG 31, Canada Census 1871, District 140, C1, Sherbrooke Town, Schedule 6, p. 3, reel C-10088; "The Paton Manufacturing Co.," *CJF*, Dec. 1893, p. 356; "The Paton Manufacturing Company, Sherbrooke, Quebec," *CJF*, 2 May 1896, p. 136.
5 Leung, "Catalogue," p. 39; *CTJ*, May 1910, p. 114.
6 Kesteman, "Histoire de Sherbrooke," pp. 168–72.
7 *CJF*, March 1903, p. 85; Houston, *The Annual Financial Review: Canadian, 1911*, p. 227; *The Canadian Who's Who, 1936–37*, p. 521.
8 Société d'histoire des Cantons de l'est, "Historique de la Paton Manufacturing Company, 1866–1978," manuscript on file in the society's holdings, Sherbrooke, 1978.; "Chronology," *CTJ*, June 1983, pp. 129, 151.

Magog Textile and Print Company

1 Alexandre Paradis, *Commercial and Industrial Story of Magog, Que.* (Magog: n.p., 1951), pp. 22–30; *CTD, 1885*, p. 260.
2 "The Print Works," *DDGR*, Jan. 1884, p. 51.
3 *CJF*, Sept. 1888, p. 287.
4 *CTD*, 1892, p. 411.
5 *CJF*, Nov. 1902, p. 327.
6 Paradis, *Magog*, pp. 36, 44.
7 *CTD, 1892*, p. 411.
8 "The Taylor System of Air Compression," *CTJ*, Nov. 1896, pp. 324–36; "Compressed Air," *CJF*, Sept. 1897, pp. 267.
9 The 1899 and 1907–08 *Canadian Textile Directory* indicate that both the print mill and the cloth mill were powered by compressed air. Paradis, *Magog*, p. 42, indicates

that in 1910 the 1897 power plant was replaced by a hydro-electric plant. However, a detailed article on the "Power Plant of Dominion Cotton Mills Co., Magog," in *The Canadian Engineer*, Feb. 1902, pp. 25–28, describes two 51-inch Hercules vertical turbines that powered the cloth mill through a direct-drive system and a 54-inch Hercules vertical turbine that had powered the print mill. According to the article, this direct-drive system was being replaced by an electric drive system.

10 Ferland, "Le rôle des déterminismes sociaux," pp. 113–14.

11 J.-P. Hétu, *Lutte des travailleurs du textile au Quebec*, (Montréal: Central des Syndicats Democratiques, 1979), p. 17; "Among the Mills," *CJF*, Aug. 1900, p. 241.

12 Hétu, *Lutte des travailleurs*, pp. 18–19.

13 Dominion Textile, *Magog: A Busy Town of Happy Homes Situated in a District Noted for its Beauty* (Montréal: Dominion Textile, [1917]).

14 See Building No. 10 in Factory Mutual Engineering Association, plan, Serial No. 73313C, Index No. 1462, Dominion Textile Inc., "Magog Consumer Finishing," 12 Aug. 1983.

Canadian Celanese Limited

1 Fred Dawson, "Celanese Canada Inc. An Historical Review," *CTJ*, June 1983, pp. 88–89.

2 Boucher, *Les 55 ans de la Celanese*, pp. 2–3.

3 Ibid., p. 1.

4 Ibid., p. 9; Dawson, "Celanese Canada Inc.," p. 88; "Chronology," *CTJ*, June 1983, pp. 132, 136, 142–44, 148, 156.

5 Canada, *Report of the Royal Commission on Price Spreads*, p. 2789; M. Martine, *Drummondville, son développement et ses travailleurs, 1925–1940* (Drummondville: Société historique du centre du Quebec, 1984), pp. 23–4.

6 Canada, *Report of the Royal Commission on the Textile Industry*, p. 26.

7 Dawson, "Celanese Canada Inc.," pp. 90–98; Mahon, *The Politics of Industrial Restructuring*, p. 54.

Montreal Cotton Company

1 *Canadian Illustrated News*, 12 Jan. 1878, p. 20; "A Canadian Cotton Mill," *CJF*, Dec. 1897, p. 367; *CJF*, Feb. 1893, p. 62; "The Valleyfield Mills," *CJF*, Oct. 1898, pp. 308–9; "A New Cotton Mill for Valleyfield," *CJF*, Jan. 1900, p. 5; *CJF*, Dec. 1905, p. 268.

2 *Canadian Illustrated News*, 12 Jan. 1878, p. 20; St-Aubin, *Salaberry de Valleyfield*, pp. 45–49. St-Aubin identifies a "Mr. Bullough" as the English investor. However, Austin, "Life Cycles," p. 238, identifies Samuel Barlow as the investor. As Ms. Austin has had access to the company's minute books, I have followed her lead.

3 "The Montreal Cottons Limited, 1883 ... 1933," *CTJ*, 30 June 1933, p. 111; "Chronology," *CTJ*, June 1983, p. 122; Austin, "Life Cycles," pp. 879, 896–98.

4 Scaled from a 1953 insurance plan. NA, National Map Collection, IP/PA/340/Salaberry de Valleyfield/1953, Sheet 20, C-128072.

5 *Canadian Illustrated News*, 12 Jan. 1878, p. 20; "A Canadian Cotton Mill," *CJF*, Dec. 1897, p. 367.

6 Lawson, "Generation, Distribution and Measurement of Electricity," p. 183; "A Canadian Cotton Mill," *CJF*, Dec. 1897, p. 367–71; *MTIC, 1928*, p. 253.
7 Ferland, "Le rôle des déterminismes sociaux," pp. 196, 255; "The Valleyfield Mills," *CJF*, Oct. 1898, p. 309; "The Montreal Cotton Company's Mills at Valleyfield, P.Q.," *CTJ*, Aug. 1908, p. 162.
8 *CTJ*, Aug. 1908, pp. 162, 164.
9 *Valleyfield, Canada: The Cotton Factory Town of Canada* (n.p.: issued by the Montreal Cotton Company, ca. 1908), pp. 7, 14.
10 For histories of the strikes *see* Claude Larivière, *Histoire des travailleurs de Beauharnois et Valleyfield* (Montréal: Éditions A. St-Martin, 1974), pp. 24–35; Ferland, "Le rôle des déterminismes sociaux"; Rouillard, *Les travailleurs du coton*; Ouimet, "L'industrie textile et les grèves de 1946 et 1952"; Baillargeon, "Histoire des ouvriers unis des textiles d'Amérique (1942–1952)."

Canada Cotton Manufacturing Company

1 Senior, *From Royal Township to Industrial City: Cornwall*, p. 228.
2 Associated Mutual Insurance Company, plan, Serial No. 7602, Index No. 2138, Canadian Coloured Cotton Mills Co., Limited, "Canada Mill," Cornwall, 25 Oct. 1906. This plan and the one dated 15 Aug. 1918 were photographed in the mill office in 1985.
3 *Canadian Illustrated News*, 26 Jan. 1878, pp. 54–55.
4 Associated Mutual Insurance Company, plan, Serial No. 7602, Index No. 2138, Canadian Coloured Cotton Mills Co., Limited, "Canada Mill," Cornwall, 25 Oct. 1906.
5 *CTD, 1885*, p. 259.
6 *Canadian Illustrated News*, 26 Jan. 1878, pp. 54–55; Associated Mutual Insurance Co., plan, Serial No. 13144, Index No. 2152, Canada Cottons Ltd., "Canada Mill," 15 Aug. 1918.
7 *Cornwall Freeholder*, 2 Feb. 1883, p. 3; ibid., 2 March 1883, p. 3; Lawson, "Generation, Distribution and Measurement of Electricity," p. 183.
8 RCLC, *Evidence Ontario*, pp. 1062–66; *Canadian Illustrated News*, 26 Jan. 1878, pp. 54–55.
9 Senior, *From Royal Township to Industrial City: Cornwall*, pp. 236–43.
10 Ibid., pp. 446–49. According to Austin, "Life Cycles," p. 553, the company was acquired by a group of investors, led by Walter Gordon, which wished to gain control of its pension fund.

Cornwall Manufacturing Company — Dundas Mill

1 Senior, *From Royal Township to Industrial City: Cornwall*, pp. 226–28.
2 Bloomfield databanks, URBIND71 and RURIND71, University of Guelph, created from 1871 manuscript Canada census schedules for Ontario industrial establishments, in a major project partially supported by the Social Sciences and Humanities Research Council of Canada; NA, RG 31, 1871 Census, District 140, C-1, Schedule 6, p. 3, Sherbrooke Town, reel C-100088.
3 URBIND71 and RURIND71.
4 RCLC, *Evidence Ontario*, p. 1068; *CTD, 1892*, p. 357.
5 Leung, "Catalogue," p. 20; *CJF*, Jan. 1904, p. 16.
6 *CTD, 1907–08*; *MTIC, 1928* and *1939*.

Courtaulds (Canada) Limited

1 Coleman, *Courtaulds*, Vol. 2, pp. 30, 36, 106–7.
2 Ibid., pp. 276, 310–12.
3 Canada, *Report of the Royal Commission on the Textile Industry*, p. 49.
4 "Courtaulds (Canada) Limited: 30th Year in Canada," *Rayon Reel*, special issue, Oct. 1955, pp. 6–7, 15; "The Story of Courtaulds in Canada," *CTJ*, June 1983, p. 100; Chronology," *CTJ*, June 1983, pp. 132, 138–39, 144–46.
5 "Courtaulds...," *Rayon Reel*, p. 6; E.S. Bates, "Canada's First Artificial Silk Plant," *Pulp and Paper Magazine of Canada*, 11 Nov. 1926, p. 1354; Canada, *Report of the Royal Commission on Price Spreads*, p. 2791.
6 Canada, *Report of the Royal Commission on the Textile Industry*, pp. 186–87.

Rosamond Woollen Company

1 "The Yorkshire of Canada," *CJF*, Jan. 1896, pp. 3–7; Reid, "The Rosamond Woolen Company," pp. 267–71.
2 The mill was surveyed by the Heritage Recording Service of Environment Canada in 1986.
3 Extracted from URBIND71 and RURIND71.
4 "The Yorkshire of Canada," *CTJ*, Jan. 1896, p. 5; Reid, "The Rosamond Woolen Company," p. 276.
5 Reid, "The Rosamond Woolen Company," p. 279.
6 Ibid., pp. 269, 272; John R. Spilsbury, *Cobourg: Early Days and Modern Times* (Cobourg, Ont.: Cobourg Book Committee, ca. 1981), pp. 10–11; *CTD, 1892*, p. 356; *CTD, 1899*, p. 438.
7 Reid, "The Rosamond Woolen Company," pp. 282–83.

R. Forbes Company

1 Karen Post Trussler, "Industrial Heritage: Definition and Developments with Special Emphasis on the Former Silknit Ltd. Textile Mill in Cambridge, Ontario," MA thesis, Univ. of Waterloo, Waterloo, Ont., pp. 44–45; Cambridge City Archives, MG 3, Introduction to the Silknit Papers; Winfield Brewster, *Hespeler Yarns* (n.p.: n.p., 1953), "The Tannery Street Mill." Dimensions are from a 1908 insurance plan in the Cambridge City Archives; employment and production statistics in 1871 are from URBIND71 and RURIND71.
2 Trussler, "Industrial Heritage," pp. 45–49; *CTD, 1885*, p. 235; the Silknit Papers (Cambridge City Archives, MG 3) contain insurance plans for the mill dated 1890, 1898, 1901, and 1908.
3 *CTD, 1907–08*, pp. 288–89; "Chronology," *CTJ*, June 1983, p. 140.
4 *CTD, 1885*, p. 235; Brewster, *Hespeler Yarns*.
5 Trussler, "Industrial Heritage," pp. 50–56.
6 Ibid., pp. 57–58.
7 Ibid., p. 56; John M. Merriman, "Three-Mill Enterprise in Galt, Ont.," *CTJ*, 9 Sept. 1955, p. 7.
8 Canada, *Report of the Royal Commission on Price Spreads*, p. 78.
9 Cambridge City Archives, MG 3, Introduction to the Silknit Papers; Trussler, "Industrial Heritage," pp. 66–71.

George Pattinson and Company

1 "Canada's First Linen Factory," *CJF*, Aug. 1892, p. 250.
2 Extracted from URBIND71 and RURIND71.
3 Cambridge, Ontario, LACAC report, Aclo Products; Leung, "Catalogue," p. 35; "Preston, Ont., Textile Manufacturing Firm to Move Operations to Jamaica," *CTJ*, 26 Dec. 1958.
4 *CTD, 1885*, p. 235; "Chronology," *CTJ*, June 1893, pp. 124–25; Canada, *Report of the Royal Commission on Price Spreads*, p. 2811.

Galt Knitting Company

1 *Picturesque and Industrial Galt* (Galt: Jaffray Bros., 1902), p. 112.
2 Cambridge, Ontario, LACAC Building Description, 11 Dec. 1982, Galt Woollen Factory, 36–38 Water Street.
3 NA, RG 31, 1871 Census, Waterloo South, D2 (Galt), Schedule 6, p. 1, reel C-9943.
4 *CTD, 1899*, p. 440; *Picturesque and Industrial Galt*, p. 112.
5 *MTIC, 1984*, p. 158.
6 NA, National Map Collection, NMC 9445, IP/PA/440/Galt/1929, Sheet 4; *CTD, 1907–08*, p. 286.

Newlands and Company, Limited

1 Merriman, "Three-Mill Textile Enterprise in Galt, Ont.," p. 2; *Picturesque and Industrial Galt*, p. 112.
2 Merriman, "Three-Mill Textile Enterprise in Galt, Ont.," p. 2.
3 Canada, *Report of the Royal Commission on Price Spreads*, pp. 2925, 2931.
4 Merriman, "Three-Mill Textile Enterprise in Galt, Ont.," p. 2.
5 Ibid., pp. 1–8; John M. Merriman, "Newlands Textiles Inc. — a new firm emerges from the former Dobbie Industries," *CTJ*, July 1980, pp. 39–42.
6 Merriman, "Three-Mill Textile Enterprise in Galt, Ont.," pp. 4–6; "Dobbie Industries Ltd., Galt, Ont. Said 'Strong and Well Diversified,'" *CTJ*, 17 Feb. 1961, pp. 25–26; J. Quantrell, archivist of the City of Cambridge, to F. Leung, 5 May 1987.

Penman Manufacturing Company

1 Merriman, "History, Development of Penmans," p. 21. Donald A. Smith, *At the Forks of the Grand* (Paris, Ont.: Centennial Committee, 1956), p. 64, indicates that John Penman's partner in Paris was his father and that they rented the first mill.
2 NA, National Map Collection, NMC 9618, IP/PA/440/Paris/1882, Penman Manufacturing Company, Paris, Ontario, 1882.
3 *Canadian Manufacturer and Industrial World*, 1 March 1882, p. 41.
4 Merriman, "History, Development of Penmans," pp. 21–22; NA, National Map Collection, NMC 9620, IP/PA/440/Paris/1924(1913), Sheet 1.
5 Merriman, "History, Development of Penmans," p. 22.
6 Canada, *Report of the Royal Commission on Price Spreads*, p. 85.
7 Houston, *The Annual Financial Review: Canadian, 1941*, pp. 812–13; Canada, *Report of the Royal Commission on Price Spreads*, p. 2925.

8 Epp, "Cooperation Among the Capitalists," pp. 414–15; *CJF*, Sept. 1906, p. 187; *CJF*, March 1914, p. 74.

9 NA, RG 31, Canada Census 1871, Paris, Subdistrict 2, Schedule 6, p. 2, reel C-9916; NA, National Map Collection, NMC 9618, IP/PA/440/Paris/1882, Penman Manufacturing Company, Paris, Ontario, 1882.

10 Canada, *Report of the Royal Commission on Price Spreads*, p. 2931.

11 Joy Parr, "Rethinking Work and Kinship in a Canadian Hosiery Town, 1910–1950," *Feminist Studies*, Vol. 13, No. 1 (Spring 1987), p. 139.

12 Joy Parr, *The Gender of Bread Winners: Women, Men, and Change in Two Industrial Towns, 1880–1950* (Toronto: Univ. of Toronto Press, 1990), p. 50.

13 Ibid., pp. 96–119.

14 Fred Bemrose, Paris Museum and Historical Society, to F. Leung, 31 Jan. 1986; personal communication, Fred Bemrose, Dec. 1990.

Joseph Simpson and Sons

1 André Scheinman, "'Berkeley Castle' Rehab, Toronto," Ontario Society for Industrial Archeology *Bulletin*, Vol. 2, No. 2 (Summer 1983), p. 2; NA, National Map Collection, IP/PA/440/Toronto/1954, Sheet 9.

2 A.R.R. Jones, "Joseph Simpson Sons, Ltd.," *CTJ*, 11 Oct. 1921, p. 539.

3 Jones, "Joseph Simpson Sons," pp. 530–40; *MTIC, 1941*, p. 155; "Monarch Knitting Purchases Simpson Plant in Toronto," *CTJ*, 14 Dec. 1945, p. 25.

4 Adele Freedman, "A nifty attempt to spruce up urban health," *Globe and Mail*, 21 May 1983.

5 NA, RG 31, Canada Census, 1871, Toronto West, D-3, Schedule 6, p. 7, reel C-9971.

6 Canada, *Report of the Royal Commission on Price Spreads*, pp. 2915, 2931.

7 Jones, "Joseph Simpson Sons," pp. 539–40.

8 "Joseph Simpson and Sons Knitting Mills," *CTJ*, June 1906, pp. 147–48.

J.R. Moodie and Sons Limited

1 "J.R. Moodie and Sons Ltd.," *CTJ*, 5 Dec. 1922, p. 518; "The Eagle Knitting Company," *Hamilton Spectator*, Carnival Souvenir, Aug. 1903, p. 74. *CTD, 1899*, p. 441, indicates that the firm was organized in 1876 and other sources suggest 1880 or 1884. The article "J.R. Moodie and Sons Ltd." states that the Sanford Avenue mill was built in 1904, but a search of City of Hamilton assessment rolls (courtesy of Ann Gillespie, Heritage Planning Unit) indicates that the company did not own the land until 1906 and that it was not until 1907 that there were buildings on it. The date 1907 is supported by a search of city directories.

2 "Chronology," *CTJ*, June 1983, p. 124; *MTIC, 1928*, p. 260.

3 *Hamilton Spectator*, 26 Feb. 1952; *MTIC, 1928*, p. 260.

4 "Chronology," *CTJ*, June 1983, p. 147; Vernon's *Hamilton Directory*, 1957, shows Robert R. Moodie as president of the company.

5 John C. Weaver, *Hamilton; An Illustrated History* (Toronto: James Lorimer and Co., 1982), p. 88; *CTD, 1899*, p. 441.

6 "J.R. Moodie and Sons Ltd.," *CTJ*, 5 Dec. 1922, p. 518; 1911 insurance plans in the city engineer's office show the building as a two-storey-plus-basement building of brick and reinforced concrete.

7 "J.R. Moodie and Sons Ltd.," *CTJ*, 5 Dec. 1922, p. 518.

8 *Canadian Who's Who, 1936–37*, Vol. 2, pp. 795–96.

The Gibson Mill

1   John Osborne, "Alexander 'Boss' Gibson, 1819–1913," agenda paper, 1974-19, Historic Sites and Monuments Board of Canada, Ottawa, 1974, pp. 3–4.
2   Snyder and Cullen, "The Marysville Cotton Mill," pp. 324, 333.
3   Ibid, pp. 324–25.

Saint John Cotton Company

1   *CTD, 1892*, p. 407; NA, National Map Collection, NMC 126803 (18/72), IP/PA/240/Saint John/1952 (1957), Sheet 23.
2   *CTD, 1885*, p. 262.
3   "St. John Cotton Mill," *CJF*, July 1887; *CTD, 1892*, p. 407.
4   "Saint John Cotton Mills," *CJF*, Dec. 1890, p. 22; "The St. John Cotton Mills," *CJF*, June 1891, p. 17; "Parks vs. Bank of Montreal," *CJF*, April 1892, p. 121.
5   *CJF*, Jan. 1893, p. 24; "Annual Meeting of Wm. Parks and Son, Ltd.," *CJF*, March 1894, p. 76.
6   "Suspension of Wm. Parks and Son Ltd.," *CJF*, Jan. 1901, p. 20.
7   "The Parks Cotton Mills, St. John," *CJF*, Nov. 1901, p. 332.
8   *CTJ*, 5 Dec. 1922, p. 501.
9   *CTD, 1907–08*, p. 256.
10 Eric Richter, "Canadian Cottons Sells Off Assets," *Financial Post*, 1 Aug. 1959, p. 12.

Stanfield's Limited

1   Ed Smith, "The Wool Weavers of Truro," *Imperial Oilways*, Oct. 1960, p. 2; "The History of Stanfield's Limited, Truro, Nova Scotia," manuscript on file, Stanfield's Limited, Truro, n.d., p. 1.
2   *CTD, 1892*, pp. 351, 365.
3   "History of Stanfield's Limited," pp. 2–3; *CTD, 1907–08*, p. 275.
4   "History of Stanfield's Limited," pp. 1–4.

Yarmouth Duck and Yarn Company Limited

1   Acheson, "The National Policy and the Industrialization of the Maritimes," p. 9; *CTD, 1885*, p. 262; James J. Wallis, "The Cosmos Cotton Company," *CTJ*, March 1914, p. 82.
2   *DDGR*, April 1884, p. 142.
3   Public Relations Dept., Dominion Textile, "Dominion Textile Inc., Yarmouth Plant, Historical Summary," manuscript on file, Yarmouth Fabrics Plant, Dominion Textile, Yarmouth, N.S., [1983], p. 3; Wallis, "The Cosmos Cotton Company," pp. 80–81.
4   *CJF*, Dec. 1901, p. 335; "The Looms are Still Humming," *Hamilton Spectator*, 4 July 1967; Lincoln, *Lockewood Greene*, pp. 306–7.
5   Wallis, "The Cosmos Cotton Company," p. 82.
6   "The Looms are Still Humming," *Hamilton Spectator*, 4 July 1967. The New England Southern Mills sold Cosmos Imperial for $1 538 133 and 800 119 shares in the new company. S. Harold Greene, of the firm of Lockewood Greene and Company, which controlled New England Southern Mills, became president of Cosmos Imperial Mills

and was chairman until he died in 1937. Lincoln, *Lockewood Greene*, pp. 559–60; "S. Harold Greene," *Who Was Who in America*, Vol. 1, 1897–1942 (Chicago: The A.N. Marquis Company, 1943), p. 484.

7 Wallis, "The Cosmos Cotton Company," pp. 80–81.

8 John M. Merriman, "The Story of Cosmos at Yarmouth, N.S.," *CTJ*, 5 Sept. 1958, pp. 22-24; "Yarmouth Industrial Fabrics Limited Builds New Weave Mill in Nova Scotia," *CTJ*, 14 Oct. 1966, p. 27.

A Select, Annotated Bibliography

For those who are interested in further reading on the history of the textile industry there is a considerable body of literature. What follows is far from a complete bibliography; however, it does highlight the major recent work in the field.

Although several aspects of the history of the textile industry have attracted considerable interest from historians, the complete history of the industry has yet to be written. Canadian historians have produced nothing comparable to Melvin Copeland's *The Cotton Manufacturing Industry of the United States* (Cambridge, Mass: 1912) or Arthur Cole's *The American Wool Manufacture* (Cambridge, Mass.: 1926). The most complete published history of the primary industry is in Chapter 2 of the *Report of the Royal Commission on the Textile Industry* (Ottawa: 1938). Among unpublished sources Gilbert Rousseau's "Évolution de la production textile au Canada dépuis ses origines jusqu'à aujourd'hui" (baccalauréat spécial, Université du Québec à Montréal, 1980) provides a broad survey of the industry from the pre-industrial period to the 1970s. The *Canadian Textile Journal* and its predecessors, the *Canadian Journal of Fabrics* and the *Dominion Dry Goods Report*, provide a basic narrative history of the industry from 1883 to the present: the centennial volume (June 1983) contains a chronology of the industry drawn from the journal's files. Another trade publication, the *Canadian Textile Directory*, first published in 1885, provides essential information on individual companies, ownership, and equipment. From 1928 the *Manual of the Textile Industry of Canada* provides much the same information. The decennial census and, after 1929, the Dominion Bureau of Statistics reports on the textile industry are also essential reading.

If readers wish to place the textile industry in the context of Canadian business history they should consult Michael Bliss, *Northern Enterprise: Five Centuries of Canadian Business* (Toronto: 1987) or, for a different perspective, Tom Naylor, *The History of Canadian Business, 1867–1914* (Toronto: 1976).

Domestic cloth production has received considerable attention as a craft form; the most authoritative work of this type is Harold and Dorothy Burnham's *'Keep Me Warm One Night': Early Handweaving in Eastern Canada* (Toronto: 1972). David-Thierry Ruddell has produced estimates of the relative importance of cloth production in Quebec homes in "The Domestic Textile Industry in the Region and City of Québec, 1792–1835" (*Material History Bulletin*, Spring 1983) and "Consumer Trends, Clothing Textiles and Equipment in the Montréal Area" (*Material History Bulletin*, Fall 1990). Janine Grant and Kris Inwood ("Gender and Organization in the

Canadian Cloth Industry, 1870," *Canadian Papers in Business History*, ed. P.A. Baskerville, [Victoria: 1989]) have established that home weaving remained an important factor in Canadian cloth production as late as 1870 and that much of this weaving was done by women. In "'Labouring at the Loom': A Case Study of Rural Manufacturing in Leeds County, Ontario," *Canadian Papers in Rural History*, Vol. 7, ed. D.H. Akenson (Gananoque, Ont.: 1990), Inwood and Janine Roelens explore some of the factors that led to the continuation of home weaving in Leeds County, Ontario.

In the thematic areas considered by this book, labour has been the object of more detailed examination than tariffs, finance, technology, or architecture. The Quebec cotton sector has been the subject of several theses, books, and articles. The testimony taken by the Royal Commission on the Relations of Labour and Capital (1888) provides a good starting point for the the labour and social history of the textile industry in Quebec, as well as in the other provinces. Réjean Charbonneau's *De fil en aiguille: Chronique ouvrière d'une filature de coton à Hochelaga en 1880* ([Montréal]: [1985]) provides an introduction to social and working conditions in a nineteenth-century mill town.

The labour unrest in the Quebec industry in the decade 1900–1910 has been the subject of two theses as well as a Royal Commission chaired by W.L. Mackenzie King. Jacques Rouillard's thesis, published as *Les travailleurs du coton au Québec, 1900–1915* (Montréal: 1974), combines business, social, and labour history. Jacques Ferland, in "Le rôle des déterminismes sociaux dans le développement des forces productives de l'industrie textile du Canada, 1870 à 1910" (MA thesis, McGill University, 1982), covers much of the same ground while emphasizing the degree to which technological developments influenced both management and labour strategies.

The strikes of 1936–37, 1946, and 1952 form the subject of several theses and articles: Ralph Ellis's "Textile Workers and Textile Strikes in Cornwall, Sherbrooke and St. Grégoire de Montmorency, 1936–1939" (MA thesis, University of Ottawa, 1985), Denyse Baillargeon's "Histoire des ouvriers unis des textiles d'Amérique (1942–1952)" (thèse de M.A., Université de Montréal, 1981), and Michele Ouimet's "L'industrie textile et les grèves de 1946 et 1952 à la Montreal Cottons Limited, Valleyfield, Québec" (thèse de M.A., Université du Québec à Montréal, 1979) all focus on the strikes. Rick Salutin's *Kent Rowley, The Organizer. A Canadian Union Life* (Toronto: 1980) discusses the strikes in Montréal, Valleyfield, and Lachute in 1946 and 1952–53 from the point of view of a union organizer. Alfred Charpentier's "La conscience syndicale lors des grèves du textile en 1937 et de l'amiante en 1949" (*Labour/Le travailleur*, Vol. 3, 1978) contains an analysis of the 1937 strike by the leader of the Catholic unions. Micheline Martin's *Drummondville, son developpement et ses travailleurs, 1925–1940*

(Drummondville: 1984) and Jean-Paul Hetu's *Lutte des travailleurs du textile au Québec* (Montréal: 1979) provide information on labour activity in Drummondville and Magog, two centres that are overlooked in most other texts. Finally Roland Renner, in "The Development of Unions in the Canadian Primary Textile Industry" (MA thesis, McGill University, 1977), provides an overview of textile union history in Canada in the twentieth century.

By comparison with Quebec, the history of textile labour in the rest of Canada has been neglected. Peter Delottinville's "The St. Croix Cotton Manufacturing Company and its Influence on the St. Croix Community, 1880–1892" (MA thesis, Dalhousie University, 1980) is a case study of a New Brunswick firm during the years of the cotton boom. It provides useful insights into labour experience and into the problems of financing and managing a cotton mill in the nineteenth century.

The experience of women in the industry is being studied by at least three historians. Gail Cuthbert Brandt has analyzed the changing employment patterns of women in the Quebec cotton industry in "The Transformation of Women's Work in the Quebec Cotton Industry, 1920–1950" (in Bryan Palmer, *The Character of Class Struggle; Essays in Canadian Working Class History, 1850–1985* [Toronto: 1986]) and in "'Weaving it Together': Life Cycle and Industrial Experience of Female Cotton Workers in Quebec, 1910–1950" (*Labour/Le travailleur*, Vol. 7, Spring 1981). Joy Parr has studied the experience of women employed by Penmans in Paris, Ontario, and contrasted it with the experience of women in the knitting industry in Britain in several articles including "Disaggregating the Sexual Division of Labour: A Transatlantic Case Study," *Queen's Papers in Industrial Relations, 1987–5* (Kingston, Ont.: 1987). In *The Gender of Breadwinners: Women, Men and Change in Two Industrial Towns* (Toronto: 1990) she contrasts the experience of women in knitting mills in Paris, Ontario, with the experience of men in the furniture factories of Hanover, Ontario. Both Brandt and Parr comment on the influence of technological change on women's employment patterns. In a recent thesis, "Women, War and Work: Female Textile Workers in Cornwall, Ontario, 1936–46" (MA thesis, Queen's University, 1990), Ellen Scheinberg has examined the experience of women workers in Cornwall's textile mills and their relationship to male management and union leadership. The experience of women, the shift from craft to industrial production, and the role of marketing in the textile industry are examined in a series of papers presented at the "Surveying Textile History" colloquium in Fredericton, New Brunswick, in April of 1989 and published in the spring 1990 *Material History Bulletin*.

Comments on and analysis of the effect of the tariff on the textile industry are to be found in most writing about the industry. The statutes and the records of imports are basic sources for the study of tariff policy. The

Canadian Textile Journal and its predecessors provide running commentary on the effect of the tariff on the industry. In two unpublished papers, "The National Policy and the Growth of the Canadian Cotton Textile Industry" (Thirteenth Conference of Quantitative Methods in Canadian Economic History, Waterloo, 1984) and "The Growth of the Canadian Cotton Textile Industry, 1844–1873: A New Industrial Career" (unpublished paper presented to the Workshop in Economic History, University of Toronto, 1981), Michael Hinton argues that the effect of the introduction of the high tariff under the National Policy has been exaggerated and that the industry was expanding before the tariff was introduced. Both O.J. McDairmid, *Commercial Policy in the Canadian Economy* (Cambridge, Mass.: 1948), and J.H. Dales, *The Protective Tariff in Canada's Development* (Toronto: 1966), provide specific comments on effects of the tariff on textiles and establish a context for studying the industry. In the late 1920s and the 1930s the Advisory Board on Tariffs and Taxation held hearings on several sectors of the textile industry; the published records of these hearings provide data and analysis of the industry.

The postwar crisis in the industry has resulted in a number of major studies by government agencies, historians, economists, and industry representatives. The National Industrial Conference Board prepared a detailed analysis (*The Canadian Primary Textile Industry*) of the postwar industry for the Royal Commission on Canada's Economic Prospects in 1956. In the late 1950s and the 1960s the Tariff Board conducted investigations of the major sectors of the primary industry. More recently the reports of the Textile and Clothing Board have analyzed the effects of tariff and other government policies on the industry. Caroline Pestieau, *The Canadian Textile Policy: A Sectorial Trade Adjustment Strategy* (Montréal: 1976), and Rianne Mahon, *The Politics of Industrial Restructuring: Canadian Textiles* (Toronto: 1984), both analyze the postwar industry's problems and the government's attempts to assist it. For a labour perspective on the postwar period one should consult GATT-Fly, *The Textile and Clothing Industries in Canada: A Profile* (Toronto: 1980).

The financial and business history of the textile industry has received less attention than its labour history. The *Report of the Royal Commission on the Textile Industry* (Ottawa: 1938) provides a good survey of the industry in the 1930s and the *Report of the Royal Commission on Price Spreads* (Ottawa: 1935) contains data on employment, wages, and sales for most of the important firms in the years 1929–33. There are also several good case studies. Peter Delottinville's study of the early years of the St. Croix Cotton Company has already been mentioned. Richard Reid, in "The Rosamond Woolen Company of Almonte: Industrial Development in a Rural Setting" (*Ontario History*, Sept. 1983), has written a brief account of one of the most significant nineteenth-century woollen mills. The Mississippi Valley woollen industry is also the subject of Elizabeth Price's "The Changing Geography of the Woollen Industry in Lanark, Renfrew and Carleton Counties, 1830–1911" (MA research paper, University of Toronto, 1979); much the same ground is covered in *The Development of the Woollen Industry in Lanark, Renfrew and Carleton Counties* published by the North Lanark Historical Society (n.p.: 1978). In "Finding the Right Size: Markets and Competition in Mid- and Late Nineteenth Century Ontario" (in *Patterns of the Past: Interpreting Ontario's History*, eds. R. Hall, W. Westfall, and L.S. McDowell [Toronto: 1988]) Ben Forster discusses the problems facing the woollen industry in the later nineteenth century with particular reference to the Rosamond company. Barbara J. Austin's thesis, "Life Cycles and Strategy of a Canadian Company — Dominion Textile: 1873–1983" (PhD thesis, Concordia University, 1985), applies Alfred Chandler's theories of distinct stages of development that are reflected by corporate structures and strategies to the history of Dominion Textile. Her study, which is the first to have had access to Dominion Textile's corporate records, includes brief histories of most of Dominion Textile's predecessor companies. T.W. Acheson's "The Social Origins of Canadian Industrialism: A Study in the Structure of Entrepreneurship" (PhD thesis, University of Toronto, 1971) includes detail on the origin of many early cotton-mill owners and information on their problems in financing the mills. The *Dictionary of Canadian Biography* also contains entries for a number of individuals such as John Gordon, Donald McInnes, and Andrew Paton, who were managers or investors in the nineteenth-century textile industry; the *Canadian Who's Who* is also a useful source of biographical information.

Although technological change is recognized as an important factor by business and labour historians, the study of the history of textile technology per se in Canada is confined to articles in trade journals. Much the same is true of textile-mill architecture; one exception is A.B. McCullough's "Technology and Textile Mill Architecture in Canada" (*Material Culture Bulletin*, Fall 1989). British and American historians have written extensively in both of these areas; to what extent their findings can be applied to Canada remains to be seen.

Index